Reflexive Practice:
Dialectic Encounter
in
Psychology & Education

Reflexive Practice: Dialectic Encounter in Psychology & Education

Angela Mary Lisle

Library of Congress Control Number: 2010906020
ISBN: Hardcover   978-1-4500-9198-5
                  Softcover   978-1-4500-9197-8
                  Ebook   978-1-4500-9199-2

To order additional copies of this book, contact:
Xlibris Corporation
0-800-644-6988
www.xlibrispublishing.co.uk
Orders@Xlibris.co.uk
300283

CONTENTS

Hawthorne Effect in Higher Education
(HE HE)

How can we make people more productive?
We could make their environment pleasant.
Eureka—you mean let them work in surroundings of their own choosing?
No, I mean let them work from home it's cheaper!

How can we ensure they'll work?
Give them an incentive.
You mean financial?
Ah, no, keep them hungry!

But won't people leave HE?
Not if you bring in a monitoring system, something based on the Hawthorne Studies
Monitoring hours of work, pace, duration, you know, monitor their computer usage
Who they talk and interact with i.e. Facebook, MySpace, Twitter, other academics . . .

. . . what their thoughts and feelings are,
Their aspirations, weaknesses, liabilities . . .
We could bring a team of psychologists in to analysis the stuff!
Is all of this ethical?

If you get people to submit to being monitored of their own freewill, why no!
We'll have consent for the monitoring process if we call it development review.
Build in competition, promotion, rewards, sanctions for poor work etc. etc.
But isn't this covert research—are there any drawbacks?

For example, how will we deal with biases and the self-interest of people involved?
How will we deal with friendships, resentment, theft of work, envy, greed . . .
All of these human traits will confound the results—
This includes the monitors as well as the monitored!

Perhaps that's why the original study was called 'The Hawthorne Effects'!
Life within the Hawthorne environment is just so contrived,
Who would want to snuggle into it!
It would be like snuggling into a Hawthorne bush,
Once you're in it, it's hard to free yourself from the thorns!

Author: Angela Mary Lisle (3ʳᵈ July, 2009)

Introductory chapter

This book offers a different view of psychology within education particularly with regards to reflexive practices as the theme as well as the application of the dialectic within psychological theory and practice. The unification of different areas within psychology and neuroscience is current and this book contains both the theory and research in this area and offers newly developed theoretical insights. The book has potential for use as an essential reader for undergraduate and postgraduate courses within the social sciences—courses such as those within education, specifically but not exclusively early year's education, social work/sociology and psychology. In terms of level of education, the book would be best suited to degree and postgraduate levels 4, 5, 6 and 7. The book takes an interdisciplinary approach and covers a number of areas within the social sciences: sociology, education, psychology and the cognitive sciences: neuropsychology, cognitive psychology, and psychophysics. As can seen psychology is the line of symmetry for these approaches to psychology within education.

The aim of the book is to examine reflexive practices within the social sciences; psychology in particular, highlighting its uses and the neuropsychology that underpins it as a meta-cognitive learning style. Central to the examination of reflexive practice is the dialectic. Indeed, when examining the dialectic nature of reflexive practice one gets a full flavour of its ubiquity and each chapter contains theoretical if not research insights which I outlined below.

At the heart of this book is the notion of reflexive practice as a self-reflexive learning style for personal and professional development. Reflexive practice is covered in a multidimensional way. It is examined as part of the personal development of a student, as personal development of the educator and as the thinking style of the individual in the agency-structure dialectic of the global post-modern human condition, and the place of early childhood education, if not education *per sae* within that international contextual framework.

In addition, reflexive practice will be examined as a phenomenon in itself, as a behaviour emergent of biology; Piagetian genetic epistemology within the psychophysical-social context of the Marxian-Vygotskian historical materialist dialectic. It takes an interactionist stance, that is, the view that ontogenetic development is an outcome of nature and nurture. Thus its discourse is mainly psychological with input from other disciplines where there is overlap of concepts or concerns with theoretical insights. Its historical roots start from the enlightenment philosophy through to postmodern philosophy culminating into psychophysics. The philosophy of methodology for example of reflexive practice is examined from the critical theory of Marx and the use of dialectics manifest within post-modernity as the reflexive turn. Both Schön's notion of reflexive practice as a critical conversation with the situation used in education and by psychologists within social work and counselling is examined. The neuropsychology of reflexive practice is also examined, and theorised as the psychophysics of brain-mind. The psychophysics of brain-mind is in addition examined in the way it connects to learning style discourses such as the visual, auditory and kinaesthetic modalities the brain exuberates. These learning styles coalesce within the active learning approach, the Marxian-Vygotskian method of learning.

A secondary thread that runs through the chapters is the notion of dialectic. The individual identity is woven with the richness senses bring; and values that emotions weave, with the evolving world, as one of the couplet agency-structure dialectic in development as a continuous journey. Thus, reflexive practice as a cycle of learning that converts into development and that is the basis for the development of identity: the ontogenetic development of the individual is examined on several plains. For example, what is the child's site of negotiation within the everyday postmodern world; or the student's site of negotiation within this rich construal of discourses and how are the professional and personal juxtaposed; compromised and/or resolved? Reflexive practice as a critique of practice and search for truths within one's social context is catalyst for agency and truth of one's real place within the human condition to bring about emancipation.

Identity formation as a social psychological phenomenon is political as well as cultural, and geographically located. In terms of polity, does parliament stand as guardian to practices within education and social welfare, or, is it but one influence inside the elaborate arena of negotiation? In the present economic climate as western societies embrace their margins; the bounded nations and otherness's; twinned sites of local, and local with global changes, of emergencies, bubble up in a glowing spectra; the UK is but one physicality of many as 'all that is solid melts into air . . .' (Marx, 'Economic', 1890). The final encounter may well be one of total eclipse or a unified glorification as global capitalism struggles for its feet, hovering beneath its own carriage on a blanket of air without the support of the industrial base.

Money—paper alone—will not support the march of capitalist accumulation. As inflation rises and gross national product falls, mindful of the fact that debit accounts are debt in the guise of growth without anything but words on paper to support them; where will the funding for education, or indeed, a welfare system come from?

What does the future hold for education and a welfare system? Is education to be a personal endeavour as the individual identity connects to the web of information the Internet offers and whilst business waxes and wanes with the move into global pockets of socialism what does this suggest of any future welfare system?

Where within Adam Smith's 'Wealth of Nations' did it suggest the state should dictate social-co-operative support to monopolistic and/or dictatorial ex-appropriation of taxes in the guise of government expenditure? The 'invisible hand' has now lost its glove: have monopolies and oligarchies become the new socialism or it just another way of working for Ford? How will the phenomenology of spirit unfold?

These questions are paramount in an ever-changing world in which reflexive practice is the only way through as the dialectic key to change.

Brief tour of chapters

One—The reflexive return of modernity: Post-modernity as a mission of progress

The historical outline of modernity, enlightenment philosophy and the reflexive practice of post-modernity marks the onset of chapter one. The question asked is, are we embraced by a *'Post-modernity, Post-structuralism or High-modernity?'* When examining the phenomena at the core of the discourse of the postmodern reflexive turn, sections sub-headed *'What Makes Post-modernity what it is, is the Reflexive Turn!'*, the work of Professor Ian Parker *'Discourse Discourse Tral la la!'* and Erica Burman captured in *'After the Piagetian Revolution: Not'*, as examples of post-modern reflection and the postmodern reflexive turn are excavated before continuing onto the meanings behind Dahlberg's *'Controlling Quality in Education: Multiple Languages of Evaluation and Reflection'*. Dahlberg develops through the work of Foucault, a notion of a postmodern education approach using alternative conceptualisations of quality that are then followed by MacNaughton's application of Foucault to early year's education to evaluate sites of identity negotiation of the child and practitioner within the early year's education sector. On a practical level this chapter helps to unravel some of the confusion about what post-modernity, post-structuralism and high-modernity are meant to be.

Standing outside of this looking in is Stewart Parker's work in the section titled *'Deconstructing the Postmodern Teacher: Technical Rationalist or Reflective Practitioner?'* which actually stands as critique to reflexive practice discourse, suggesting its mission as a conveyor of truth is overstated. The chapter ends with a notion that reflexive practices lead to several perspectives, the conglomerate of which reveal the whole as a patchwork perspective of reality thus truth: My conclusions however not Stewarts, who prefers the notion of language games. As one subject in a chain of language to another (Nietzsche), I am always mindful of the Hegelian spirit in the process of becoming, never to be objectified and therefore to stand as a hologram somewhat like Descartes' phantom: will the ghost solidify or vaporise? The quandary leads nicely into chapter two where the philosophy of reflexivity as a research method is deliberated.

Two—All hail reflexivity!

The title of chapter two suggests the rejoice of many at the thought of, or discovery of, a discourse that allows us to salvage a notion of truth many hold dear—one in which all discourses play a part as stories intermingle like individual dictates to reality. Action research as a form of social inquiry stands in defence of reflexivity as we ask, *'What is it and what is its purpose?'* Critical psychology and reflexivity form part of the theoretical underpinnings to action research and once this is established within the chapter, it then moves forward to look at the individual in a scientific community of practitioners *'From wo/men the scientist to the scientific community'*—action research, critical theory and transcendental realism, are outlined including Habermas' theory of hermeneutically critical-emancipatory interpretivism. Abduction is also discussed as a method of social inquiry that unites action research, critical psychology and social constructionism with the reflexive practice cycle. The problems involved in this unification are assessed. Teaching and Learning in an atmosphere of reflexivity, involving doubly double hermeneutics, grounds practice and the reflexive practice cycle can be shown to be as useful to practitioner educators as it is to social works or those within counselling as a way of understanding and dealing with practitioner work on a daily basis: Or anyone who reflects on practice as a means to improving it. Indeed, it can be shown that within the execution of a laboratory experiment, the natural scientist actually engages in, yes you got it, reflexive practices using the reflexive practice cycle: plan, act, observe and reflect, if necessary, re-plan. This is the joy of reflexivity, hence the title of the chapter, 'All hail reflexivity!'

Three—Reflexive Practice: Maintaining interaction in the zone of proximal development

Having fully digested the discourses of reflexive practice in the latter two chapters, in chapter three, the reader is presented with a small-scale study using reflexive practice teaching as a methodology. The purpose as with teaching practices generally is to assess and/or examine the teaching and learning process, such as the learning achieved by student-participants and how it takes place with learning enhancement as an outcome. It is suggested that part of the teaching and learning process will be to develop self-reflexive learning and self-monitoring skills of students to allow them to develop into self-reflexive and independent learners. The presage factors that reveal themselves during the teaching and learning process are discussed as are the insights gained through the practitioner-educator reflecting on the teaching process. It is suggested that dialectical reflection/observation, and critical analysis and evaluation, of both teacher and students leads to a more fruitful educational encounter. Insights from this chapter are further investigated in chapter four, five and six. The theoretical framework for the enhancement of the teaching and learning process is based on Marxian-Vygotskian psychology: social constructionism. The analysis section however introduces insights using theory and research from cognitive psychology and connectionism.

Four—God said let there be light: The psychophysics of brain-mind

Clarifying Marx's dialectical historical materialism, and its biological and sadly for some, reductionist underpinnings, fills chapter four. The subject matter of this chapter was at one point felt to be too biological for general social science use, but as knowledge progresses and develops, it appears such diversity is expected as we move towards a more diverse approach to psychology and education. Thus neuron cells with synaptic connections, the dopaminergic modulatory system, first and second order messenger system, and the central nervous system, complete with the Marxian notion of dialectical historical materialism make up the theoretical framework for brain-mind as brain/biology conducts electrochemical messages—ideas, which on a parallel plain material practices and the sensory experiences they entail, produce ideas. Ideas in turn, which guide practice: the dialectic of brain-mind is what takes place in the individual as practice and theory—both actions of the individual—lead to the development of concepts and ideas. One might suggest the dialectic of brain-mind is the dialectic of top-down and bottom-up cognitive processes. The natural sciences have learned a great deal from the social sciences through interdisciplinary investigates and cross fertilisations. I hope this chapter can be put to use the same way.

Five—Assessing learning styles of adults with intellectual difficulties

Chapter three was a small-scale study. Reflexive practice as a self-reflexive learning style was explored and the cognitive and meta-cognitive processes discussed. In a similar way, chapter five outlines an experimental study of the usefulness of a computer assessment package for assessing learning styles. The learning styles assessed were the visual, auditory and kinaesthetic (VAK). This field experiment in itself is not ground breaking but the insights drawn reveal the contingencies involved when theoretical knowledge is watered down and teaching practice becomes robotic and lacking in reflexive practices. This proposition does not refer to the teacher-assessor who assisted the experiment however, who was actually a dedicated practitioner, it refers to the wider use of VAK to assess learning styles in primary schools before primary school teachers were expected to be in command of the theory behind the learning style system and its uses. The VAK learning styles approach for example was in extensive use across the UK and throughout the education system and it can be show that without practitioner knowledge of its theoretical underpinnings it can be used inappropriately and *may* cause underdevelopment of learning modalities that are not integrated into a self-reflexive learning plan. This led to a move within academia to stop using the VAK learning styles assessment approaches to student aided learning. However, having fully grappled with the theory behind the VAK learning styles, I am of the opinion that it is not the learning styles that are wrong, it is the way they are applied. For example, the key is not to single out one learning style above all the others as the one and only learning style for that particularly student; it is to use it as a leaver into learning whilst at the same time (if possible, for example if the student is partly sighted or hard of hearing these modalities are harder to develop) developing the other learning styles either through direct self-instruction or via multi-sensory teaching—Sprenger (2003) for example, in *'Differentiation through Learning Styles'*, develops a framework for using the VAK approach alongside individual learning plans. This chapter stands as testimony to the notion that both theory and practice are essential elements of a psychology of education.

Six—Neuro-cognitive psychology and education: Mapping neuro-cognitive processes and structures to learning styles, can it be done?

The sixth chapter continues the interdisciplinary theme. However, this time reflexive practice is viewed through the theoretical lens of the cognitive sciences. Putting things in context, the mapping of neurophysiology to learning styles, an outline of synaptogenesis, the schematic illustration of multi-sensory interactions of reflexive practice and its grounding as educational pedagogy, and reflexive practice as a brain modulator are illustrated using diagrams such as an adapted version of Morton and Firth's Model of brain/mind/behaviour interrelations (1995). The Reflexive Practice cycle showing the dialectic of brain-mind and foci of attention using reflexive practice as an equivalent to working memory (Baddeley et al) are explored. The reification and scepticism associated with such highly theoretical propositions is also explored—the conclusions reached? Once again, the theoretical and experimental work of the cognitive sciences informs the social sciences—a unification of cognitive sciences and education is the outcome. As always, the unification is perhaps one sided as educators struggle with the thought of learning 'heavy theoretical knowledge' and these issues interfere with advances in this area. Nonetheless, advances have been made through the work of Doctor Howard-Jones and Professor Geake, but to name a few who embrace the unification.

Seven—The Consequences of crossing disciplinary boundaries: Cognitivism, connectionism, constructionism and emergent intelligence

Whilst educators are reluctant to engage with theory, within the area of cognitive sciences such as psychology there is a flurry of activity as more and more research and theoretical discoveries emerge, in particular, within the paradigms of artificial intelligence, robotics, neuroscience, and neuropsychology. It appears that no matter how hard we try to hold back technology and the marriage between disciplines, the more virile they become. Chapter eight therefore looks at the developments within the cognitive sciences as the brain meets the machine and takes over! The way developments in one field have led to developments in the other is remarkable, even fascinating when you consider the innovations: just how does the mind control a computer mouse for example and who would have thought computer simulations could produce theoretical insights to evolutionary cognitive psychology, as Pinker's theory (1997) suggests it does. Thus, this chapter whilst outlining the developments within the cognitive sciences, and as discoveries from laboratory work are taken into education practice—we witness developments in brain based teaching, the revelations from both areas are equally insightful to education and the cognitive sciences generally. In addition in this chapter, I develop theoretical insights locating mind-brain processes such as the rehearsal loop much like Nyberg & Tulving et al (2000) make suggestions about neurological networks underlying episodic memory and Ranganath & Cohen et al (2005) suggest areas of the brain associated with the links between episodic memory and working memory maintenance: dorsolateral prefrontal cortex and the hippocampus. The biological processes that underpin the process of ontogenetic development are also explored.

Eight—Agency-structure in social spaces: Reflexive practice & personal development planning

As we move from one chapter to another, the interplay between meta-cognition or reflexive practice as a way of modulating learning whether in education or on a person level becomes more of a mission as we encounter the complexities of life in a postmodern world. As the students had in the latter chapter, we all have sites of negotiation for identity development. These sites of development become more and more complex the more complex society becomes.

How do we as individuals develop identities that suit the economic system whilst maintaining a balance between working life and social life? What exactly is expected of an early year's pedagogue/practitioner in the postmodern international world imbued with a multitude of perspectives? This chapter embraces 'Education in an International Context' and the role of a postmodern early year's pedagogue/ practitioner within it.

Nine—The future of psychology and education

Identity development on a personal as well as a professional level involves some form of self-actualisation. How do we achieve self-actualisation in the present global system of identity development? Chapter nine contains discussions about identity development using the humanistic approach to self-reflexive identity development. Within education, it manifests itself as the student-centred learning approach where the educator takes the role of facilitator. By exploring identity development through reflexive practice what transpires is a notion of self-reflexive learning and development as the process of becoming, where self-actualisation is the carrot before the cart as the 'phenomena of spirit' unfolds.

Managing ourselves as self-reflexive learners is one way of developing 'model' citizens. In primary education students are introduced to citizenship in the form of multiculturalism in the postmodern metropolis and its insertion of the rights agenda. Personalised learning takes the form of individual learning plans or self-reflexive learning logs. In secondary education the rights agenda becomes fully integrated into the internal workings of the school polity as students develop a syndicate through which they achieve a unified presences as a student pressure group. Along the path of development, students are instructed to keep personal logs, or diaries mapping their development much like a personal biography; a narrative that they themselves have mapped. It is expected as part of formal learning, and students will record on the Intranet where personal development planning is logged and assessed either by the student or educator, their biographical/personal narrative. Facebook for example is a personal form of logging or blogging that is recorded and changed as identity develops. There are advantages and disadvantages to recording personal development on an Intranet or Internet site and these will be debated. In the formal context, students write short-term goals, medium term goals and long-term goals with milestones to pass and objectives to be achieved. Each student has the potential to map her/his own future professional and personal development—a plotting of self-actualisation if you will. Just how feasible is this? Plotting self-actualisation using self-reflexive learning and self-management is critically assessed.

Chapter One

The reflexive return of modernity: Postmodernism

Modernity

I want to begin this chapter firstly by discussing what post-modernity is, what it is not, and its various insertions across the social sciences and humanities. To do this, we first need to address what modernity is, because post-modernity has to be something that modernity is not: Something more than, or different to it to merit the name post-modernity.

It was initially thought that modernity was recognised in the arts as a change in society, a movement captured by the modern artists of the time. Baudelaire (1859-60) when he wrote 'The Painter of Modern Life' gave birth to the term 'modernity'. He used it to mean the present—'now'. Art works that portrayed 'now' the present as opposed to the past were regarded as paintings of modernity (Derek Sayer, 1991).

But long before this, philosophers signalled the initial development of modernity starting with the 'enlightenment'—the development of empiricism and positivism within the social sciences based on the natural science model of investigation and the development of the industrial and the democratic revolutions. Indeed Stuart Hall (1992) in 'Formations of Modernity' outlines the formations of modernity as processes involving social, culture, political and economic changes. In terms of cultural change for example, John Locke (1632-1704) opposed the 'divine rights of kings' and the infallibility of the absolute truth of religion. His paper 'Essay Concerning Human Understanding' (1690) discusses the insertion that all knowledge is based on facts, things that all human beings can apprehend through their senses. It marked the onset of empiricism and positivism in Britain. Locke's thoughts were influenced by the work of Greek philosophers such as Aristotle's 'Metaphysics', particularly, physics (senses) 'how could anyone know if he were not furnished with the capacity of perceiving by sense?' (Aristotle, 384-322 BCE, in Rev. John H. M'Mohon, 1879). This is the idea that knowledge is acquired through the senses, by empirical/experiential means. And Plato's ideas on reason, which account for the fact that humans can choose what to do through logical thinking—we can perceive things and use this knowledge to reason and guide actions to successful conclusions. Inductive reasoning of the knowledge of things perceived through the senses is the onset of empiricism and positivism. So, empiricism and positivism together involve experiencing the world via the senses and using reason—logical inductive and deductive reasoning to determine our actions in the world around us. This way we can be reasonably positive about our empirical experiences.

A second paper 'Two Treatises on Government' (1690) written by Locke had an enormous influence on politics in that it is documented in historical, philosophical and sociological literature as contributing to the development of the French revolution. Locke had to leave Britain in view of his beliefs—he went to France and met with David Hume (1711-1776) who was like-minded in that he also held rational believes about society based on reason. The French Revolution went down in history as the 'triumph of reason over religion'. It involved the spread of political ideals such as 'liberty, equality and fraternity'. In America, this manifest itself in the American Independence movement as the liberation of America from British influences—a movement towards 'fraternity, freedom and justice', hence the Statue of Liberty in New York. Here then, we have a concept of modernity that involved the use of empirical experiential knowledge to reason positively about the 'human condition' and emancipate humanity from traditional knowledge that had become outdated and not beneficial to society generally, only those who held power in terms of that traditional knowledge, property or land rights in terms of kings-man-ship or Lordom. Thus not only did this cultural change lead to political change, it also resulted in social change—the onset of the demise of the aristocracy and more freedom and equality in social relationships. Hall (1992) very rightly points out that the process of change was not necessarily the sole influence of culture but a combination of factors in all spheres: cultural, political, social, economic and I would suggest perhaps even territorial. This stands in opposition to the single cause modernisation theories that took as the motivating cause one or the other composite forces for societal change. For example, Marx suggested economic relations to be the main causal factor for societal change and Weber culture.

Sociologists then as a referential of modern society similarly adopted the notion of modernity and became known as modernisation theorist. For Marx and Engels it was seen as characterising unique social relationships compared to pre-existing societal arrangements. This had important economic consequences as well as social and political ones:

> 'This notion of modernity was anticipated by Karl Marx and Friedrich Engels in *The Communist Manifesto*, a work written at the beginning of that 'Year of Revolution', 1848, when *ancient regimes* momentarily looked set to crumble the length and breadth of Europe.' (Sayer, 1991, p. 9).

A process of industrialisation swept the continent of Europe and elsewhere, starting in Britain. Modernity marked a distinction between the present social relationships, and those of the past social relationships of feudalism. In feudal society the social relationships between the land owners—the lords and barons, and the serfs—peasantry who lived and worked on the lord's land; were that of landed lord and the serfs who were his property/slaves. In return for working for free on his land, the lord gave the serfs/peasants food and dwellings. The lord would also protect them but would call upon them in times of war to do battle at his side.

The serfs/peasants where allowed to work the land in return for food—the crops they had grown for example; the lord keeping the surplus crops as a form of taxation. The lords and barons were the aristocracy across Europe who secured their position in life on the grounds of the ownership of land and property and their past gallantry in battles against unwanted visitors—'barbarians' (as they were referred to in earlier literature on the topic, for example, Marx). Few wo/men were free—it was in effect serfdom—peasant slavery. The lord not only fed the peasantry he also gave them common land to live on and use. Overtime the serfs and burgesses bought up common land as the demise of the aristocracy ensued.

Burgesses were free wo/men—freemasons who roamed from one town/village to another, exchanging goods such as vegetables and wheat for the serfs, who were not allowed to cross the boundaries of one lord onto another lord's land. The burgesses were almost like merchants. They would take wheat from one serf village, keep some of it for their troubles, and take the remainder to the next village and exchange it for fruit say that s/he would then take back to the first village. This signalled the beginning of a second change in the social relationships, in that, bartering became common. The next change occurred because, if a villager could not afford to give the burgess some of the food, the burgess would carve a debt notch in her/his walking stick to remind her/himself of the debt. Some of these debts were repaid in kind with possessions such as metal objects like tools or jewellery. The burgess could then exchange the metal objects or jewellery, sometimes pieces of gold and later coins, for food or anything else s/he wished to purchase. Thus spawn the beginning of the modern monetary system. Coins were just at valuable as jewellery and became our modern day money; an observation made by Sir I. Newton!

The introduction of gold and other precious metals thus contributed to the change in social relationship as well as the burgesses' influence (i.e. the geographical movement of burgesses from one village to another) because the burgesses started exchanging gold coins for goods rather than bartering one good for another so that the exchange of value became based on coins/money. This therefore marked the very beginning of modernity for Marx—a society in which people could sell goods for money that could then be used to purchase different goods. It was the beginning of the free market economy. The cotton industry developed at this time because serfs/common wo/men would make thread or wool on spinning wheels to weave into cloth. Each household in a village would own a spinning wheel and the burgess would buy surplus weave/cloth produced by the households as well as the surplus vegetables they grew on the common land. It was the beginning of manufacturing—the cottage industry.

Rather than the power in society being based solely on the ownership or non-ownership of land and property, it was now also based on the exchange of goods for money—coins regarded as having equivalent value to the goods. The money could be used to buy anything—machinery for example. The burgess got wealthier and bought land on which to build the first factories. Those peasants/commoners who did not own land would travel to the factories to work. In the end, the factories could produce cotton cheaper than the cottage workers and so put the cottage industry out of business.

At this point, the relations in society had changed in that wo/men started to sell their labour power for money. The relationships between one wo/man and another wo/man therefore were based on monitory value—the exchange of value in a free market economy because by this time, wo/men were free. They no longer belonged to a lord or lived on the lord's land, they were free to live where they chose and work in factories if they so wished. It was a society in which at the base, was the cotton and woollen industry in which relations were monitory. This entailed the exchange of value in terms of work in factories for money for the proletariat-serfs/commoners, or if you owned the factory, expropriation of the surplus value produced as profit—capital gained—for the factory owner to keep on account that s/he owned the factory and the machinery. And at the superstructure, the relationships were that men were free but either extremely poor—proletariat-serfs/commoners—or extremely rich—the factory owners and the land and property owners. Unequal relationships based on the unequal distribution of goods and money.

In fact, although wo/men were free, Marx felt that the arrangements were worse under the capitalist system than that of the feudal system because factory owners could pay any amount for the labour power of the proletariat-serfs and usually paid the very minimum a man could live on. A sum that would keep her/him alive long enough to make the factory owner profits and if the labourers died it did not matter because they were lots of poor landless people to take their place. Under the feudal lords, wo/men were not free but they did not die for a living wage; they were fed and housed in return for working the land.

The relations under the capitalist system had become those based on exploitation of the most extreme kind (Marx, 1848, 'Communist Manifesto'). Whilst the factory owners became richer and richer, the poor became poorer and poorer. Capital gain was the main characteristic of this societal type. It was what Marx called capitalism. A new *modern* form of social relationship based on capital gain in a free market economy: modernity. The unequal appropriation of surplus value (good and profits) produced was accepted on account of the law of ownership: The legal ownership of the means of production (hence the move by past Labour parties to nationalise companies thereby making the goods and profit more equally distributed via the state, but the lack of competition makes nationalisation a non-obtainable option).

For Marx Weber (1920) in 'The Protestant Ethic and the Spirit of Capitalism', capitalist society became more and more technical, rational and bureaucratic as industry grew. As capital increased, technology increased to beget even more capital.

Given that science can still influence government to some degree for example with claims to truth over problems like global warming, social problems (paedophilia and marital breakdown) and economic crisis and solutions (inflationary prices and pay-freezes), philosophers have got it wrong. Empiricism and positivism are still there but even-tempered through notions of scrutiny and examination via the relevant scientific community, and through media coverage, the populace at large. All three political ideological regimes want to operate in the middle ground!!! Is this postmodernism? I do not think it is because all three political regime types want to operate in terms of liberal values—the enlightenment project has been high-jacked by Joe Bloggs, everyone's doing it! It is the height of modernity as Giddens suggests (Giddens did however reject positivism in favour of interpretivism and hermeneutics but I shall deal with this in the next chapter).

For example, Neil Smith (1992) in 'Geography, Difference and the Politics of Scale' discusses 'the geographical turn'. Influenced by the work of Foucault (1986) and others such as Soja (1989) Smith presents a notion of post-modernity, as a society where spatial differences are the sites for agency. Smith suggests the 'spaces of difference' is a way of putting 'space' or context with its unique characteristics back into critical theory. Smith further suggests that it stands opposed to Giddens' structuration theory in which agency is lost because of the inarticulate notion of front and back binarisms that do not really project a visual understanding of the individual spaces of difference. Geography is important however when considering agency whether we see the geography as physical space or metaphorical intellectual space. In terms of physical space for example, Giddens refers to the North-South divide within the UK as well as class geographical localities. In terms of metaphorical space, 'the space of difference' (Foucault 1986, post-modernity as 'the epoch of space') or 'site of difference' (Michele Barett, 1987; cited in Smith, 1992) is of a particular characteristic of the difference, usually the salient characteristic (age, gender, ethnicity, race, class or disability) which becomes salient precisely because needs associated with that characteristic are not met under present political, cultural, economic and/or social relationships so agency within the spaces of difference act as pressure groups to vocally protest and procure beneficial changes for their group.

Giddens' structuration theory refers to the process by which 'class' as a social position bestowed via our occupational status, and position within the social structures, becomes real and reproduced in everyday life as lived social positions of people—agents. The relationship between structure and agent is dialectic. Agents can affect structure and structure can limit agency. Giddens calls people agents, because he sees them as having the propensity for action—doing something that will make their social position more comfortable and bearable (although he does put straight-jackets on his agents given he sees structure as more powerful than the atomistic type of agency he sees before him). In the height of modernity, the social positions people occupy are numerous and interlaced with other characteristics such as age, race, ethnicity, gender and disability. What has emerged is as Smith puts it 'a mosaic of geographic localities with intricacies bound together in spaces of difference' (Smith, 1992, p. 67). Basically, each individual has a social position that is geographically located and imbued with economic, political and cultural arenas that people socialise through.

The socialising arenas are the mechanism through which agency comes into being: Giddens' localities—described by others as 'spaces of difference' and 'sites of difference' through which groups or individual agency pressure the government for action to be taken to improve social well-being. Or at least through the localities or arenas, agency can communicate the problems that will eventually surface to a level that a third person can take action. Smith rejects Giddens' structuration theory suggesting that 'Time-space is insufficiently integrated into structurationism' (Smith, 1992, p. 67). There is not the space here to argue Giddens' point (or at least modify it); it will be done in a later publication, when I unite Giddens' structuration theory with the social identification approach to inter-group relations. For now, I want to continue with the basic theory of agency-structure as a dynamic prism through which we can view the reflexive turn: The tool of sites/spaces of difference within the social systems arenas.

Agency can affect structure and structure can affect agency in localities—'spaces of difference'. The spaces of difference are thus context dependent (located geographically, physically and metaphysically in terms of the characteristics of spaces—individual identities, given that we take our identities from the social, political, economic, cultural and geographical arenas) and are time related. The spaces of difference nonetheless, have become so eclectic that as agency goes, the power to influence structure in any major way can be lost according to Smith (1992). The spaces have become atomised with less power to influence government policy because a smaller group has less than the optimal amount of pressure at hand. I see things differently because from the characteristics that form 'the space of difference', one will become salient which we will also have in common with others who occupy a similar position (is this Marx's consciousness or what I refer to in chapter 4 as the global consciousness of mind thus social-cognition with the help of GABA gamma aminobutyric/ rays brain modulation?). Therefore, the salient characteristic/ difference of space will be the characteristic that orchestrate agency.

The Salient characteristic that moves agency will be made salient through 'a reflexive conversations with the situations in which we find ourselves' (Schön's, Reflexive Conversation with a Situation). I examine this concept in a later chapter when looking at the agency of students, staff and others in the development of social spaces within the early year's service sector: education, health care and welfare, that is, the development of early year's practitioner statue as professionalism in social spaces. When uniting the notion of spaces of difference (locality/sites) to that of the reflexive turn, we get rather an energising picture in which all social agents can from their individual localities/spaces or sites engage in reflexive practices. Has reflexivity become omnipresent? If so, Marxian consciousness is not lost, it is still there, labour has not 'dimed' the brains of the labouring classes to the degree that they cannot still reflect on their site/spaces or localities of difference and voice their needs.

Karl Marx was one of the main advocates of activity theory, the agency of the working classes; his main premise was that ideas for social change come from alienated material practice and the critique of such practice. What Marx meant by this, was that the human species 'agents in localities' or 'spaces of difference' engage in activity as part of the ongoing cycle of needs in a material world. At times when human creative experience becomes alienated—difficult and uncomfortable, even detrimental to health and well-being, the psychological experience of alienation emanating from the problematic material practice leads to thoughts of and about changes in that material practice and the locality of, sites of or spaces of difference. Through change, i.e. acting on solutions to problematic material existence, material existence becomes less alienated and the psychic tension reduced because the problem is confronted. Both individual 'needs' and 'common needs' can be or are met through putting into practice the ideas developed from the alienated material practice and human psyche is objectified through this process which is the dialectic movement of Marx's historical materialism: the historical development of human essence (including his faculties) and society in terms of changed social structures: The dialectics of Giddens' agency-structure.

To recap then, what characterises post-modernity, as the term is being used, is the reflexive turn—the acknowledgement that we do need to scrutinise, to look back at what we have achieved so far along the road to progress to evaluate the results in terms of truths, AND the consequences of truths in terms of the social, political and economic consequences, as well as the texts written with the various interpretations and the meanings researchers and people give to the context in which they find themselves. The main characteristic therefore is *the ubiquity of the reflexive turn*. Everyone is doing it! The common wo/man is no longer without his/her faculty of conscious thought! The toil is no more! (Would you put critique in writing please and email it to me so that I can address each one in turn: aml483@tutor.open.ac.uk)

Within sociology, it is acknowledged that historical societal change from feudalism to modernism occurred in all of the social systems: the political, the economic, the social and the cultural, and that the changes were interlinked in terms of dynamism and construction. Philosophers are more concerned with the cultural changes in empiricism and positivism and one might suggest that these changes were the bedrock for the others. What appears to characterise all change is this reflexive turn. The binding of metaphysics to physics in an ever spiralling movement of reflexive action: the reflexive turn at the height of modernity is visualised as a spiral of continual action: constant relative motion of the dialectic of theory and practice, physics and metaphysics as we engage in the reflexive turn. All hail reflexivity!

What makes post-modernity what it is, is the reflexive turn

It is suggested that the reflexive turn started in the 1930s with critical rationalism. In was presented to us by Popper (1934) in 'The Logic of Scientific Discovery'. Popper was particularly concerned with the use of logical positivism in the social sciences especially the way observation was being used on which to formulate theory. For example, 'pure observable facts' are imbued with interpretations that are subjective not objective, and observations can be distorted. For example, the

Romans (maybe even the Greeks before them) observed that the world was flat and the stars hung from a metal-plate in the sky. Theory in other words, thought to be the sole progeny not ancestry of observable facts is in fact constructed when we lay on the objective facts our interpretations of them (Blaikie, 1993, p. 25). Hermeneutics—the interpretation of scripts, particularly the various interpretations of the 'Bible' also took impetus at this time, especially since it was becoming apparent that theory does not always correspond with facts. Hermeneutics which actually dates back to 18th century French, 'hermeneutikos', from Greek meaning 'expert in interpretation' (Etymological entry, Collins Concise Dictionary: Plus, 1989, p. 585) was re-established but with a difference.

Hermeneutics was now not just wrapped-up in the discovering of the best interpretation, it was also to involve the discovery of the context of the written text—the historical-cultural-temporal moment in which it was written complete with the author's worldview, for example, beliefs about things such as the nature of the roundness or flatness of the planet. Thus, a notion developed whereby text were examined for the worldview of the authors and interpreters—this was very important because if you lived in Greco-Roman times you may very well believe that the world was flat and that if you sailed off into the horizon you might just fall off the end. Thus someone with this belief would have a very different worldview to someone who believed the world to be round as we do now.

So then, we can see that one's beliefs have an impact on the interpretations we come up with and the theories we build as well as Popper's notions about the subjectivity of interpretations. The transcendental ultimate realities generated by the 'Hermits' of Greco-Roman times may be very meaningful and have some correspondence with 'a reality', but it appears it is not always the case that 'a reality' is 'the reality'. Sometimes what we think we see or hear or feel is distorted in the case of the flatness or roundness of the planet, by distance. The reflexive turn then is an acknowledgement that we can get it wrong and we need to examine what we have done or what has been written in the past to see if it has any bearings on the present in light of the ongoing accumulation of knowledge. This is a faculty we all possess and use when we engage in introspection, or self-analysis, and not just the analysis and evaluation of the objects in the world.

The reflexive turn in the social sciences is applied to anthropology (Richard Fardon, 1992), technology (John Bowers, 1992), developmental psychology (Erica Burman) language and texts; and to different meanings produced from texts and observations. All of which are generative of context, space and time. This notion of the reflexive turn has now entered most social science disciplines if not all. Ian Parker for example (1992) in 'Discourse Discourse: Social Psychology and Post-modernity', examines the way firstly, the reflexive turn was suggestive of the rigorous critique of the social psychological discipline itself and now to the way discourse *per sae* is examined. I shall now examine the reflexive practices within psychology, care and education.

Discourse discourse tral la la!

Ian Parker (1992) suggests that the reflexive turn during the 1960s and 1970s was aimed at evaluating social psychological theory and methods. This still continues of course but not with the same energy because much of the unravelling of distortions in theory and methods has been tackled. He witnessed a move towards the examination of discourse in text and narration; particularly the narratives of ordinary wo/men. Parker calls the shift in the object of investigation, 'the turn to language'. Parker highlights the way earlier advocates of 'the turn to language' Wetherell's (1987) 'Discourse and Social Psychology' and Harre and Secord (1972) and Gauld and Shotter (1977) were not taken seriously—not even as a 'fad' in mainstream social psychology, which insisted and still does 35 years on, in halloing the laboratory experiment with all its abnormalities.

Intellectual debates regarding meta-reality and such like were ignored or not taken seriously; the sand did not seem to shift beneath their feet. Parker suggests this to be a political move, aimed at maintaining the mantle of science. Whilst donning the mantle of science is useful and even desirable, the question remains, should this be the only method of investigation or is there a necessity for other forms of investigation. And on this note, I must agree with Ian, there is more to life than what takes place in a laboratory and one can in fact benefit from the research of the other. This much has been revealed throughout the history of scientific investigation itself. A mixture of methods will produce differences in perspective and sometimes findings but this all adds to the build up of knowledge that is multi-dimensional and I think if done with rigour, knowledge that is much more valid than that obtained using only one method such as the experiment. Point accepted (Kelle, 2001) that in some cases the diversity of characteristics of the data can depending on the mix of methods produce data with internal contradictions due to some incompatibilities inherent in the mixed methods approach. (See Udo, Kelle, 2001, *Sociological Explanations between Micro and Macro and the Integration of Qualitative and Quantitative Methods*').

The need for discourse analysis as Parker suggests, is immense. For example, does writing a science paper in the 3rd person singular actually make the research more scientific? Well not really it only makes it *sound* more scientific! Discourse analysis also opens up the debate around notions of ethics. For example, experiments such as Zimbardo's (1973) 'Stanford Prison Experiment' and Milligram's (1974) 'Obedience to Authority' have been and are subject to rigorous scrutiny because although they shed light on some shocking human tendencies towards the macabre, they were not ethical. In the Zimbardo experiment, managers—appointed prison officers abused their power by totally de-humanising the managed prisoners.

Prison officers would bray on doors and shout at prisoners to remove any coats/garments hung behind doors if managers could not see the prisoners through the door windows. They were allowed no breaks, were made to stay in their cells/rooms, and eat at their desks. They were told an 'open door policy was in operation' and that they had to leave room doors open thereby removing any privacy. Verbal ridicule was used when prisoners were assessed for parole at review meetings. Prisoners would be cross-examined by two managers (prison officers) and shouted at; their responses would be twisted and turned against them. Any attempt to rectify an untruth was regarded as arrogance or weakness and managers would retaliate with punishment such as solitary confinement. Mental cruelty was the norm, inflicted on the prisoner put in solitary confinement. Other prisoners were encouraged to, and all of the managers (prison officers) would; laugh at and ridicule the solitary confined until broken (i.e. request the psychological torment stopped). But the managers got out of hand and continued the psychological torment knowing the solitary confined was in tears and pain. This was regarded as a weakness that any one of management 'calibre' would not do: Crying was for the weak. The other prisoners were encouraged to 'grass on the solitary confined' if they discovered anything 'anything at all they had on them'. So the other prisoners got extremely inventive, suggesting the solitary confined lacked manners—would join in conversations without being invited for example. Or the solitary confined would move furniture in the room without asking permission.

Zimbardo stopped the experiment only when physical abuse got out of hand, although the psychological torment was just as damaging. So, what started as a request for a 'level playing field' turned into a psychological torture chamber for any prisoner the managers felt did not 'fit in'. Either because the solitary confined was conscious of 'the laws and proper procedures' and was therefore deem to 'get above station', or their ideas were claimed and mangers did not want the prisoners to get recognition for them, the managers wanted recognition for themselves and were in a position to do this because of their power differential. The solitary confined would be de-humanised and put in the 'prisoner status role'. They would not be allowed to leave the torture chamber without references from the managers who would not give any knowing the solitary confined was in pain and liable to retaliate. They wanted the solitary confined to break—to succumb to psychological breakdown—psychosis or neurosis which ever occurred first. After all, the managers wanted a level play field on their terms.

Some theories or pieces of research are perhaps not so alarming but they are demonstratively wrong in their 'claims to truth' exaggerating findings far beyond their scope of being. Some academies have principles that they hold above the norms of humanity. Then shout from their ivory towers—'kill the virgin she's positively feral!' at every new discourse they find alien to the existing culture of the institution, regardless of ethics, truth or humanity. Therefore, Parker advocates the use of discourse analysis to deconstruct social psychology texts because it is one way of uncovering discrepancies in the text and disciplinary knowledge claims. We see it as reflexive in that truth claims are scrutinised including the data on which they are based. The reflexive gaze is also applied to texts *per sae*; continuing on the lines of Foucault (1980) for example, the critical appraisal of documents particularly bureaucratic ones containing 'medico-administrative knowledge' Foucault suggests from the 19th century onwards, has revealed some interesting political relations within institutions and the way they are supported by academic discourse and theory whereby the latter is regarded as 'truth' and 'reality'. I am referring to in particular, Turner's (1987) notion of 'the medicalisation of the human body', particularly females' in terms of menstruation, pregnancy and childbirth. Turner (1987, pp. 37-8) suggests that the doctor has replaced the priest as custodian of social values. Health care is localised in the community car system and has become the agency of surveillance and control.

The Human Genome Project for example, has legitimised the genetic basis of human pathology as if it were 'the truth' when in fact there are several theories that could just as easily explain ontogenetic development of human pathology; the forerunner to phylogenetic development (Such a theory will be diagrammatically illustrated in chapter 4). This is alarming. As Foucault (1980) and later Turner (1987) also points out, the emerging discourse of the 19th century 'the medical discourse' has rendered women hysterical, 'the hysterical women in need of an hysterectomy' and also women as unable to go through childbirth without being hospitalised.

The act of childbirth has been so medicalised that paediatricians will no long wait the full duration of pregnancy, they want the pregnant women in hospital on the date the baby was diagnosed as being 'the true' date of its birth. If a woman goes over the date diagnosed then she will be subjected to the medical procedure of being induced! Caesarean sections are becoming more and more common and in fact may even affect the phylogeny of a given populace if it is over used. Women who have natural births for example, are genetically programmed for this. If something has gone wrong—perhaps women are expected to have too-large-a-baby because the medical model suggests a particular birth weight desirable, thereby putting the mother at risk; to counter this the medical model suggests a caesarean section. Indeed, how can we possibly not have a science dedicated to revealing these distortions in the natural sciences?

A final concept Parker draws attention to is relativism. For example, can research done in one particular socio-historical; cultural-political-economic-territorial context be generalised to another. The answer is not always, and sometimes not at all! In other words, research and truth claims generative of it are relative to that particular worldview and the socio-historical, cultural-political-economic-territorial context. We need the reflexive gaze with all its analytical devices to examine claims of truth if we are to achieve the mantle of science. For after all, without 'true' undistorted claims to truth; science is nothing more than personal stories or narratives, much like the 'grand narratives' written in sociology i.e. Marx's and Weber's modernisation theories and in orthodox medicine i.e. psychiatry where blood-letting was at one time seen as a way of curing hysteria—regarded as a women's disorder.

These days, a women's uterus is still removed but for reasons it is *deemed* acceptable such that she may wish not to have more children or 'would have a healthier life without one?' This is not to suggest that theorists like Marx and Weber were not remarkable men of brilliance; it is just a way of illustrating how changing and shifting society is and one can only catch a glimpse of it. As Marx said (1948, '*Communist Manifesto*') 'All that is solid Melts into Air!' As far as the claim to truth that a woman is healthier without a uterus then perhaps one should ask WHY rather than just accept it, which is what the reflexive turn is all about.

But to return to Parker's argument surrounding narratives, he was reiterating the work of Lyotard (1984a) 'that "meta-narratives" of modern enlightenment culture have given way to little stores which constitute post-modernity, a multiplicity of language games . . . In place of truth, we have perpetual reflection on the impossibility of truth' (Parker, 1992, p. 84). Parker further explains this position as a move towards a fragmented localised picture of meanings and experiences that reveal 'signs of truth reflective of the social context'. Parker regards discourse analysis thus, as a way of 'grounding a critical view of language/personal stories', and this makes it a 'postmodern endeavour':

> 'Reflexivity appears to provide the answer. We turn around and reflect on our language and ourselves. Reflexivity is used to denote our deliberate awareness of our place in things and our difference from others. To reflect thoroughly enough on your activity as a researcher is to problematise your own position as distanced observer, and then to dissolve any space between the topic and the resources you bring to bear upon it. The crueller critics of this state of things say that this is part of a move from parody to pastiche (Jameson, 1984). If you were to reflect on everything what could be more radical than that?' (Parker, 1992, p. 93).

Indeed, this for Parker is a 'depoliticised' stance for it is not about critique for its own sake, much like perspectives under the rubric of psychology might jostle for a position (space of difference even) within the discipline of psychology itself; it is about grasping the true nature of our actions and the context we find ourselves in so that our understanding has bearing on the actual lived context. Lastly is the notion of 'critical distance'. The idea that we should 'stand outside of' the cultures we live', including the social science cultures. This way we will hold a 'critical eye/reflexive gaze' more readily for even our own social psychological practices.

After the Piagetian revolution: Not

This is precisely what Erica Burman (1992, 1993) has done with practices in Developmental Psychology, using the notion of discourse analysis as the postmodern critique—the reflexive analysis of language, Erica has united the two by applying discourse analysis to developmental psychology, particularly Piagetian developmental psychology, from a critical distance. Firstly, Burman draws attention to the fact that assertions about modernity being superseded by post-modernity mask the reality, which is that actually, we are not postmodern in terms of the theory we use in institutions such as the education system. The theory we use to guide practice in education and the care of children generally, for Burman still entails: 'traditional power structures and relationships [that] are either left intact (or still being reproduced) by postmodern culture; and secondly, such [theories and the] theorists are wrong to celebrate post-modernity. For when postmodernism does start to inform, for example, family relations it is not progressive' (Burman, 1992, P. 95).

I must say in a ways I agree with Erica, theory is used to perpetuate inequality particularly when supported by claims of truth about the genetic nature of intelligence for example, and I feel that perhaps also as Erica does, Piagetian theory, because it is a unification of philosophy and biology—'genetic epistemology', it is taken for granted as an assertion that intelligence is innate to the point that each individuals' ontogenetic development can be predicted as uniformally developing at stages within specific unites of time. The whole theory is reflective of the enlightenment philosophy—it is as Erica puts it 'teleological, patriarchal and imperialistic' (Burman, 1992, p. 96). What is perhaps even more important for me, is the way Piagetian theory is used to justify one particular approach in education, that of the 'child-centred approach'. The child-centred approach although in its purest sense has good intentions at heart—we all learn better what we choose to learn and not what we are told to learn; but to practice this approach as 'the approach' because of the influence of Piagetian psychology in education, is a falsehood with a particular nasty twist. Children will learn, and many will learn what they want to learn and not what is in their best interest to learn or what we may want them to learn. And I have just committed an immortal sin here because I have gone against the very philosophy that a critical postmodern reflexivity is about. But I am a pragmatist—I was a child of the 1970s and not the 50s and 60s and I can therefore see the sense in learning how to read and write before leaving school even if it might not be what the child wants to learn at that particular point in time!

To get back to the debate concerning genetic epistemology, it is not that this aspect of the theory is wrong, it is the fact that such theories are taken literally including the stages of development which we now know are misleading and culminate into bad practice within education. The actual concept of genetic epistemology is useful—it illustrates the way an individual can develop genetically within his or her own lifetime. It is the practices that develop from it that are poor constructions of its true essence. For example, we may be born with a brain physiology that is pre-programmed to acquire knowledge of things in a particular way, but during the course of our own lifespan we can develop those structures including the behaviours associated with them. Therefore, the concept of ontogenetic epistemology actually goes against the notion that intelligence is fixed at birth and that it will go through set stages of development. The concept itself is correct, the stages are wrong. Crystallised intelligence for example is the development of language and social skills and research has shown it to develop with age well into retirement age and beyond for those who keep their minds active. It was Piagetian formal operational thinking that was thought not to develop if it had not done so by the age of 11 years, hence the 11 plus examination which purportedly 'creamed' the most intelligent pupils from general education putting them into grammar schools. The Piagetian notion of a time-stage related specific formal operational thinking ability has since been shown to be a misconception. It is through the reflexive-turn, the critical gaze of social psychologists like Erica, untruths and distortions come to the eye.

Similarly, the fact that stage theories are used to support the practice and overt preoccupation of classification and segregation, as Erica says of Foucauldian observations:

'If the history of developmental psychology demonstrate its role as (in a paradoxically conspiratorial terminology) an administrative technology of classification and segregation (of which the Piagetian notion of stages forms merely a contemporary version), what implications does this have for our understanding of its possible effects and functions?' (Burman, 1992, p. 97-98).

This shows to Erica, you and me, that the mechanisms of intervention and social regulation are still there inherent within the version of Piagetian education practiced in the education system of the UK; encrusted in practices aimed specifically at 'gate keeping'; excluding those deemed undesirable from acquiring the strategies essential in the art of formal thinking and therefore from the higher echelons of Dante's dream world (Hell, Purgatory, and Paradise). Such undesirables include women, or anyone alien to European shores; therefore classification reinforces 'The Frontiers of European Identity' (Cohen, 1994) if not the Nordic/Anglo-American male and patriarchal identity. One way the reflexive enterprise has tried to counter the unequal distribution of intellectual identity is to batten the gates requesting equality in terms of gender, un/marital status, class, ethnicity, race and disability but at times with little impact and knowledge of the fact that the battle is a continuous one if equality is ever to be reach or maintained.

Within the family for example there is the continual assertion of equal conjugal-roles. A spin-off of this is the notion that fathers could take-over the task of commuting children to and from school and a cry by women within the early years education sector for the insertion of 'the male role model' into primary education. What a fascinating proposal! What is a male role model and why particularly do we need one in primary education? If we are to achieve equality within the sexes, then why are we re-enforcing the differences between existing female and male roles? What is it that men do in primary education that women cannot or will not do? I can see that there is a male backlash to the female sex equality campaign but do we really want to re-enforce gender-role differences? Erica suggests blurring the distinctions between existing traditional female and male gender-identities 'through notions of androgyny' empowers men because women are further exploited through the exaggeration of their feminine sexual identity. This seems to be the only aspect of traditional female identity males are willing to see females join in equal status with. As Erica also points out, advertising companies use 'pop psychology' to enhance the sale of their produces, and also, it is used to sell a particular identity that men find desirable—*of the female*—one that is dreamed up from hours of fantasizing over the type of women they want to engage in the sexual act.

Thus movements towards equality have resulted in further sexual exploitation usually for the very young inexperienced females who have not the experience to understand that actually, females say no because it is one of the only forms of empowerment we have. I do not suggest a return to 'traditional' gender-role distinctions either. What about all the other identity characteristics we could unleash as part of womanhood such as formal operational thinking for example, industriousness, heroinism, bravado, strength and so on. The move therefore towards equality has resulted in a shambles. The battle for equality is far from over and the reflexive gaze will continue—it is an essential and not an extravagancy.

In its extreme form the construction of intelligence and identity itself, is corporate business: The socially constructed nature of childhood and its influences upon development. There are several fundamental influences that effect childhood identity constructs; social status, economic status, political climate, geographical location and cultural heritage, in addition to family dynamics, family structure, childrearing practices, the education system and position within the family. Play too has its influences on the child's identity and it is socially meaningful and socially constructed on a daily basis. Audrey Curtis (1994) describes the differences in play and toys between cultures. In non-western cultures, children make their own toys or they will engage in the adult roles that Western children learn through playing with toys. In some cultures, the child will actually mother a younger brother or sister, whilst in Western cultures, children play with toys such as dolls and toy prams that are produced for them by large, multi-national corporations. Steinberg, Sharon and Joe Kinchloe (Eds) (1997) in *'Kinder Culture: The Corporate Construction of Childhood'*, examine this relationship.

In Western societies play has manifest itself as a means to enhance child development over the past century or so but does it really always enhance development or slow it down? Identity is also prescribed through advertisements. Boys are always pictured playing with cars, and girls with dolls. Some toys are unisex and educational i.e. Fisher Price. The cloths industry is terribly sexist and prescriptive. Most girl's cloths are pink, sparkling and cute. Boy's cloths casual but de-sexualised. Play in the education system is under continual supervision and Bruner (1993) would argue a product of culture much like children's identities. It developed mainly under the Piagetian legacy;—conservation theory. Piaget remains the dominant psychological resource for professionals yet why not Vygotsky or Bruner? Piaget's impact on Developmental Psychology is so great the others are rendered invisible (Burman)! Well almost, the 'new' Early Years Foundation Stage Practice Guide (May, 2008) has incorporated into it, elements of the Reggio Emilia approach. Thus, citizenship and social skills, with a more co-constructed curriculum timetable rather than Piagetian stages is envisaged. It has been 5 years or so in the making and has been the outcome of discussion by practitioners, trainers, academics up and down the UK, and of course education ministers.

Piaget was interested in genetic epistemology not children according to Erica, who suggests Piaget saw the child as 'the epistemic subject'. He was not trained in psychology and his PhD thesis was rejected for being too eclectic! His work focuses on the individual and the social and cultural factors of education are ignored. Yet his work has been used as standardised assessment in education even though he forcefully argued against this. His work was initially a counter reaction to empiricism, for example, IQ tests, which comes across in his early work that consisted of semi-structured interviews. Later Piaget's work was redeveloped to look at children's actions and not what they said or thought. It appears Piaget realised children's responses in interviews were prone to suggestibility as many of his advocates also discovered (Donaldson and McGarrigle, 1974).

There has been a return to notions of 'listening to the child's voice' within education, and as part of the Children's Right Agenda (2004) but it appears that it will not be accepted as 'the method' only one of many because children are regarded has having no concept of right or wrong therefore truth and non-truth before the age of eight years. One can see the sense in asking a child if s/he knows something rather than presuming s/he does or does not from workbooks, drawings or from direct observation using tick boxes and charts. Vygotsky (1978) believed Piaget's method to be one of the most important contributions to the field of Developmental Psychology but this side of Piaget's work is lost and even though some see the clinical method as a useful tool for capturing the essence of children's thinking processes it is regarded as too intrusive and not essential to educational practices. As Dahlberg (2007) points out, direct observations are useful but only when taken as one of a number of methods of observing children's mental processes or the process of learning itself.

Burman further points to the fact that scientism has influenced developmental psychology using work such as Piaget's because children are measured against the scientific ideal 'man the scientist'. This view of the child is one in which the child is a biological organism that is naturally curious and likes to explore the environment around it, interacting with it, thus learning and development are bi-products of the child's natural curiosity. Whilst this may be so, it remains a romanticists dream to think that all children within a particular social context will develop at the same rate or even develop the same skills of language and numeracy.

The entirety of the child's environment, their emotional temperament, self-esteem, as well as other context variables will affect the child's development and learning. Thus, Erica accords agency to the child rather than allowing him/her to be treated 'as if' s/he was just another variable in the production process of workforce educating, and suggests a movement towards focusing on the process of education rather than focusing on the subject—the child. Despite the critique nonetheless, Piaget's work remains as a formidable force in education, but is become one of many 'voices' or theoretical approaches. It is the invalueability of reflexively examining our own discipline that such untruths are revealed many thanks to Parker and Burman.

Controlling quality in education: Multiple languages of evaluation and reflection

The education system is quite bureaucratically organised. The enlightenment project has left its mark of utilitarianism and progression. Progression is measured in terms of *value added* or one might say *added value for money*. This is identifiable by the level of education each student has reached at a set age range and is weighted against the amount it costs for that level of education. The level of development reached in the Foundation Stage, is measured by developmental mile stones using the Foundation Stage Profile (equivalent to base line assessment), which buttresses Key Stage 1, then Key Stage 2; leading onto Key Stage 3 (these form Piagetian stages of development measured via Standard Assessment Tests). Then there is level 1 Basic Skills and level 2 GCSE that are equivalent to Key Stage 4, level 3 is NVQ and Advanced GCE; level 4 first year degree (HE certificate), level 5 is second year degree (HE diploma), and level 6 is HE degree.

At each stage or level will exist a form of assessment either an examination or course work equivalent said to measure that level of development, and at each level valued added can be calculated in terms of the increase in measured ability/ development. The utility of provision as one enters HE can be measured in terms of employability skills developed such as transferable skills, research skills, as well as subject knowledge skills that are demanded in the employment market. In terms of quality of provision, as well as level of development reached, the calibre of teaching staff, the enrichment of the environment, types of planning and assessment, extent of library provision and technology provision for example make up some of the quality indicators as well as things like degree content and learning outcomes, pastoral care, retention projects, career services and campus facilities, most if not all—plus more—of which are monitored by Ofsted and the QAA and some would suggest are highly bureaucratised and overly technical.

In 'Beyond Quality in Early Childhood Education: Language of Education', Dahlberg, Moss and Pence (2007) look at these influences in terms of their representation as measures of quality and suggest that they no long measure what is regarded as quality within education. These authors suggest the incorporation of 'meaning making' that has broader application and tends to encompass the differences we have in multi-racial, multicultural societies, and coupled with technical rationalism would move us closer to what quality is thought to be by the majority of those involved in the education system.

The discourse of quality within education is according to Dahlberg et al (2007), a controlling factor: Quality control was an industrial concept brought into education 'to control the quality in education'. It was adopted globally as part of the globalisation of western culture, marking what was thought to be the dominant indicator of a good education:

> 'The discourse is instrumental in rationality, neoliberal in values, technical in practice and managerial in discipline. It tells a positivistic story of early childhood education and care as a technology that can help fix many faults in post-industrial society, without society having to address its underlying structural flaws of inequality, injustice and exploitation.' (Dahlberg et al, 2007, p. vii).

In addition to this, the discourse of quality in education, suggests the delivery of subjects that are equally educated, with quality guaranteed, in view of the pre-set learning outcomes 'as indicative of readinesses for full time school in the early years, or the employment market in post-compulsory education. It was meant to represent scientific management at its best. Hence the title of Dahlberg et al's book—'*Beyond Quality*'—is an attempt to move away from the dominant discourse of quality as technical rationalism to one that more readily addresses the needs of postmodern societies in terms of education. In the early year's sector, some have suggested the adoption of traditional practices that have worked in the past, such Reggio Emilian pedagogical practices. But a move towards 'languages of evaluation' is thought to be more appropriate and encompasses the ingredients of the postmodern world, as one characterised by difference and diversity, with an eclectic mix of practices to meet its needs. Is it a substitute for the assessment process and structure of technical rationalism? Quality as structured assessment with value added development will remain on the agenda, but it will be one of a number of discourses that measure quality within education. The discourse of evaluation, 'languages of evaluation' signify multi-lingual multi-disciplinary practices that will coalesce.

In truth, the influences we see as that of the Reggio Emilia approach, are based on the work of Loris Malaruzzi, and his concept of 'the hundred languages of expression; the role of the atelier, the use of documentation in group learning and the value placed on space and time and relationships between the child, its family, and the community including the school within the community (Thornton and Brunton, 2005). To adopt this form of learning and evaluation alongside the existing quality control of the Piagetian influence, would be a return to or unification of Piaget's later work in which the clinical method is used in addition to direct observation and documentation to record and monitor the child's thinking processes but with the addition of recording the child's universal development within the community setting. Piagetian stages are not so ardently adhered to (if at all) within the Reggio approach, although this is not necessarily regarded as s better proposition; but would be used to record and monitor not to judge as normal and abnormal but engaged and achieving or disengaged and working towards a particular stage or level.

This framework allows the child to develop at its own pace and is a freer system that allows the child to be curious and engaged rather than authoritatively engaged. Because when all is said and done, Piaget did not suggest his stages to be cast in stone and the theory of conservation although based on mathematics and 'universal' epistemic biological processes i.e. proprioceptual measurement of the organism in space and time; it is cultural and each culture has its own numeration system the development of which is linked to experiential perception of environmental context of depth and three dimensional objects in space and time.

It is ontogenetic, the outcome of schema development as an adaptive propensity of the organism in the three dimensional environment of space and time. Therefore, the child will adapt i.e. develop in relation to its environment and its natural curiosity of objects within that environment. So, unless it is intended that children should be controlled like rats and mice in a laboratory—the school, the stages of development are only signifiers and not laws. Thus, as many in the early years sector as well education generally know, child need space and time to grow at their own velocity and a mixture of evaluation indicators is far better than just one—Piagetian stages and the quality indicatory they generate. It signifies a move toward as Dahlberg et al point out, a multiplicity of languages/discourses of evaluation. Indeed, the new

Early Years Foundation Stage Guidance document (May, 2008) although maintains a similar curriculum, focuses on creative expression driven by curiosity and language development within a community atmosphere and the essential social skills and knowledge of the world including citizenship, to allow the children to grow, develop and function in a multi-cultural, multi-racial global and technical social world.

The group observation method entails the documenting of meaning making as it occurs throughout the process of learning. As Rinaldi (2001) argues, it becomes a spiral of documentation, observation and interpretation: the spiral of reflective evaluation. For example, the child's contribution to a group project will be recorded as it is worked on as well as that of the other members of the group. In essence, what is being recorded is meaning making during the process of learning. Children and adult are therefore co-constructors of the learning process and the meaning and development it engenders for them as individuals. Through this method, the child's thought processes are in view and recoded (Thornton & Brunton, 2005; Dahlber et al, 2007). According to Dahlberg, the process of meaning making and the co-construction of interpretation is more democratic than many quality control indicators. The co-construction of meaning and its interpretation, which under Reggio also takes into account values and contextual factors that are then open to view by the child, parents and other community members, becomes a spiral of reflective interpretation. This way, two sets of tools are used:

> ' . . . the templates embodying predefined norms and setting out criteria for their measurement. Rating scales, check lists, standards protocols, procedures; detailed systems of inspection—these are the methods and tools of quality . . . [as well as] Meaning making takes a quite different approach: it works with pedagogical documentation and reflection, and through listening (Dahlberg et al, 2007, p. ix).

And together they form a dualistic role of complementing each other and can be used to measure the others' validity and reliability: In short the triangulation of documentary records, Piagetian type indicators, and various other observation methods like the Reggio group observation method. This type of assessment is part of ongoing practise within the early year's sector and although those who contributed to the development of the new early year's foundation stage guidance see it as a better alternative to the one it supersedes, some working within the early years sector are dubious of its success. Private Childminders for example, come under the rubric of Ofsted and up until now, documenting the development of the children they care for was not compulsory. Nonetheless, documentary evidence of children's development is generated throughout the care period and so the actual evidence of development is there it is just a matter of collating it and putting it in a portfolio for parents to see and Ofsted to examine. Drawings, photographs, shopping lists, audiotapes, computer-generated evidence plus much more can be collated as evidence of the child's competence at a particular task. It became compulsory in 2008 and now it is signalled will be dropped again because childminders have not got the time or the resources to fund the collection of documentation expected, or the time to write up all the entries expected by Ofsted. Although this section of the early year's work force have access to education so they can engage in self-development in terms of professional status, for example there is a pathway for practitioners through which they can obtain a Foundation Degree in Early Child Studies, in terms of time and resources the group are deficient.

So what does all of this mean for education? According to Dahlberg, if all including childminders came under Ofsted, it would lead to a more qualitative experience and a richer child: that is as it would appear on paper. Perhaps the recording of early year's practices from three onwards within nursery settings might be just as fruitful but how this would affect children who stay with private childminders until the age of five remains to be seen. There is a movement away from the discourse of 'problematization in the early childhood field' (Dahlberg, 2007, p. 6) and closer proximity to the reality and truth in early year's institutions through the recording of the co-construction of knowledge and identity of children engaging in creative meaningful practices. In addition to this, the method has the potential to lead to other emergent meaning making and co-constructing operations such as those of social relationship patterns involved including those of management and community.

Dahlberg when discussing quality within early year's education draws attention to Foucault's notion of power relations as bi-polar ruler-ruled, master-slave, teacher-student—ascribed roles in existence before the sixteen hundreds. In some ways this has now changed to that of governance. Under the new power relations, we can be governed and we can govern ourselves and may govern others. Power is achieve through disciplined conformity, using normalisation as a persuasive mechanism of one's claims to truth. The individual is constituted through these relations as either holding power through truth claims or knowledge claims or not holding power and therefore succumbing to disciplined conformity. For Foucault, power and knowledge are linked. Because some people are in a position to say whether knowledge is true or untrue, they hold power and thus command the discipline of others. The thing about discipline is that it can be used to self-regulate—self-govern. So power is achieve with the least amount of effort over others who do not have knowledge claims to truth. And this is the main problem as far as Foucault is concerned, because truth is power. Regimes of truth—discourses (knowledge claims of truth) transmit power relations by the claims to truth. Thus, to undo the power relation one must counter claims to truth be revealing them as untruths.

The discourses one finds of self in the web of others can show how our actions are produced and our identities. So, the child who is written about as 'a good reader' or 'strange' will become what they are labelled. The child who is written about as a poor speller will be acted towards as a poor speller and others' actions towards her/him guide his/her actions towards them. It is a case of the self-fulfilling prophecy (Rosenthal & Jacobson, 1968). To counter this, Foucault suggests the shaping of our own subjectivity which he calls 'care of the self' through self-reflection (Dahlberg, 2007). Through thinking about self and one's actions, one can see the true self and this knowledge of self can be used to counter the knowledge claims of others about oneself. This can occur through the co-construction of and meaning making of the learning process given that both identity and power are constituted through the co-construction process. Rather than being created by a powerful other in the learning process, one is creating self, thus leading to a richer child. At the same time, the power relations are thought to be in full view and malleable by all those involved: it becomes a process of negotiated identity rather than an ascribed identity. It does have its drawback however it is the practitioner who in the end decides what will constitute evidence of development as s/he will always have the last say.

The reflexive turn to politics

Glenda MacNaughton (2005) similarly in *'Doing Foucault in Early Childhood Studies: Applying post-structural ideas'*, unravels Foucauldian ideas to similar ends, by applying the Foucauldian concept power relationships within the early years sector, to those between the student and adult including those of management and practitioner roles. Thus, the child, the practitioner and management are examined through the Foucauldian lens. Glenda makes no excuses for her politics. And rightly so, early year's care and education has for far too long been seen as women's work, is usually done as unpaid labour by many 'wives, daughter and mothers', and is work that is taken for granted as menial. Thus MacNaughton (2005) says:

'I invite you to reflect on how your politics affects your positions on the politics of knowledge in early childhood, because the recognition that knowledge is inseparable from politics is what 'Doing Foucault' in early childhood studies seeks to achieve'. (MacNaughton, 2005, p. 3).

This involves identifying the 'stories' that are silenced or marginalized and giving them political space through sharing the responsibilities that unfold within the power, knowledge and truth relationships. MacNaughton see educators as activists, in a position to right social injustices. The activist stance operates through the production of action research and critical reflection, both of which can be recorded and reflected on so power relations, knowledge and truth claims can be examined and are open to view by parents and the community, in this, and she echoes the sentiments of Dahlberg et al. Through uniting practitioners' observations through shared reflections within practitioner communities, MacNaughton suggests ' . . . in [the] Foucauldian sense, from the 'bottom-up' [we can] introduce change into the larger structure of power in which our work is embedded'. Thus, from this point of view, the practitioners are signified as the 'bedrock' for growth within the early year's sector. It is regarded as a qualitative activism that will ripple outwards from the chalk-face centre to the outer relations of government policy makers.

Reflective practice in this sense is seen as a mechanism for controlling one's own learning—self-reflexive learning—leading to self-discovery, and use of the knowledge learned to activate changes at a higher level of power; in that it aims to put pressure on policy makers, thus inform policy and thus can be seen as a form of self-management or self-governance as Foucault termed it. Using critical reflection in this way is over against the dominant ideology that operates in society. It is a Habermacian-Gamancian type of political activism, aimed at fragmenting unequal power relations supported by the unequal dominant ideologies. The ideologies include those of developmentalism and other academic knowledge regimes of truth that mask inequalities such as those that sustain an understanding of children and youths as subordinate and less privileged and less powerful than adults. An understanding of the ways ideology operates will lead to an understanding of what needs to change, why and how:

> 'By asking questions such as, 'who benefits from what I do and know?', 'How and why do they benefit?', 'Do I want this to continue?', 'Why do I take this particular action or use this particular knowledge?', or 'whose interests does this knowledge or action support?' (MacNaughton, 2005, p. 11).

Ideological changes could including the curriculum, for example, is it fully mutli-cultural or partly? Also, practices *persae* including things like routines and in-door and out-door play, and the ideologies supported by academic knowledge claims of truth (Burman, 1992; Dahlberg, 2002, 2007; & MacNaughton, 2005). Discourses that subjugate and marginalize 'the other' in mainstream education whether the other is in terms of class, gender, age, race, culture, disability or family background. All these different 'othernesses' have claims to truth and each one as a regime of truth should have authority equal to others. Discourse such as developmentalism occupy privileged space with authority of truth claims and operate to mask the truths of otherness, concept mechanism such as *normalisation* through comparison, *exclusion* through truth claims or boundaries to normality, *classification* using normality claims to differentiate, *distribution* hierarchically using normality claims, *individualising* through normality claims to separate groups, *totalisation* using truth claims to divide and rule, and *regulation*, using truth claims of rules to induce conformity. For example, each stage of development has rules about how the child should act—regulation aimed at conformity. So, officially sanctioned truths such as those of normality are used to govern actions of both adults and children.

Disrupting the regimes of truth using power and knowledge tactically can, according to MacNaughton, free the child and practitioners from its/their effects. So how can the regimes of truth be disrupted or overthrown? One can actively seek multiple perspectives so that we do not listen to a one-sided argument. An example MacNaughton highlights is that of unofficial truths about desirable family types, the nuclear family for example, and how listening to the stories or truths of parents such as lone and single parents, gay parents and re-constituted families; the practitioners can help to liberate them from a subordinate, subnormal position granted to them by the normalising discourse of nuclear family type with two adults and 2.4 children. Listening to the other perspectives will disrupt the dominant regime of truth. Further tactics include, seeking meanings not always apparent, by 'overlaying your own truths with marginalized meanings as a way to develop meanings and actions that are more equitable and just' (MacNaughton, 2005, p. 47). The following vignette (figure 1) will act as an illustration of how power relations between child and educator, and educator and mentor can be distorted and wrapped in hidden meanings and politics that underlie the relationships.

Vignette 1

Mrs Rue Hellan (Mrs RH) has worked in education for 20 years first as a playground attendant then as a classroom assistant. She decided to train as an early year's practitioner because she felt she already knew the job after spending a long time in the local primary school working part time whilst her own children were of school age. The mentor, Mrs Piggling (Mrs P), is a full time SEN co-ordinator who trained first as an early year's practitioner and she looks after 20 SEN children and mentors two staff. Alice Deone (AD) is a very bright ten year old whose mother and father have divorced and she lives with her mother; a part time secretary, and visits her father and his new wife on Sundays when he is not working in London. Andy Shifty (AS) is a bright boy who lives with his mother and father in the local village, with his brother Jack Alex (JAS) and parents. Andy's mother workers in the village café and his father run a market stall. Their neighbours Lily and Shames Promise work for Willy's parents in the local public house, and Andy and Jack take care of Lucy during the evening when they are both at work. Willy Corsa (WC) is Andy's friend and they walk together to school every morning. Willy's parents own a public house, and Willy would like to drive a BMW when he's old enough. What follows are the reflective evaluations of Mrs RH regarding observations she made of the female child, AD.

I find AD a strange child. She wrote a little book on lose paper tied together with paper clips. AD said that her book was about things to do when caring for her doll, Prudent, that she refers to as if it were a real baby. AD said she wrote the instructions for AS who baby-sits for his next-door neighbour, Lily, with his older brother JAS. AD said she wrote the book because AS had told her he and his brother did not know what to do sometimes when Lucy, Lily's daughter cries for her mother. I felt that to write instructions for a baby-sitter was a good idea so I set that task for AD's class. AD got very tetchy and grumpy about this. She said it was her idea and that I had taken it from her. She claimed that the group had not contributed to the task and that it was all her work. I felt she was getting too big-headed about it and thought she showed a bad attitude towards a member of staff and class members.

On reading the reflective entry Mrs P asked Mrs RH how she had dealt with the situation. Did she praise AD initially for the instructions she has written? Mrs RH said she had not, that she thought AD had written the instructions at home and 'by the looks of them had probably copied them from a book or the Internet'. Mrs P asked Mrs RH why she thought AD got up-set, to which Mrs RH said 'She's a bit 'upperty' that way . . . she thinks she's good at everything and she's very bossy. None of the other children get a look in. I think she needs pulling down a peg or two. We need a level playing field in that group and she upsets the cart.'

Mrs P asked 'How do you think the situation should be dealt with?' To which Mrs RH said 'Well if we allow the other children space to develop their writing skills then maybe they will not get accused of stealing AD's work and they will all be equal. The mentor Mrs P asked 'How do you propose to do that?' To which Mrs RH replied 'We'll create a situation in which AD has to listen and watch the others so she can appreciate that other class members can contribute and have abilities too'. The mentor Mrs P asked Mrs RH 'How do you feel AD will feel about this?' to which Mrs RH replied, 'well it will help AD to fit in because at the moment she sticks out like a sore thumb'. Mrs P thought that Mrs RH had got some of the points right with regards to creating an equal situation and so allowed Mrs RH to continue to with her proposals. After all, Mrs P had enough to worry about she had to write 20 SEN children Personal Education Plans.

Two weeks later: Mrs RH had found it essential to record observations of AD; the situation had become according to Mrs RH, progressively worse. AD is aggressive and tetchy. She will not sit and listen and interjects all the time when the other children are talking. She will no longer contribute to group projects, for example, a group poster for a display at the local church. Her manners are appalling—she invades personal space of others by sitting next to them very close when they are trying to eat at lunch times. One of the children has taken to eating in the adjacent dining room. She keeps bending her head round to stare in the faces of children when they are busy, distracting them from their work. She is becoming clumsy and knocks into things, spilling children's pencils cases for example on the floor. Today I asked the whole group who would like to use the white board and AD ran to the front of the class knocking WC off his chair without being told she was chosen to do the board work. I think AD is aggressive and a danger to the other children. She appears to have no social skills and such psychological problems are affecting her work, which has deteriorated as a result. It has become messy, with scribbles and blotches of biro-ink, although she may actually be masking a spelling problem. Her reading is poor. When she read to the class a day or so ago she got words mixed-up and tantrumed when the other children laughed at her. I think AD might need assessing for special needs.

On reading these observations the Mentor Mrs P asked Mrs RH 'what do you think has cause AD problems to erupt like this?' Mrs RH replied 'The child comes from a broken home. The mother is not very maternal an AD appears withdrawn. She will not make eye contact with staff. I think she might have autistic tendencies. She is also frightened of men and screamed when the caretaker entered the toilets to clean then, the poor man didn't know where to put himself. I invited AS and WC to play with her today but AD refuses to play with boys. It could be because she has no father figure at home. Lately she will not play with the girls either and she thinks they are cruel. She told the playground staff member that all the children were against her and that she wanted to go home.'

The mentor Mrs P asked 'Did you ask AD if she thought the children were cruel?' To which Mrs RH indignantly said 'No, but you can see it in her face and you can tell what's she's thinking from her facial expressions'. Mrs P asked 'How can you tell if what you think she is thinking is real?' 'Well it's her body language—she has an unusual grimace.' At this point three girls who were listening in on the conversation between Mrs P and Mrs RH started running around them both shouting 'Alice is a thinking, we know what you're thinking, you're thinking, you're thinking, we know that you're thinking . . .' The two women ignored this. But later Mrs RH held a meeting with the children in AD's absence telling them that although they might be able to 'pick up' on what AD was thinking they hadn't to let her know. One child asked is it OK to laugh at it? And Mrs RH said yes.

At a meeting between Mrs RH and Mrs P. Mrs P wanted to know if Mrs RH had talked to AD one to one quietly about the anger problem, to which she replied she had not. So she was instructed to do some one to one counselling with AD before inviting AD's mother in to discuss AD's behaviour problems. Mrs RH indignant again, said, 'well it's plain to see AD needs treatment; Mrs Babbage (B) will tell you the same.' To which Mrs RH called Mrs B from across the playground. 'You noticed AD's strange behaviour didn't you Mrs Babbage?' Mrs B said, 'AD's strange behaviour?' 'Yes' said Mrs RH, 'you know her awkwardness?'

To this Mrs B went into full flow—'well I suppose she doesn't like to mix at the moment. She seems to be having social skills problems. She's not communicating properly. She doesn't seem to understand body language.' To which Mrs P said, 'body language?' 'Yes' said Mrs B, I've seen her stuttering in group discussions. She doesn't seem to time it right when she interjects—she doesn't seem to know when to listen and when to speak. I think you need to speak to AD Mrs RH to find out what the problem is.' Mrs P left the two other members of staff in the playground to return to the classroom to prepare for the afternoon class.

A further two weeks later, Mrs RH recorded a discussion freestyle she had with AD, talking about AD's problems. The report read: AD will not open up. She seems not to trust anyone and is very suspicious about the meeting. I asked AD if she was all right, if she was having problems at home and AD said she was not. She went very quiet and looked thoughtful and dazed. Mrs B was at the meeting. When I started talking to Mrs B, AD asked if she could leave. Imagine—it was proof of her insolence and insubordination. I told AD I thought she had social skills problems and that she did not understand body language, particularly the way she interjects when people are talking like she had just done. AD said she did not see it that way at all. She even had the audacity to suggest that it was *my* story *not hers* and that I was developing the story line to suit my way of thinking. The child has obviously been talking to her mother to come up with suggestions of that nature. I have decided to put AD on report. I think she has definitely got psychological problems and is heading for a nervous breakdown. I think she needs medication and I suggest psychiatric treatment. In addition, even the children have noticed strangeness; they said that they know what AD is thinking. She has an insolent, mad, grimacing look of a paranoid schizophrenic and I would not be surprised if she has it in her to commit bodily harm to someone, even murder! I feel we are in danger of our lives as staff members having to work with her and would like her to be removed from the school.

Figure 1

Critical questions

When the mentor read this she was lost. Nearly six weeks had passed since the first discussion and Mrs P was overcome with her own work and had not really given Mrs RH dealing with AD much thought. She could not understand the problem and felt something had gone terribly wrong but did not have the time to deal with it. What should the mentor do in this situation? What is the actual problem here? How was Mrs B implicated? What affect is the situation having on a) AD, b) Mrs RH, c) Mrs B, d) the other children and e) Mrs P?

Power relations between child and educator, and educator and mentor can be distorted and wrapped in hidden meanings and politics that underlie the relationships. They cannot be disrupted until the ruptures that form in the discourses can be torn apart to reveal the hidden meanings and politics that underlie the relationships. MacNaughton in her book talks about the concept of being 'tactically marginalized', who is being tactically marginalized in the vignette? What is happening in terms of power relations? Is the marginality class related, age related, sexist, racist, ethnic, or to do with ability? Why is Mrs RH acting the way she is? What is the normalising or abnormalising discourse used? What is the source of the exclusion discourse? How is the victim being classified? What is the distribution mechanism? Which discourse is used to individualise and separate off the victim from the 'normals'? How is the totalising ideology used to get others to conform to it? What regulations are used to limit the thought of others about the rules governing the problematised behaviour? Who is the perpetrator and who is the victim? How can we defragmentalise and decontextualise the vignette to render the truth visible?

Once the scenario is fragmented according to MacNaughton, one experiences an epistemological shudder, a new way of looking at things. It has become a useful tool for researching, analysing, and revisiting everyday interactions to explore equity and social justice issues. The regimes of truth are shattered and fragmented leaving bare the oppressive ideological practices. In addition to this, the vignette shows a multiple of interrelated characteristics that are linked that are made salient as characteristics for exclusion: race, class, age, gender, ethnicity, disability and ability. Using Rhizoanalysis the links in politics of these characteristics can be linked to community discourse, text in books and other texts on the Internet to see how they interact to subjugate and exclude. Once the texts are rendered visible, they can be deconstructed, whether the text be everyday 'teacher talk' or practices governed by academic knowledge truth claims. Once the cracks appear in the text, the power relations will be disrupted and deconstructed. MacNaughton also suggests we should privilege 'truths' that produce greater social justice. But who can say which they are? Shouldn't we just favour 'the truth?' For example, when asking the question 'What regulations are used to limit the thought of others about the rules governing the problematised behaviour?' psychiatry is a very powerful discourse that can and does affect law and just as important, lay/naïve psychology as we have witnessed in the vignette.

The identification of mental illness in terms of diagnosis is based on a medical model of illness developed in the west over many centuries. Ingelby (1982) regards its roots in objective physical knowledge of how the brain works as 'extremely shallow'. As Kuhn states, theory does not occur in a vacuum but is influenced by ideology present in the scientific milieu. The social construction of mental illness reveals itself quite blatantly in the political abuse of psychiatry in the Soviet Union when dissidents were diagnosed as schizophrenic because of their beliefs. Homosexuality is another case of the social construction of mental disorder, or deconstruction, it is no longer regarded as a mental disorder, and in both cases political forces determined the criteria of what constituted the illness. Furthermore, western psychiatry can be used as a means of social control by people in power. Under Section 136 of the Mental Health Act (1983) the police are empowered as are social workers, to remove to a place of safety (i.e. mental hospital/prison cell) any person they judge to be mentally ill where the police ordinarily have no power of arrest (Middleton, 1989 & Tanweer, 1992). This law is unique—it permits the detention of people by the police who have no professional qualification to diagnose mental illness. On what do they or for example, a member of staff in a school (i.e. Mrs RH) base judgement? In the 'Politics of Experience' (1967) Laing puts forward the conspiratorial model of schizophrenia. He argues it to be a form of violence perpetrated by some people on others. The knowledge has also become part of everyday language and is thus used as 'lay/naïve psychology' to maintain a particular definition of reality, usually the perpetrator's own. Szasz (1970) echoes this sentiment. Therefore, just as the label schizophrenic can be constructed and deconstructed the layers of social reality can be peeled away to reveal the truth that resides within. But would it be as MacNaughton suggests 'a truth' that produces greater social justice? I think that 'the truth' is just and will always remain so, and MacNaughton's suggestions concerning the disruption of oppressive 'regimes of truth' using power and knowledge tactically, can free the child and practitioners from its/their effects.

This section thus reveals the power of reflexive practice and the essentiality of what Dahlberg et al (2007) would like to see in education, that is, languages of evaluation applied to education practices. MacNaughton's work too brings to life the meaning of power relations as envisaged by Foucault and the necessity of reflexive practices to the undermining of oppressive practices within institutions.

Deconstructing the postmodern teacher: Technical rationalist or reflective practitioner?

Stuart Parker (1997) has a view of the postmodern education system as one marked by two interlaced cultures: technical rationalism that came to us from modernity—the enlightenment project, and reflective teaching, which for Stuart, is an offshoot of the reflexive turn of post-modernity. Like most authors, Stuart sees technical-rationalism as imbued with the 'higher authority of natural and universal laws there to regulate their domain of reality'. Reflective teaching is viewed as an instrument to fine-tune the process of education. It resides on the same polarity as critical thinking, action research and reflection leading to democracy. The dilemma in reflective teaching however for Stuart is that reflective teaching can spiral down into a web of relativism in which 'anything-goes'. What is more intriguing for Stuart, is that reflective teaching is used to sustain and support the technical rationalism of the enlightenment project, and adds to bureaucracy and one's place within it. The different stories of relativism's subjects can also be distorted and what counts as truth and reality can vary from one story to another governed by the bureaucratic characters of technical rationalism. Technical rationalism as far as Stuart is concerned with its '*Managerialism*, [has] *one right answer*, has no such relativistic worries; it simply doesn't tolerate difference' (Parker, S., 1997, p. 4). The result is a conglomerate of distortions in which '*anything-goes*' as long as the bureaucrats permit that particular story.

Thus, Parker believes we should deconstruct reflective teaching accounts/ stories, as well as those of action research, critical theory and liberal philosophies in education. To Parker they have the same thrust in terms of methodology and politics, which is where I part company with him because as far as I can see, technical rationalism as described here by Stuart is not what enlightenment thinkers had in mind when talking about rational thought and empirical thought as means of progress. The synthesis of reflexive practice and scientific management as technical rationalism can be a bad mix as we witnessed in the latter section. So although reflexive practice is a way of improving practice its function is not straightforwardly that of increasing profit. Its function was the development of the teaching and learning process to enhance learning.

Reflective practice is not just a classroom practice either and can be used to evaluate other practices in education including personal development and ones place within education and one's relations with management. For example, the layers of management can have different goals. Not all managers have utility or value-added or quality as their priorities. Some for example pay-lip service to these and can magically produce evidence to support their claims to truth about the quality of provision in their institution. Thus, just how technical and rational is the bureaucratic rule of management, in that, does it actively pursue equal and qualitative learning through a learning process that is efficient and sustainable? Well, it appears to be based on the 'invisible hand' of self-interest—every wo/man for her/himself in a free market economy, which unfortunately it is not always economical or free or beneficial for all concerned. Where one manager or teacher for that matter may strive for quality, efficiency and sustainability, another might equally be happy to mosey along, playing 'divide and rule' or 'piggy in the middle', thus exuding distortions, doubts and lack of autonomy for the teacher in the classroom.

In addition to this, people have different views about what is or what is not good practice in education. Do we base the process of learning on the Piagetian ideal, 'the child as the scientist', and allow a process of learning based on exploration 'explorative learning'; or do we accept the Vygotskian notion that some children's learning needs 'scaffolding'—a supportive framework of instruction-led learning. Similar to this is the behaviourist learning theory in which learning takes place best in small chunks that is pre-organised as a supportive framework so that each new chunk of learning builds on the previous chunk and is set at a level achievable and formatively assessed so that the learning is reinforced for the student who can then also assess what they have learned along the way and add to it, thereby giving the student control of their learning: Instrumental learning/linear basically, or over a longer period, Bruner's spiralling curriculum. Piagetian practice is longer in duration—stages of 2 to 4 years and the child can get lost in the process.

To support Piagetian practices therefore in education, assessment has to be administered through a supportive framework of smaller discrete chunks which is therefore, a mixture of all three theories, if not; then Vygotskian and behaviourist learning practices/processes using Piagetian theory of conservation as the indicative content. Some practitioners opt for a facilitative pedagogy in an atmosphere of student-centredness.

Views of learning affect management styles and management styles as we have seen are built on self-interest, and not necessarily on government policies such as those pronounced by Gordon Brown in December 2007—the practice of creative learning (Piagetian) with fewer SATs and more individual teacher assessments (behaviourist linear-learning?—the Practice Guidance for the Early Years Foundation Stage, May 2008). Whilst I agree that creative learning is the ideal option, in practice it takes too long and some children get lost along the way and become stigmatised which affects their self-esteem and thus their ability to learning. And as this story suggests, each manager will produce styles of management based on his/her own experiences, needs and beliefs, and of course, individualised training package. Therefore, the technical rationalism of the enlightenment is tempered by each individual's self-interest, values, and beliefs and coupled with reflective practices will temper those of management in return and possibly anyone who is involved in education, both at the chalk-face and beyond.

If reflective practices do not bring management to bare the way they are meant to temper the processes of education then education will not be equal, qualitative, effective, efficient or sustainable. Thus, whilst Parker see technical rationalism as a way of justifying bureaucracy and manager's place within it, reflective practices in education will accord the tempering of management to support a more equal, qualitative, effective, efficient and sustained education system and support teaching staff rather than treat them like technical methods-of-production to gratify their own ends. People do not end up in a boat together because they are all friends, they pay passage and eligibility fees prescribed before entry and will not suffer at the hands of the incompetent willingly. It therefore leads to me say that Foucault's notion of self-management is a more appropriate option.

Reflective practices in education can take on many forms. Parker (1997) discusses the reflective teacher as an individual entity attached to the classroom. Parker suggests that each individual is concerned with means and ends as part of the rational process of teaching; each individual having different means and ends and operating in different contexts, so that the values, theories and resources they use will be emergent of that particular context and experiences of the individual. The 'imperative' of reflective teaching and action research is to change the process of teaching and learning as a way of improvement without 'claim to universality or permanence'. 'Its motivation is not the increase of knowledge of how children learn but the improvement of the reading in these particular children . . . in specific, idiosyncratic context'. This for Parker 'distinguishes reflective teaching/action research from positivist forms of investigation' (Parker, 1997, p. 39). Traditional reflective teaching was/is also a very personal thing; a tool for improving individual practice by highlighting areas for improvement in one's own teaching practice. As Parker points out:

> 'the autonomous individual must be able to turn this responsibility inward upon herself to achieve integrity through the rational self-knowledge which enables a *person* to determine his or her true nature, genuine self and real interests, and to keep faith with them . . . Autonomous free will is, in other words, a will that is rationally conceived' (Parker, 1997, p. 44).

Technical rationalism for example penetrates concerns about the time of a teacher-student encounter, the aims and learning objectives, the process, the relationships between teacher and students, the environment and resources, the assessment strategy and teacher-student ratios. But for the reflective practitioner, the elements of the teaching-learning process do not always obtain just because we may follow the rules. A truly reflective teacher will know when to change one of these elements to achieve the learning objectives desired. This is what distinguishes the technical rationalist from the reflective practitioner. The technical rationalist will follow the rules to the letter despite any changes in context variables. The reflective practitioner will think on her/his feet—Schön's (1984) 'thinking-in-action', and again afterwards, 'thinking-on-action' knowing that different context demand different approaches.

The problem here is that whilst this may be so, it is only one aspect of reflective practice. As a teacher-researcher in the social sciences for example I am concerned to both emancipate the individual and the process of learning with its theoretical base. Therefore, although initially my reflective teaching practices are geared towards the improvement of the process of learning and the teaching practices that I am involved in, reflective practice of that process can produce theoretical insights just as enlightening as that of my personal reflection of myself as a teacher. And any theoretical knowledge contribution that emerges—grounded theory—will be scrutinised by the scientific community for what Parker calls distortions of the truth/reality, and rightly so, although I'm not sure if Parker is suggesting such a thing can exist or whether he is suggesting a community of articulate rhetorical debaters is more fun? Whichever the case, Parker does suggest that an ideal speech situation is very difficult to achieve and that even when we think we may have reached this ideal, another theory can come along and completely remove the existing paradigm—Khun's paradigm shift. The more stories we examine—due to our understanding of spaces/sites of difference and relativisms, the more the distortions of reality can occur. But we need all of the stories to piece together the separate elements of truth. Distortions which can be subjective biases and:

> 'effects of ideology, custom, habit, tradition, coercion, authority and institutionally imposed and maintained definitions and expectations; the very forces which result in the kind of anti-critical turn of mind whose symptoms include routinised and unresponsive behaviour' (Pollard and Tann, 1994; p. 8-9 cited in Parker, 1997, p. 54).

Hence, to render inoperable the distortions Parker suggests Habermas' critical theory as a pathway to the ideal speech situation; a situation in which claims to truth are critically appraised and evaluated as true representations of reality in a scientific community. In this respect, reflective practice much like technical rationalism is in search for truth: the reflexive return of modernity. In chapter 2 I examine this concept under the banner 'All hail reflexivity!'

In chapter 3, my reflective teaching practices are put on view. Like Parker's technical rationalism coupled with self-reflexive learning I firstly plan a programme of study, deliver it, observe the delivery and then undertake some reflective evaluations of the teaching sessions. Reflections concerned with improving the process of learning, maintaining interaction and focus—the motivation of the students; improving student self-monitoring skills and therefore self-managed learning skills, thus emancipation, increasing the knowledge base of the learning process, thus self-appraisal skills, problem solving and countering the technical rationalism that renders the individual practitioner a 'ghost in the machine' (Weber, 1920). Technical rationalism seeks only the advancement of the requirements of the post—reflective practices may have the same thrust but because the individual is given more autonomy and control that which is learned will help further the development of the individual's tailored needs.

In addition, whilst Parker views the reflective practices of individual teachers as a way of accessing the lived experiences (in the form of narratives put on view) of classroom practices—a way of objectifying the context of learning for the observers within the scientific community; the reflective process is a means to an end for enhanced practices and emancipatory relations for teachers and pupils—NOT JUST technical rationalism but the holistic development of the individuals concerned.

Does a true plus a false statement equal truth or falsehood?

Does reflective practice lead to accuracy in truth/meaning-making and understanding for those involved and/or those who read the narratives as secondary sources? Parker suggests that truth plus truth i.e. for teacher and student/s will equal greater truth. But the generation of truth and falsehood can add up to either truth or falsehood; false statement plus false statement can become a greater falsehood, a truth and/or truth-false dilemma. Therefore for Parker, we can never really say that we have acquired lots of truth, or a mixture of true and false statements the whole of which collapses back into a conundrum of distortions! But the reflective practice spiral of understanding should generate something that resembles a truer picture if it is the focus and not falsehood:

> 'Reflexive rhetoric about meaning and doubts about truth bottom out not in essence but in decision . . . to continue with our questioning would be nonsensical, boring or passé' (Parker, 1997, p. 122).

It appears we have the autonomy to live in doubt if we so wish—it is our decision. But Parker also suggests that some narratives can be shown to be better than others 'by virtue of their point-to-point correspondence to nature's own stores' (Parker, 1997, p. 142). With this I agree. If knowledge is truly empirical—obtained via the senses—literally—sensory osmosis—see my discussion on Lockes' ideas (chapter 2 & 4)—then actual essence contributes somewhat towards 'the recognition of the truth-reality' and what it means and this will eliminate doubts for those who as Parker say, do not want to live in doubt.

One more point about the new breed of student reflective practitioner, or as Parker calls them—teacher deconstructors—'teachers and student teachers will become deconstructive in their reading of educational texts, in their situating of received wisdom, in their creation of values, in their evaluation of courses and the statements of bureaucrats and politicians' (Parker, 1997, p. 142). So in terms of deconstruction then 'anything goes'?—Students will aspire to a level of critical autonomy in thinking.

To summarise, can we really tackle politics in education? Are the discourses of technical rationalism really those that prevent emancipation? For example, the technical rationalist austere type of system does not stand-over against the marginalized or underclass, it is the distortions of it that make it appear that way! The reflective practice spiral of action and the ideal speech situation will lead to greater autonomy and holistic development for individuals and will help to sustain a situation in which distortions are dealt with and eliminated. Dealt with through reflective practice as a form of introspection/self-analysis in which the reflective practitioner is freed from self-delusion via critical practices. Referring to Habermas' work, this as well as communicative competence can eliminate distortion if validity holds on 4 accounts: 1) dialogue is intelligible, 2) the prepositional content is true, 3) the speaker is sincere and 4) it is appropriate for the speaker to discuss the speech/dialogue content. Parker reiterating Habermas argues that:

> 'If successful, then, a transcendental argument will be a supremely powerful argument, as it will show what must be assumed in any thinking about experience, reason or language, and will precipitate conclusions which are unassailable by reference to the particularities of context or situation. The conclusions will be absolutely and universally true' (Parker, S., 1997, p. 59).

If this is not the case, then the style and tone of the discourse—its differences—will contain within it, its own subversions, distortions, half-truths and hidden agendas and therefore the deconstructive momentum of its demise: Precisely as Glenda Mac Naughton (2005) outlines in 'Doing Foucault in Early Childhood Studies'.

Playing 'Off the fence!'

> 'Isn't the dude straight-forwardly a hypocrite in the use he makes of the very devices which are the hallmark of his opponent's system of beliefs and values?'

> (Stuart Parker, 1997, p67)

> 'You are troubled at seeing him spend his early years in doing nothing but play. What! Is it nothing to be happy? Is it nothing to skip, to play, to run about all day long? Never in his life will he be so busy as now . . ."

> (Jean Jacques Rousseau)

Throughout this book I have used reductionist as well as social constructionist arguments to support my thinking—I have never been able to 'jump off the fence' to either side of the divide. Instead I have interwoven the two polarities and I think sometimes to the outrage of one or the other. I have also used the social constructionist argument to critique itself whilst underpinning my own ideas with reductionist research such as that developed in neuroscience—I have indeed developed a theory in neuroscience that explains diagrammatically constructionist ideas concerning the ontogenetic development of cognition. Like Parker, I have derided the phoniness of some who purport to be critical of insincerity in debate and argument but who then regress into the 'anything goes' scenario as far as truths is concerned. My aim in this is a striving for a transcendental argument that emancipates in the long term and as well as the short term rather than deluding to a state of affairs that maintains a status quo for fear of consequences that may or may not transpire, and yet whilst maintaining that status quo leads us further down the path in obscurity and danger of extinction. Literally!

The paradox is solvable despite its puzzling nature—if science is what it is meant to be, a means of obtaining truths then why do we entertain the insincerity of obscurest-delusion? The delusions of creating a pure social science are miniscule to that of confabulated delusions and insincerities. If there is a trade-off between hypocrisy and obscurest-delusion then hypocrisy appears to be the lesser of the two evils when the hypocrisy chosen leads to furtherment of knowledge that is emancipatory. For example, it might be hypocritical to couple together social constructionism with neuroscience i.e. connectionism (see chapters 3, 4, 5, 6 and 7) because of the reports about the unethical treatment of laboratory animals and human participants during neuroscientific experiments but I have witnessed seemingly harmless social constructionist research create harm unwittingly. For example, Rosenthal and Jacobson's 'Pygmalion in the Class' revealed the way teacher's expectations could unintentionally influence the self-esteem and learning of the child leading to the self-fulfilling prophecy, but the research itself was unethical—one group of children was treated 'as if' A grade and another 'as if' C grade. The C graders therefore not achieving the grades they may have had they not taken part in the research and been labelled C graders.

If obscurest-delusion was to be emancipatory then why should it be wrapped in obscurity, delusion and insincerity? The linguistic-turn as a language game is fun—we all like to play . . . but seriously, shouldn't we decide what is at risk when maintaining a particular construct of reality for fear of what might happen should we reveal the truth? Hence like Parker to reveal truths through deconstructing obscurest-delusions is a better alternative to gamesmanship involving linguistic-turns whether the gamesmanship is a part-time preoccupation or a full time job—I'm not trying to apologise for synthesizing social constructionism with neuroscience's connectionism and constructionism because the two had to be brought together at some point because of the knowledge that will now flow that is emancipatory. This will be revealed in chapter 8, 'The Consequences of Crossing Disciplinary Boundaries: Cognitivism, Connectionism, Constructionism and Emergent Intelligence'.

As Parker suggests, deconstruction ignores content in a discourse and addresses the structures that enable the content to be expressed. It is a strategy used to displace an argument that can be shown to have no secure foundations. When I undertook the study of my reflective practice in the chapter that follows, there were so many introspective behaviours meta-cognitive in nature that I could not find a rational foundation for other than to look at the meta-cognitive behaviours in a reductionist way. You might find the narrative of my reflective practice flamboyant with lofty ideas and a fondness for doing that which we are taught not to in the social sciences—to try to prove our own theories rather than disprove them. The synthesis I engaged in to prove what I thought was correct I feel still holds true, although perhaps looking back my approach was probably naïve. Knowing what I did about social constructionism, reification and laying claim to evidence that was not fully visible I should have held a more restrained expedition of the support to the grounded theoretical content. Instead, I chose to committee myself further by adding more theoretical support underpinning my entire thesis with all the knowledge that would support it. Was it the right thing to do? As it happens, my knowledge of neuroscience and reflexive practice as a meta-cognitive process were hard to separate as most of the connections and theoretical suggestions I make have face validity. For example, even reflexivity as a research process has face validity and as I discuss in the next chapter is used by those who believe the social sciences should follow the natural science method as well those who believe social sciences should be more qualitative.

Chapter Two

All hail reflexivity!

Abstract

This paper looks at the problems associated with the validity of social inquiry, and suggests that action research as a research strategy brings together the retroductive and abductive strategies leading to greater validity. The epistemological and ontological problems involved in uniting realism/retroduction and social constructionism/abduction are explored. On conducting action research in higher education where situations develop in which teachers are reflexive practitioners, and students are reflexive students, dialectically reflecting on the teaching and learning process, and the subject matter of social sciences, the possibility arises for the existence of doubly double hermeneutics. Information obtained from the social encounters involving doubly double hermeneutics can then be used to construct further plans for the teaching and learning process. These plans are the models; similar to the models retroduction involves. In addition, it is suggested that not only is reflexivity the process of action research but also the ontology, epistemology, methodology and method of social inquiry. Furthermore, the reflexive practitioner's interests motives and values are part of the reflexive process of the research, with a concern for the emancipation of the subject. It is suggested that these emotionalities are what Locke described as ideas of succession, ideas, which emanate from the ideas of reflection and sensation as modes of experiencing the world. Lastly, in a situation of 'communal reflexivity' we have something resembling Habermas' 'ideal speech situation', which it is believed is what is involved in the process of critical social theory and reflexivity.

Keywords Reflexivity, Realism, Action Research

Action research as a form of social inquiry

'Action/Research: its use and even its awkwardness serve to conjure forth that most intractable of questions for social science: what is the relationship between theoretical and practical knowledge...how can theory be more integrated with practice?...[A]ction-research requires a reconsideration of longstanding issues in the theory of social inquiry—concerning reflexivity, rationality, validity and ideology; and secondly that a proper resolution of these issues in the theory of social inquiry will be found in the (reformulated) practices of action-research, since action-research addresses 'head on' social inquiry's fundamental problems—the relationship between theory and practice, between the general and the particular, between common sense and academic expertise, between mundane action and critical reflection, and hence—ultimately—between ideology and understanding' (Richard Winter, 1987, p. vii—viii).

For Winter, action research is the integrating mechanism between theory and practice because through reflexive practice, i.e., planning, acting, observing, reflecting, and revised planning, theory is entwined with practice. The reflexive practice of action research is not about research *per se* it has purpose—to produce ideas or theories for change based on that reflexive practice. It is about learning from the reflexive process and putting that which has been learned into practice with the aim, in education, of improving the teaching and learning environment. Educational action research for this reason is advocated as a mode of practice on a general level (Elliott, 1991).

In addition, because action research involves dialectical critical reflection, Winter suggests this will solve the epistemological dilemma of interpretation: Action research involves inter-subjectivity leading to greater validity. Winter's theoretical elaboration of action research's own mode of inquiry is presented as an object of theory. Winter uses the Kantian: '[T]ranscendental exposition' of a concept as an exposition which shows the necessary assumptions for the concept to be "possible" (Kant, 1933, p. 70): Hence his famous *a priori* categories of space and time as conditions for the possibility of conceptualizing consciousness (pp. 72-8)' (Winter, 1987, p. 3).

Thus for Winter space and time become the *a priori* conditions for conceptualising consciousness, and transcendental knowledge, but that knowledge is limited. The limitations of such transcendental knowledge 'the mode of our knowledge of objects' which is also said to be *a priori*, Winter believes remains a problem because: '[O]f the inevitability of the "illusion" by which "we take the subjective necessity of a connection in our concepts…for an objective necessity of a connection of things in themselves (pp. 299)"' (Winter, 1987, p. 30).

Indeed, Winter suggests that Kantian 'analytic thought' is impossible without 'synthetic thought', because of the nature of cognition itself, which implies *a priori* attenuation, categorisation, comparison and accentuation of incoming data. *A priori* forms of intuition and categories of understanding are facilitative to illusion even with transcendental exposition or Kantian categories of logic and understanding because of the biases in perception. I would suggest however, that self-reflexivity can transcend the problem of illusion, which I will discuss in more detail later, but to continue with Winter's reasoning he suggests: '[M]y intention is not really to prescribe *a priori* grounds for identifying an object ('action-research'), but rather to provide grounds for identifying a mode of knowing such an object' (Winter, 1987, p. 3). Dialectical reflexivity for Winter, becomes the mode by which inquiry becomes intelligible. Language is reflexive. Meanings are communicated via speech, and because action research is dialogic activity, language becomes the medium of dialectic reflexivity for self and others: In the teaching and learning situation, between reflexive practitioners and reflexive students.

According to Winter, this leads to theoretical grounding epistemologically and ontologically, and overcomes the problem of illusion. The knowledge produced by dialectic reflexivity, producing inter-subjectivity, becomes objectified and the ontological problem is solved because 'being' is not questionable in Descartes' sense as action research involves 'being-with' others. As Winter states:

> Dasein's being is Being-with, its understanding of Being already implies the understanding of others…it is through the dialectic between self and other that consciousness can develop towards 'self-consciousness', i.e. the comprehension of its own reflexive nature…between two self-conscious Beings…the true nature of one's own Being is thus only achieved by confronting another in a 'struggle' whose prize is simultaneously freedom and truth' (Winter, 1987, p. 14).

Thus for Winter, we know ourselves through being-with others, and the dialectical reflexivity involved in action research delineates the mode of understanding (the knowing as giving and taking of meaning between individuals).

According to Winter's adoption of this Cartesian interpretation of Heidegger's Dasein, it is the dialectical reflexivity of action research that makes is more objective. The inter-subjective understanding and meaning of 'Being-with', achieves greater validity through the contestive nature of dialectic reflexivity. Not just dual or a plurality of reflexive practices but a dialectic interchange between reflexive individuals which allows those involved to acquire an objective understanding of being and the nature of that being in that particular social encounter.

Another theme that runs through Winter's analysis is the notion of freedom. According to Winter, action research frees the individual because; competing ideas of reality and knowledge meet each other face on. This line of thought comes from Hegel. Experience and meaning is always situated (spatiality) because 'both theorising and consciousness must be situated for either to be intelligible' (Winter, 1987, p. 15). But by a 'careful sense of responsibility towards truthful understanding', Winter uses the Heideggarian notion of time here, 'The temporality of future possibilities into a time-less present of unchanging certainties' is possible. For Winter the outcome is: 'Grounds for its implicit commitment to an unending dialectic of developmental and reflexive understanding' (Winter, 1987, p. 16).

It is clear that Winter sees action research as emancipatory. Dogmatic theorisation by the individual becomes a 'playful sphere' for creating meaning and understanding, which may not transcend culture and tradition but does open up 'a plurality of possibilities' for future action and theorising.

So, what does this mean exactly for educational work in particular and action research generally? Well, it entails validity for research, because of the inter-subjectivity of dialectical reflexivity therefore, a deeper understanding of the meaning the teaching and learning process has for participants. The purpose of reflexive practice is to improve practice, to improve the teaching and learning process. Because of this, it has an emancipatory element for the student and the practitioner; and aims to improve the educational setting on a general level.

I would suggest however, that reflexivity 'is more than grounds for identifying a mode of knowing such an object',—action research and the reflexive consciousness. Reflexivity *is* the theory and the practice of action research. Reflexivity as consciousness is 'being' and as 'being' is an analysis of the nature of that being. Being is theory and the process of being is the practice. Action research is Being-with others in the reflexive process of being.

Heidegger's (1962) ontology 'I am, therefore I think', epistemology, does not question material existence like Descartes' epistemology 'I think, therefore I am', ontology. Thus for Heidegger by making sense of the subject/object epistemology he is doing ontology. Heidegger's Dasein, 'Das' the, 'Sein', intelligibility: the intelligibility, consciousness thus becomes the epistemology. To 'step-out of' Dasein, is to '*be*' without '*ing*', epistemology, to 'be' without intelligibility.

Heidegger in his later work, refers to Dasein as a consciousness much like the 'Being-with' inter-subjectivity of 'consciousnesses', in the sense that Winter uses it, but also consciousness as in 'Being-there', being in everyday human existence (Dreyfus, 1991, p. 13). The later 'Being-there' is the intentionality of consciousness, grounded in the rhapsodic temporality of Dasein. In both senses outlined—'Being-with' involves intentionalities and 'Being-there' intentionality in the singular, as does 'being-in'. The intentionality of 'Being-in' is the mental content of being; the way consciousness relates to objects by virtue of existence 'being-amidst' other ontological/epistemic humans (Taylor, 1997).

Heidegger points to the fact that Dasein, or 'being-in', human existence in a world, can also operate as an intelligibility of objects regardless of intentionality almost like 'being' on automatic pilot. And he talks of a state of indifference which he regards as the 'debris of our everyday practical world left over when we inhibit action' (Dreyfus, p. 47, 1991). But Heidegger suggests that regardless of the mode of Dasein (Being-with, Being-there or being-in), we live in a world of objects thus knower/subject and known/object always negate some sort of interchange thus we give/take meaning with intentionality and intelligibility (Dreyfus, p. 48 to 59, 1991, Taylor, 1997).

Dasein is thus a mode of transcendence of the subject/object arrangement. Not necessarily a bridge between them, the subject/object distinction becomes for Heidegger, a 'comportment' in which 'everything *is*', and the subject/knower always acts relative to the objects/the known with intentionality not indifference because Dasein imbues *a priori* knowing to the knower. For Heidegger understanding and meaning without intentionality is meaningless, not necessarily even, a reflexive clarity (Descartes).

It is suggested however, that 'Being', can be 'to be', existence as a pure consciousness regardless of, sometimes in absence of Dasein. If we think of Dasein as the transcendental semi-cultural community psychical understanding of human existences in an existential world, Heidegger's 'everything *is*', ontology-epistemology, then the naive curiosity of the new-born driven not by thirst or hunger but '*is*', 'be' without the 'ing', is the benign, the pure experiential mode—aesthesia—ideas of sensation and succession without ideas of reflection based on pure perception and feeling, 'to be' without 'ing': Emotivity, 'being' without Dasein.

To be without 'ing' (epistemology) is to be without Dasein, *a priori* intentionality and intelligibility, to be without *a priori* knowledge of the world. Yet to be in a world denotes space/existence and it will soon become space in time therefore space/existence as 'to be' with 'ing'. Once this occurs, we have 'being', the ontology-epistemology relationship in a form of 'Being-without' others' Dasein. Thus, the epistemology that comes from being without other's Dasein is transcendental knowledge directly from 'the intelligibility', consciousness, 'being'. Descartes reflexive clarity of being in the form of pure subjectivity, consciousness, is the bearer of transcendental knowledge.

According to Winter's dialectical reflexivity we get the introduction of a contestive arena where 'everything that *is*' in the Heideggerian sense, is contested by reflexive participants until a point is reached where the definition of reality of the social encounter leads to the emancipation of participants because of the compromise of inter-intentionalities. With Descartes' reflexive clarity, the definition of reality is reached through the reflective turn: of ideas of sensation succession and reflection, and can be with or without intentionality. Both forms of being/ontology and knowing/epistemology are possible in the Heideggerian sense, the later, amounting to a residue category he equates with disengagement (or disenchantment) with Dasein.

According to this line of thought, the temporality of being and the spatiality of it may not be transcended instantaneously, but through the continuousness of action research overtime and via reflexivity or dialectic reflexivity, both time and space may possibly be transcended, thus leading to the true emancipation of truth and reality. Action research is a spiral process of planning, acting, reflecting and revised planning (Winter, 1987; Zuber-Skerritt, 1992). The main principle is that participants learn from the exercise and put that which is learnt into practice leading to improvement in practice. It is a continuous process of action and reflection overtime. The transcendence of time and space will become clearer when we discuss Habermas' critical-emancipatory interpretivism and Harre's ethogeny. But first let's look more closely at reflexivity and how self-reflexivity and not just dialectical reflexivity transcends the problem of illusion.

In defence of reflexivity: what is it?

Reflexive come from the Latin 'reflectere' bend back: meaning to be directed (reflected) back to the subject or thing. We can analyse this meaning by breaking it down into two meanings. One meaning is that of reflection: long considerative analytic critical evaluative thought. The other meaning is that of reflexion: through observation (sensing) acquiring a mirror image of our actions, almost like a reflex arc. The first meaning describes the process, after the mirror image of our actions impinges on 'the mind's surface', (Dasein as in 'Being in', 'Being there' and 'Being-with'). The second meaning is related to conscious awareness itself, as direct experience is received from external sources: a reflex action to stimuli (being as aesthesia).

So, we are doing two things here: reflecting, as in thinking analytically, critically and evaluatively ('Being-in', 'Being-there' and 'Being-with' with or without intentionality) and 'reflexing', receiving an image then projecting future actions like a response to a given stimuli (being as in aesthesia without intentionality).

If we bring these two meanings together, then reflexivity becomes a process of analytic, critical, evaluative monitoring of the actions of self and others in order to or not to, modify ongoing actions. Reflexivity becomes the critical analytic interpretive and evaluative process between stimulus (receiving an image of our actions) and response (projecting future actions).

In the reflexive process of action research, all the senses are used together. The traditional ones: seeing, hearing, smelling, tasting and touching with reflexivity: ideas of reflection, consciousness, sensation and succession: the emotivity of the soul. We are drawing on all the essential facets developed to understand and master our environment. We are not just 'reflexing' we are reflexive.

Ideas of sensation Locke regarded as the immediate content of perception such as: the sky is blue, the sun is shining and I am warm, that which is given in sensation or by means of the bodily senses 'they are simple ideas of "sensible qualities" and "physical objects"'(Chappell 'Locke', 1994, p. 36), the perception of sensory experience both internal and external. For Locke, ideas of reflection were ideas we have whenever we reflect/introspect on what we are doing. 'The mind gets these "by reflecting on its own Operations within itself": these include the ideas of "Perception, Thinking, Knowing, Willing and are all the different actings of our Minds" (E II. Vii. I and 9: 128 and 131, cited in Chappell, 1994, p. 36).

Thus for Locke, reflection and sensation are each modes of experience. In addition to this, Locke suggested that we have simple ideas of 'succession', which are neither ideas of sensation or mental operations, but are experiences such as pleasure or pain. They 'convey themselves into mind, by all the ways of Sensation and Reflection' (E II. Vii. I: 128, cited in Chappell 1994, p. 37). In other words, for Locke, they come from a combination of the two, both reflection and sensation.

I would suggest however, that ideas of succession are the emotive experiential valves placed on 'ideas of sensible qualities and physical objects'. They are a direct response to stimuli both internal and external. If experience is painful we avoid it, if it is pleasurable we are more likely to do again. It is a survival mechanism. It is combined with reflection, because through reflection we acknowledge the value of experience 'ideas of sensible qualities and physical objects'. Thus, Locke's ideas of succession are the evolutionary experiential emotive middle ground between ideas of sensation and ideas of reflection.

Work done in biopsychology confirms this. The limbic system in the brain serves as a meeting place between the cortex and older parts of the brain, hypothalamus and thalamus. From the cortex the limbic system receives interpreted information about the world, Locke's physical objects, and from the hypothalamus and thalamus it receives interpreted information about the body's internal states, homeostasis, motivation, and emotive experience, Locke's 'sensible qualities'. This information is integrated in the limbic system and relayed back to the cortex, the cortex being responsible for reflection.

These are the brain structures involving Locke's ideas of sensation, succession and reflection in the reflexive turn. Through sensing and placing a value on that sensory experience, i.e. pleasurable or painful, in relation to the body's internal states: homeostasis, motivation and emotional arousal, we build up experiential schemes on which to base future actions (Heidegger's Dasein and the intentionality of 'Being-in'). Reflection is the cognitive process of remembering and critically analysing experiential schemas complete with sensible and physical object experiential values to guide ongoing action. Here is one element for change/no change of future actions.

Descartes' reflexive clarity needs to be based on evidence/objects for it to be regarded as anything other than Kantian perceptual illusion. In action research, reflexivity becomes Descartes' reflexive clarity: Locke's ideas of reflection, sensation and succession, in the form of critical analysis and evaluation of sensory information. Ideas of succession are the aesthetic antipathy of 'being' with intentionality due to the influence of being 'Being-in', 'Being-there', 'Being-with' others in the Heideggarian sense.

The empirical evidence of ideas of sensation, is evaluated by ideas of succession, sometimes in the mode of aesthesia, or aesthetic antipathy, or antipathy, then the reflexive turn in the form of ideas of succession and reflection, critical analysis and evaluation, of ideas of sensation is reflexivity in full circle. Reflexivity can thus be based on being, on aesthesia, without intentionality or aesthetic antipathy, 'Being-in', Being-there' and 'Being-with', with intentionality.

It is the oscillation between sensation and succession (perceiving and critical emotion) and reflection (critical analysis), the oscillation between 'Being-without' (transcendence) and 'Being-in' (Dasein) that transcendental knowledge is forthcoming. Thus, Locke's ideas of sensation succession and reflection in spirals—reflexivity—are the root to reflexive clarity, when emotivity is in the aesthesia mode.

The reflexivity of action research involves the continuous monitoring of the teaching and learning process in a cyclic manner and with heightened conscious awareness because it is a deliberative process. A deliberative process of reflexivity to achieve reflexive clarity of the teaching and learning process with the intention of improvement, improvement of teaching practice and learning for students. For example, we start with *ideas of sensation,* the students can see the diagram on the board, and they have told me they understand it. I am not content however (*ideas of succession*) because I would really like them to explain it to me in their words so that I know they have truly understood it: *Ideas of reflection.* Based on past experience I know that students say they have understood something to hide their embarrassment of not knowing. So I *act* accordingly, I ask the students to explain the diagram. If it has been explained correctly, *ideas of sensation,* my *ideas of succession,* contentment, in *reflection* will guide my ongoing action, move onto the next topic.

In this instance, the reflexive clarity of the reflexive process can be based on being (the aesthesia mode) or 'Being-in', 'Being-there' and 'Being-with' with or without intentionality. It is with intentionality however, the intentionality to achieve fusion of horizons between the teacher and the students, the improvement of the teaching and learning situation. The traditional model of action research: plan, act, observe, reflect and revise plan, is the same cyclic process (Winter, 1987; Zuber-Skerritt, 1992), involved in reflexivity to achieve reflexive clarity. Reflexivity is a cyclical process of sensation/sensing, succession/evaluating and reflection/critical analysis. In this manner, reflexivity becomes both theory and practice of action research, the theory is reflexivity as 'being', 'Being-in', Being-there' or 'being-with', in the process of reflexive clarity, the practice.

The main contention to reflexivity is Kant's notion of illusion. Dialectical reflexivity transcends illusion because it involves inter-subjectivity. Gregory (1966) suggests illusions occur because perception is not determined simply by stimulus patterns, but is a dynamic searching for the best interpretation of the available information, and involves inferences. Illusions can also be an example of mistaken perception (Coon, 1983). Action research though, is a continuous process of reflexivity, over the period of an hour or two, which builds into weeks, months and sometimes years. I fail to see how in a process of continual reflexivity anyone could be susceptible to illusion. Reflexivity transcends illusion—plan-act-observe-reflect-and-revise-plan in spirals overcomes the problems associated with misperception and misinterpretation.

If for example you continually regard the lack of understanding of students, of information you are teaching them as their lack of intelligence and not perhaps your teaching method, then you are deluding yourself. This is not illusion but delusion. It is self-inflicted illusion. A competent teacher however will search ever possibility until they find the reason for the lack of understanding. This is the true nature of reflexive practice and the root to reflexive clarity. Reflexive practice therefore rules out the possibility of illusion. The reflexive practitioner produces hypotheses or plans of action, observes and reflects on the actions to see if they confirm the hypotheses and if they do not, then further hypotheses/plans of action are produced and so forth until a plan of action is forth coming which solves the problem. During this process of sensing, succession and reflection any illusion would be resolved.

It is the socio-political, cultural-historical situatedness of being as Dasein, 'Being-in', Being—there' and 'Being-with' with or without intentionality which remains unresolved and which I will discuss in detail later. But nonetheless, it is I suggest the reflexivity involved in abduction and retroduction that has led to some of the greatest scientific discoveries we know, discovers that transcend both the socio-political, cultural-historical situatedness of being for them to be discovered in the first instance, any intentionalities being reflexive clarity.

Critical psychology and reflexivity

In what way is reflexivity the theory behind action research? Nick Heather wrote:

> '[F]or psychology to be reflexive, I mean that any theory of human behaviour must be able to explain how theories of human behaviour come about, because the making of those theories is part of the human behaviour that the theory sets out in the first place to explain…the activity of scientists in theorising, experimenting and observing, etc., is not different in kind from the ordinary activity of other men and women and, indeed, from the activity of scientists when they are not wearing scientific hats . . . psychologists make observations about observers, experiment with experimenters and theorise about theorisers' (Heather, 1976, p. 28).

Heather goes on to explain how George Kelly's 'Personal Construct Theory (PCT)' gives us a theory of wo/man which is reflexive. It can account for itself and the objects observed: Thus when asking the question, 'in what way is reflexivity the theory behind action research?' the answer is three fold. Kelly's 'wo/man the scientist' as a reflexive entity gives us a theory that accounts for itself—epistemology, the object of study—ontology, and as the deliberative process of reflexivity, action research, reflexivity, becomes a methodology and part of the method. What more could a social science ask of any theory! It has truth value, can be used to predict future events and past events, difference in perception and evaluation can be put down to differences in values, motives, interests or biology and culture. It has internal consistency and again when linked with action research 'wo/man the scientist' as a reflexive practitioner generates research. It's useful and changes behaviour, but as yet behaviour remains situated culturally but may through the continuousness and the careful sense of responsibility for truth and emotionality transcend the constraints of time, thus spatiality.

From wo/man the scientist to the scientific community

According to Kelly's PCT, we are all scientists. We put our own interpretations on the world of events and from these personal theories, go on to produce hypotheses, predictions about future events. From a repertoire of personal constructs, according to Kelly's notion of 'constructive alternativism', we have no way of knowing the exact nature of physical objects or reality, we only know that it exists, thus we place a personal construct on the world of events to explain it.

The personal constructs and theories we have are schemas. Templates of events (episodes of social encounter in the classroom for example), behavioural repertoire (ways of acting in those social encounters); experiential schemas built upon over our lifetime, or in relation to educational action research, over our teaching careers. From this repertoire of experiential schemas, theories and constructs, we choose the ones we think best fits the world or social reality or behaviour we are confronted with at the time to explain. Kelly's 'wo/man the scientist' in other words, uses all three forms of ideas, the ideas of sensation, succession and reflection on which to base future actions. With action research however, we *consciously* plan, act, observe and reflect on episodes of social encounter and ways of acting in those situations, in a much more purposeful and deliberate manner: we plan to transcend to gain knowledge. The values, motives and interests, Heidegger's intentionalities, are part of the process. Another aspect of action research is the notion of dialectical reflexivity, that is, not Kelly's 'wo/man the scientist' but 'the scientific community'—a community of reflexive practitioners/research partners and students.

All hail reflexivity!

There is irony here. From the enlightenment period to the 1960s, or there about, many social scientists were adamant that science would not be based on subjective reasoning and here am I asking you to go full swing into such a methodology that uses full blown rationality—reflexivity, as the ontology, epistemology, methodology! We have just gone through a period in social science history where nothing could be taken-for-granted (Berger and Luckmann) because of the socio-political, cultural-historical biases in perception and interpretation of objects: the social construction of reality. Now I am suggesting we use the essence of that very phenomena effected by those biases as the glorious tool capable of overcoming those very biases. I suggest this *is* fighting fire with fire! Reflexivity is the way forward, and it appears to be the process chosen by many in the social sciences, and not just social constructionists.

Action research, critical theory and transcendental realism

Note the similarity between action research as a reflexive practice and the retroductive (transcendental realists research strategy, Harre and Bhaskar) and abductive (the research strategy advocated by Habermas) strategies of social inquiry. The retroductive and abductive strategies of social inquiry are based on cyclic processes not the linear logic of induction and deduction. Reflexive action research is a cyclic process. Action research involves building models for action, 'plan-act-observe-reflect-and-revise plan'. It is a combination of abduction and retroduction—'Abduction is the process used to produce social scientific accounts of social life by drawing on the concepts and meanings used by social actors, and the activities in which they engage' (Blaikie, 1993, p. 176). The retroductive research strategy involves the building of models in order to explain observed regularities. Action research brings retroduction and abduction together as a methodology. We are using the same methodology and method Kepler used when he discovered the elliptical orbits of plants. The only distinction being, we are applying it to the social world. Our abduction involves obtaining the meaning and understanding social actors have of their world so we can understand that world better from their point of view as well as our own, evaluating it based on the mutual understanding of meanings and values and then changing it.

The process would be as follows. We start with inductive reasoning, which begins with a singular statement and concludes with a general statement. For example:

1) *This group of students are first year students and have little knowledge of the discipline thus need teaching using the traditional method—lectures.*
2) *All first year students have little knowledge of the discipline thus all first year students need teaching using traditional methods.*

If we were to use deductive reasoning, we would start from a general statement then conclude with a particular statement, which is the reverse of inductive reasoning. Both these methods may be based on prior observations but they do not leave room for the unexpected or the exception to the rule. Many students have done private study for example. Thus, the linear logic of these methods falls down. Action research however, retroduction and abduction, are based on cyclic or spiral processes of reflexivity, the linear logic of these methods is looped into a cycle or spiral of action. From observation, we make hypotheses about connections such as in two above, which we then test using induction and deduction. The abductive strategy will also entail asking the subjects for their understanding and meanings, to see if the theory is correct, for example, asking the students what they know about a topic and how they would like to go about learning the topic. Then the theory as in two above will be accepted or rejected on this basis.

Abduction is about hypothesising and testing and re-testing, just like action research, plan-act-observe-reflect-and-revise-planning. It is a continuous process of dialectical reflexivity (interactive discussion between teacher and students) and change. Sifting through experiential schemas of episodes of classroom encounter to synthesis the teaching strategy, conditions for the teaching/learning process and learning style which are more enabling to the achievement of fusion of horizons in that social encounter. The outcome is fusion of horizons and further experiential schemas, models, plans of action on which to base future episodes of social encounter in the classroom.

The retroductive strategy of social inquiry involves induction, deduction and abduction, as well as building models to explain phenomena, for example, building models of social episodes of encounter: Planning for future teaching/ learning sessions based on observation, evaluation and reflection. Action research is a form of retroduction. Plans for action are based on observations, evaluations and reflections of episodes of social encounter in the classroom. Theories are produced, i.e., seminars would be the best way of teaching this topic or group etc., and then the practitioner acts in accordance with these observations and theories. Again, these actions are observed and reflected upon and further planning takes place, including a diary or report, which will be kept for future reference. It is a continuing spiral of action, and planning based on observation, evaluation and reflection, and the recording of the entire process: The process of action research, and the process of teaching and learning. The plans for future action, drawn from these processes are the final product, the models of retroductive reasoning.

The planning and revised planning at each stage of planning involves a model for a particular episode of social encounter in the classroom. Over numerous cycles of planning, acting, observing, reflecting and revised planning, you build up a catalogue of episodes of social encounter, which have been critically analysed and evaluated by you as a reflexive practitioner, sometimes your peers, and the students involved in the teaching and learning process. These models or plans of action contain teaching strategies, learning objectives and outcomes, group size and level of development and so forth. Not just based on one individual's interests, motives and values, but those of all involved, because all those involved have analysed and critically evaluated and reflected upon the teaching and learning process, the episodes of social encounter. This is full-blown reflexivity, which incorporates the ideas of sensation, succession and reflection.

Transcendental realism/retroduction: action research

Bhaskar (1983) one of the leading transcendental realists who advocate retroduction was critical of the unity between retroductive and abductive strategies because of biases of social actor's interpretations of their actions:

> '[I]t is important to distinguish the meaning of an act (or utterance) from the agent's intention in performing it. The meaning of an act is a social fact which, to the extent that the act is intentional, is utilized by the actor in the production of his performance. But the reason that the act is performed by the agent is a fact about the person which cannot be read off or deduced from its social meaning' (Bhaskar, 1983, p. 292).

What Bhaskar is saying here is that there is a distinction between the meaning of actions and the motives, interests and values that affect actions, for example, if a parent smacks a child it could have a number of meanings depending on the motives. It may be that the child was disobedient therefore the motive would be corrective, it may be that the parent wants to frighten the child to prevent it from disclosing something that the adults do not want others to know about. Therefore, the motive would be selfish on behalf of the parent/s.

With the dialectical reflexive process involved in action research, the meanings and motives for actions are continually open to discussion by 'the scientific community', or the collection of reflexive practitioners/students. Indeed, in higher education generally, students are asked to assess each module. In many cases, the students are involved in the reflexive process of action research, evaluating the teaching and learning process and are invited to offer solutions to any problems that might develop. It is a democratic process of dialectical reflection to reach a compromise of intentionalities: inter-intentionality. This overcomes the individual biases of socio-political and cultural-historical meanings, beliefs, motives and interests. These motives *are* what spur action research on. Students it is assumed enter higher education to learn. Thus, their motivation is improved learning by contributing to the democratic process of dialectical reflexivity.

Action research or deliberative reflexivity which units these two strategies not only overcomes the hurdles of finding the truth of meanings and motives, but because we can build models for future action, it may be the key to discovering what Bhaskar calls the real domain of reality. The underlying structures and mechanisms that exist and which make up this reality. Habermas' hermeneutically critical-emancipatory interpretivism allows insight into some of these underlying structures and mechanism, namely the epistemic worldviews of subjects/socio-political, cultural-historical unity, units (Marx's practical-critical activity as the fusion point in dialectical historical materialism: see chapter 4). The bias that might occur in conducting action research is group thinking or social cognition. I am thinking here of Kuhn's notion of the scientific community, as an example of group thinking/social cognition. The solution to this problem can also be found in Habermas' critical theory.

Habermas: hermeneutically critical-emancipatory interpretivism/abduction: action research

Habermas' critical theory is one variation of social and cultural hermeneutic science. The mode of experience is 'communicative experience'. Like action research, the researcher is a 'reflexive partner' understanding meaning derived from communication with the social actors using the strategy of abduction. It is a dialogic venture thus overcomes the problem suggested by Bhaskar, i.e., the bias of social actor's interpretations, meaning and motives. As Norman Blaikie states: '[T] he process for understanding this socially constructed reality is 'dialogic', it allows individuals to communicate about their experience within a shared framework of cultural meanings', (1993, p. 53).

In the same manner as action research, this process means that the reflexive practitioner, the researcher/participant by his act of reflexive practice in collaboration with others, overcomes the intransitivity of monologic science processes. The process becomes a dialogic dialectically reflexive process. In addition to this, Habermas' critical theory involves three forms of knowledge: 'It includes: interpretive understanding of systems of belief and modes of communication using the methods of historical-hermeneutic science, the critical evaluation of these; and the investigation of their causes by the methods of empirical-analytic science' (Blaikie, 1993: p. 55).

The historical-hermeneutic aspect to Habermas' critical theory is the key to overcoming the problem of group thinking, or the social cognition of a given 'scientific community of reflexive practitioners'. Winter overcame this problem by introducing the notion of a 'playful sphere' for creating meanings and understanding, in which there are winners and looser in the game of truth placing and reality knowing. Thus, this particular problem then for Winter, remains really. We are still left with competing realities and competing truths, not only within a given 'community of reflexive practitioners', but between them. In other words, the 'playful sphere' allows freedom of interpretation but not necessarily freedom of 'the truth' and 'the reality'.

The same problem remains with Habermas' critical theory, it does not provide a foundation for emancipatory science: One in which truth and reality are free from interpretations, interests and motives because 'he needs to find a way of establishing the truth of the critique' (Blaikie, 1993). The motives, values and interests of action research are part of the research so this problem is resolved. Habermas resolves the problem of competing truths and reality, or competing interpretations by introducing the notion of 'critical discussion' and 'rational consensus' between 'scientific communities', in what he calls the 'ideal speech situation'. But what is the ideal speech situation? Action research by its very nature involves critical discussion culminating in rational consensus. In a community of reflexive practitioners/ partners, and reflexive social inquiry, we have the fertile ground for an emancipatory science.

Critical psychology, social constructionism and reflexivity

Critical psychology at present is about critical analysis and evaluation of the subject matter of the discipline. Indeed, within the height of post-modernity, the emphasis is on reflexivity. Looking back at the narrative of social theory in an analytic, critical and evaluative manner: what was the author's worldview, motives and interests when writing the text, theory or conducting research? What are its uses? What alternative does it obscure? Does it fit reality? Deconstructing texts, theory and research *is* critical psychology or to use the post-modern assemblage, social constructionism. Constructing, deconstructing and reconstruct theory and research based on rigorous critical analysis and evaluation: reflexivity.

The notion of a scientific community proposed by Kuhn where 'truth becomes a matter of community consensus' is transcended via the process of construction, deconstruction and reconstruction. Incompatible worldviews, or different and competing worldviews produced by different scientific communities or reflexive practitioners, become part of a catalogue of worldviews which enter a global arena (especially at the height of post-modernity) of reflexivity in which intentionalities, motive, valves and/or interests are critically analysed and evaluated for truth, reality and value. When involved in the process of construction, deconstruction and reconstruction what they are engaging in is 'hermeneutically critical-emancipatory evaluative interpretive activity. This is the closest the social sciences have come to Habermas' 'ideal speech situation' in which there is freedom of truth and reality. Is this a matter of Berger and Luckmann's social construction of reality? Are we as reflexive practitioners and teachers of critical social theory constructing but another perspective, worldview with which to view the World and if so is it any better than those we already have?

I see reflexivity as the means of obtaining a true reflexion of reality. Theorists from many spheres have transcended upon different aspects of the reflexive process as a means of obtaining this truth. Reflexivity is about change. Change becomes the only constant in the process of construction, deconstruction and reconstruction until freedom of truth and reality is achieved. It is a cyclic process much like action research, retroduction and abduction. I see reflexivity as a process, a methodology, ontology and epistemology: as a realisation or acknowledgement of the very facet that exists reflexivity, which can be used to discover other truths about reality: The ultimate unity between empiricism, rationalism and emotivism. Emotivity being the ability to place value on objects and it emanates from the core of human essence.

What are the problems involved in this unity?

In uniting different research strategies, we encounter several ontological and epistemological problems. There are similarities and differences between the various perspectives that advocate either the use of abduction or retroduction. The main dichotomy is between the realists who advocate the use of retroduction and the constructionists who advocate the use of abduction. Critical psychology has much in common with its post-modern assemblage, social constructionism.

In terms of ontology, it is far to say that realists such as Bhaskar and Harre, critical theorists such as Habermas and feminists, structuration theorist Giddens, and social constructionists view reality and the identity of the subject as socially constructed and reconstructed. Both Bhaskar and Giddens however, belief this reality to be embedded in the social structures, Giddens in particular, and operating at a level beyond the understanding of ordinary wo/men and as far as Bhaskar is concerned, above and beyond the comprehension of social scientists. Bhaskar suggests that structures and mechanisms exist, and that we cannot directly see or have knowledge of them.

The social structures Giddens refers to are the culturally embedded patternings of social relations that have become institutionalised and thus exist as if cast in stone. These institutionalised social relations are the culturally determining forces operating against the freewill of the individual, but which the individual is over-against thus the dialectics of agency-structure. Bhaskar's structures and mechanisms however, are a combination of those Giddens refers to and mechanisms that operate in the universe referred to as 'ultimate reality', *the reality*.

Bhaskar suggests that there are three domains of reality, the empirical consisting of events which can be observed, the actual, consisting of events which occur that we might not be aware of, and the real which consists of structures and mechanisms which produce these events. The empirical domain relates to Locke's ideas of sensation, the actual can only be achieved through reflection and succession and the real can be achieved by synthesising information from the empirical and the actual: reflexivity.

Habermas himself indirectly, as do feminists, acknowledge the fact that social structures can operate, at times, beyond individual freewill, but like Giddens have belief in the reverse—that individuals can directly and indirectly influence social structures. Habermas and critical social theorist's of all manifestation, aim to emancipate the subject from the influences of those structures. 'The autonomy of individuals' is their goal.

Some realists such as Bhaskar are more interested in the technological scientific understanding, and some might suggest that such a unification of dichotomised viewpoints is impossible. I suggest not. The taking from each of these perspectives the elements that connect into an internally consistent whole, is a move forward and perhaps one that will result in a perspective that brings us closer to Bhaskar's actual and real domains of reality.

I suggest that the differences could still be subjected to 'community consensus' as in the tradition of social constructionism, made up of pragmatists, but should function alongside the elements that form the unified whole. Be the unification theoretical or the practicalities of research strategies. Even pragmatists such as the social constructions must have some understanding of 'the reality', not necessarily just competing reality. Social and institutional discourses admittedly are socially constructed, deconstructed and reconstructed and constantly changing. But there are themes and continuities in the constructive processes that are influenced by events. I suggest that these patternings and the events that influence them are the key to Bhaskar's and feminists 'singular reality'. We are approaching a point in social science history in which we see not only themes and patternings of a social constructed reality but also themes and patternings of a socially constructed social science research. Thus, although societal events and social researches are situated spatially and temporally, a compilation of knowledge of these should help us to transcend the spacio-temporal bounds of the relativity of research if not societal events and happenings.

As far as epistemology is concerned, all positions seek understanding. All seek understanding of social actor's meanings and understanding of the subjects' social realities. By uniting realism, critical theory (Habermas and the feminist), and social constructionism, including critical psychology, through action research we will get a deeper understanding of the process of social construction with its many realities and perhaps move from the linear logic of competing realities, to discover the themes (structures and mechanism) of those realities. The cyclical process of reflexivity is thus a move toward the real domain of Bhaskar's *reality*. Thus, we arrive at an ontology that draws on the similarities of realism, critical social theory, structuration theory, feminism and social constructionism, consisting of:

1. An ontology as a social reality and subject which is socially constructed, deconstructed and reconstructed in a cyclical process, but which has underlying patternings and mechanisms which can be discovered by recognition of those patternings and through this recognition of patternings, discover the mechanisms that operate beyond our present consciousness of them.

2. We get an epistemology which consists of penetrating the frame of meaning and understanding social actors have of their human condition and in the same instance the understanding of the frame of meanings social scientists have of the subject matter so we achieve multiple hermeneutics.

3. We get a methodology and method of social inquiry which aims to facilitate the understanding and meaning of that ontology and epistemology which is the process of deliberative reflexivity involved in action research. *Planning* (or theory production) *acting* (testing that theory or hypothesis using induction, deduction and abduction), *reflecting*, critically analysing and evaluating the data collected, and *re-planning*, producing new theories for testing, or planning actions based on the observations recorded and analysed. This latter planning stage being the model building retroduction involves.

4. The method of action research like any other research is the way these observations are recorded and the way data is collected. It is the rigorous process of reflexive practice that is its distinguishing feature, dialectical reflexivity in educational action research.

5. The aims of this action research being, to discover causal mechanism, i.e., cause and effect chains of culturally embedded patternings of social structures, in order to understand, thus control those mechanisms and activate a process of emancipation.

Teaching and learning in an atmosphere of reflexivity

In the educational action research I am proposing, 1 to 5 would all be part of the same process: Reflexivity as the ontology, epistemology, methodology and method. Number 1 above entails the locating of the zone of proximal development as the mechanism or foci in Marx's dialectical historical materialism—the fusion point of brain-mind in the space time continuum of four dimensional events: The creation of ideas from material practice. The material practice of reflexively radical practical-critical evaluative activity (DRRP-CEA): deliberative dialectical reflexivity.

Number 2 would be the same deliberative process of the process itself, the dialectically reflexively radical practical-critical evaluative activity of, reflexively hermeneutically critical-evaluative interpretive activity which leads to doubly double hermeneutics. There is the double hermeneutics of the teaching and learning process and the double historical hermeneutics of the subject matter of psychology. The methodology and method would be the same deliberative dialectical reflexive process: the continuous monitoring of the teaching and learning situation to achieve fusion of horizons which leads to 5, doubly double hermeneutics and double emancipation.

Reflexively radical practical-critical evaluative activity is the distilled form of Marx's practical-critical activity. The activity Marx put forward as a way of understanding the world and changing it. It is the combination of Locke's ideas of sensation, succession and reflection in a cyclical process of reflexivity: Sensing, practical; and succession and reflection as critical-evaluation, all together become practical-critical-evaluative-activity.

It is radical because of the way reflexivity turns this activity into a continual spiral of activity: continuous monitoring of the teaching and learning process to maintain fusion of horizons at the zone of proximal development, Vygotsky's zone of proximal development. In addition, practical-critical activity is Marx's dialectical historical materialism: The methodology of producing ideas from material practice. In this way, reflexively radical practical-critical evaluative activity is emancipatory. We get emancipation on two levels, firstly the emancipation of the subject, improved learning, and the emancipation of the subject matter of the social sciences: truth-reality.

Doubly double hermeneutics

'The social sciences operate within a double hermeneutics, involving two-way ties with the actions and institutions of those they study. Sociological [and social psychological] observers depend upon lay concepts to generate accurate descriptions of social processes; and agents regularly appropriate theories and concepts of social science within their behaviour, thus potentially changing its character' (Giddens, 1987, p. 30-31).

Giddens (1987), suggested that double hermeneutics was at the core of social science research. Double hermeneutics being the researcher's immersion in with the subjects under investigation, to the point whereby, the researcher knows enough about the subject's subculture to be able to function as part of that subculture. It is about understanding the subject's worldview and being able to function in that socio-political, cultural-historical unity. It is about observing and reflecting on the social situation until the researcher can function within it effectively. During the process, there is a two-way interchange of meanings and understanding and exchange of languages: The technical language of the social sciences and the lay language of the subjects. What develops is 'mutual knowledge'. Giddens calls it double hermeneutics because the interchange is dual. The researcher gets to understand the subject's worldview, and the subject gets insight into the worldview of the researcher. It involves empathic interchange.

Habermas' hermeneutically critical-emancipatory interpretivism when brought into the equation with action research, and practised alongside it, overcomes the bias of interests, motives and interpretations of the subject matter of social theory and the teaching and learning of social theory, which therefore leads to double hermeneutics *and* historical hermeneutics. There is the double hermeneutics described by Giddens, of dialectical reflexivity and dialectical historical hermeneutics. Gadamer regards historical hermeneutics as: '[T]he fusion of horizons that takes place in the understanding as the actual achievement of language' (Gadamer, 1989, p. 378).

Thus for Gadamer, hermeneutical understanding is historical understanding: The bringing together of the horizons of the past and the horizons of the present: In a classroom situation if this is achieved for all participants, then each one achieves historical understanding or hermeneutical understanding of the author, theory, or research being studied. Critical discussion and rational consensus of the teaching and learning process entails overcoming the individual bias, individual epistemic worldview, motives and interest, of the teaching situation. Critical discussion between teacher and students, and reflexive practice thus leads to rational consensus of the reality and truth of teaching practice, this gives us mutual knowledge at the teaching and learning process level: double hermeneutics. However, during the teaching and learning process of the subject matter of psychology, we overcome the epistemic worldview of theorists and social researchers by critical discussion involving the historic-hermeneutics of a given author or theorist. It is dialectical historic-hermeneutics due to the critical discussion between participants. This is the second level of understanding that is also double hermeneutics.

It becomes emancipatory because through dialectically reflexively radical practical-critical evaluative activity of dialectically reflexively hermeneutically critical-emancipatory interpretive activity we achieve a critical evaluative understanding of the author, theorist or researcher that brings us closer to reality and truth. Thus, we get doubly double hermeneutics. We also get double emancipation. The emancipation of the truth and reality of the author and the emancipation of the teaching and learning process: Deeper learning for the students, better practice for the teacher. The author's worldview and interpretation of truth and reality is not only open to critical evaluation and analysis but also, the worldviews of participants. We get Gadamer's fusion of horizons between the theorist and us as interpreters and the fusion of horizons between participants in the critical discussion. Discussing known events and contingencies that influenced the author and the interpreters of the author gives us the epistemological worldview, interests and motives of both the author and interpreters: doubly double hermeneutics.

The first and second purposes of my action research were related. If using action research to achieve Vygotsky's zone of proximal development is possible, then in the same instance; we achieve doubly double hermeneutics. This in turn should lead to: A, improvements in the teaching and learning situation; thus improved practice, B, improved learning, spontaneous scientific concept formation and therefore develop a deeper understanding of the subject matter of social theory; leading to better evaluations of the subject matter being learned. And C, A, and B should lead to the emancipation of the truth and reality of social psychology: Double emancipation.

However, this differs from the 'ideal speech situation' Habermas was referring to because it involves the critical discussion between reflexive practitioners and students in one locality. But it does show how that 'ideal speech situation' could be manifest. At the very least, it shows how we can overcome the spacio-temporal bounds of relativism, because although all knowledge is relative, there are bounds to the relativity of knowledge: space and time, and thus the generality of that knowledge. Hermeneutic understanding of social situations in the ways described here with the documented spacio-temporal boundaries gives insight into those boundaries therefore helps us to overcome them.

Through this process of DRRP-CEA and DRHC-EIA, which leads to doubly double hermeneutics, incompatible worldviews, or different and competing worldviews produced by different scientific communities or reflexive practitioners, become part of a catalogue of worldviews. These experiences can be documented and build up into a catalogue of worldviews and classroom episodes of social encounter.

In addition, linking DRRP-CEA and DRHC-EIA to transcendental realist, Harre's notions of ethongenics would produce the following. According to the principles of ethongenics, the social world is primarily made up of episodes of individual encounters which we need to construct homeomorphs for (models of social encounter in which the subject is the source i.e. action research models). And which we need to construct paramorphs for (were the subject and source of the model are different). Once these episodes of social encounter (i.e. documented pieces of action research), are published, we end up with iconic models for episodes of individual encounter and a catalogue of worldviews, which when put together means, we will be able to reproduce any given social encounter complete with subjects' worldviews—At least in the teaching and learning environment anyway and as Harre says:

> 'It is through imagined paramorphs and their connection with their sources, multiple, single, semi or fragmentary, that theoretical terms gain part, and a vital part, of their meaning. A scientific explanation of a process or pattern among phenomena is provided by a theory constructed in this way' (Harre, 1970, p. 46-7).

In other words, it is through building such models that we gain insight into the processes we engage in and the fragmentation of relativism is transcended. Action research is quite a unique model of action. It is a methodology for social inquiry and a model for producing models—plans for episodes of social encounter based on observation of social encounter, and reflections of social encounter to produce further plans, models.

We could build these planed models of episodes of social encounter into a matrix to predict future social relations in given episodes of social encounter complete with the psychological units—worldviews. In fact, is this not what researcher do all the time? In conducting research and interpreting research, we are documenting episodes of social encounter. If we do this through the process of DRRP-CEA and DRHC-EIA then we will overcome the socio-temporal fragmentation of relativism thus freeing 'the truth' and 'the reality'. Validity will be true validity.

Our homeomorphs of episodes of social encounter and epistemological worldviews will be based on the true understanding and meanings of social agents including other contingencies such as world events of economic crisis, political climate, socio-cultural historical climate etc., with a deeper understanding on a scientific level. Because of this, research will have generality and we will be able to offer solutions to problems and prevent them, therefore emancipating the subject not only in education but also in action research in all its manifestations.

In relation to educational work, this two-fold reflexivity (reflexivity of teaching and learning and the reflexivity of critical social theory) gives us doubly double hermeneutics. There is the double hermeneutics I have discussed associated with the fusion of horizons between authors and interpreters. There is also be the fusion of horizons between reflexive practitioners, and once more pieces of action research are conducted and documented within higher education, and the research put forward for critical discussion by other 'communities of reflexive practitioners', we have multiple hermeneutics.

What we have is the means to transcend spatially and temporally: the true freedom of truth and reality. The interests, motives and values of interpreters however associated with the teaching and learning process may spur it on, but the interests, motives and valves of social science subject matter generally will remain openly contested in the communal reflexivity of critical social theory. Intentionalities will either be compromised through the dialectical reflexivity of the global scientific community, or will be transcended.

Conclusion

Reflexivity is the theory and practice of action research, the ontology, epistemology, methodology and method. It is Heidegger's ontology-epistemology 'Being-with', Dasein, 'the intelligibility': consciousness and intentionality of improving, in the educational setting, the teaching and learning process. It is the deliberative process of reflexivity thus involves the cyclical process of sensation, succession and reflection over time with the aim of achieving reflexive clarity thus gaining transcendental knowledge of the mechanisms and patterning of social encounters and the social relations in those encounters.

Reflexivity transcends illusion because it is based on ideas of sensation, succession and reflection in cycles leading to reflexive clarity. The understanding of the meanings of the social situation is *a priori* because of the *a priori* of intentionalities: Dasein that make up 'Being-in', 'Being-there' and 'Being-with'. However, because reflexivity is the conscious practice of reflexive clarity, it allows you to go beyond the surface mean of social situations to acquire transcendental understanding of the patternings and mechanism.

The competing interpretations of reality that may develop are incorporated into the dialectical reflexive process thus part of the process of achieving reflexive clarity. The intentionalities, motives and interests are continually open to examination and form part of action research, the goal being emancipation of the subjects. It is Marx's practical-critical activity: The critical analysis and evaluation of material practice to produce ideas for change: dialectical historical materialism.

Action research is a cyclical process, the same cyclical process involved in abduction and retroduction—it units the opposing camps of realism and social constructionism in their many guises. Through this unity, we have the framework for methodological activity that can in theory transcend the spatiality and temporality of meanings and experience, thus the fragmentation of relativity.

Doubly double hermeneutics is possible; the construction of homeomorphs of episodes of social encounter, psychological units, and socio-political, cultural-historical unity, units, which can be built into matrices from which paramorphs can be constructed, is possible. It is revolutionary activity. It leads to double emancipation in education, the emancipation of the subjects, improved learning, teaching and education and because it involves dialectical reflexivity of the subject matter being taught: dialectical historical hermeneutics, it leads to the emancipation of the subject matter of the social science.

In addition, it gives us insight into Habermas' 'ideal speech situation' because DRRP-CEA of DRHC-EIA, I suggest, is the cognitive mode of that ideal speech situation. Therefore, dialectical reflexivity (or quadratic reflexivity as more than two people are part of a scientific community) leads to the emancipation of the subject matter of the social sciences through the multiply hermeneutics involved in a 'global scientific community'.

Once the DRRP-CEA of DRHC-EIA technique is mastered however, the possibilities are infinite. Within higher education, it leads to the location of students' zones of proximal development (Vygotsky's zone of proximal development) thus emancipate the student's intellectual capacity. In action research generally, it will lead to validity and reliability.

Chapter Three

Reflexive practice: maintaining interaction in the zone of proximal development

Abstract

In this study, dialectical reflexive practice is used to maintain student-teacher interactions in the zone of proximal development. The zone of proximal development is the development-and-learning unit of the child or learner and I suggest that it is also the fusion point of Marx's dialectical historical materialism: the creation of ideas from material practice. Reflexive practice, as a concentrated form of activity, leads to a heightening of consciousness awareness and becomes the 'tool' and 'result' methodology of pin pointing and maintaining interaction in the zone of proximal development, encouraging learning which converts into development. Transcriptions of two taught sessions were evaluated for evidence of deep learning. All students achieved deep learning and reflexive practice skills. The curriculum model used was the learning outcome-led model: the congruency between learning outcome, approach to learning and assessment.

Keywords Reflexive Practice, dialectical reflexive practice, zone of proximal development, concept formation, deep learning

Purpose and background to the study

Reflexive practice in education is 'learning-in-practice' (Elliott, 1991; Eastcott, 1992; Newman & Holzman, 1993; Chaiklin & Lave, 1996). According to Kolb's (1973) learning cycle, concrete experience is reflected up on and actions based on these reflections convert into knowledge and learning. Thus, reflexive practice as a cognitive style is beneficial not only to teachers but also students (Kolb et al, 1973; Schön, 1983; Ronald Barnett, 1992). The reflexive practice of action research is likewise 'learning-in-practice' and I am placing it within the theoretical framework of activity theory, because action research in education has become devoid of its roots. Kurt Lewin (1946) coined the term 'action research' and his original spiral of action plan-act-observe-reflect-and-revise-plan has been adapted numerous times in educational research (Winter 1987; Kemmis & McTaggart 1988; Elliott, 1991; Eastcott, 1992). Lewin's background, developmental psychology, in turn can be found in the experimental developmental studies of Vygotsky (1962).

Vygotsky following on from Marx was an activity theorist (Newman & Holzman, 1993; Chaiklin & Lave, 1996). The main premise behind activity theory is that we learn through actively engaging with the world in social contexts. Contexts are important to activity theorists because each context brings with it a set of rules and constrains on action (Biggs; 1990; Newman & Holzman, 1993; Chaiklin & Lave, 1996; Engestrom; 1996 Allan, 1997). With reflexive practice however, the rules are the practice of reflexive activity aimed at improved practice and learning, therefore, when both teacher and students are reflexive practitioners, the rules are congruous with the practice. That is, we reflect on practice in order to produce ideas for improvement, which may entail change in practice. Hence, activity theoretic: The rules clearly are that change might well be the norm. Reflective practice is the activity of producing theory: activity-theoretic. The constraints involved in teaching and learning nonetheless are variable and harder to control or eliminate (Biggs, 1990; Chaiklin & Lave, 1996).

The unification of the reflexive practice of action research and activity theory, in particular, builds on Newman & Holzman's adaptation of the Marxian-Vygotskian methodology: The practical-critical activity of enhancing development through instruction led learning in the zone of proximal development (Newman & Holzman, 1993). The reflexivity involved in action research I suggest is the methodology of exacting/pin pointing the learner's actual level of development and maintaining student-teacher interaction in the zone of proximal development to initiate learning that converts into development. Therefore, reflexive practice as the daily practice of action research is a way of learning though practice to improve it. I hope to demonstrate this, in this study.

Reflexive and reflective are similar but different concepts. Being reflective involves thinking about practice but being reflexive involves thinking about practice and also contains an element of continuity such that the practice of thinking works back on the reflexive practitioner to enhance practice or learning. Thus, much like a reflexive arch, being reflexive entails critically thinking about practice in order to draw insights from it that can be put back into practice to improve it.

The main research question is: 'Does dialectical reflexive practice maintain teacher-student interaction in the zone of proximal development?' If the research question is validated, then it offers support for the view that reflexive practice leads to improvements in teaching and learning, that is, if those *are* the intentions of the reflexive participants and also given the constraints of teaching and learning. Secondly, if the research question is validated, it offers support for the existence of a social encounter in which doubly double hermeneutics is possible. Double hermeneutics is communicative activity in which participants—teacher and students—understand each other's worldviews enough to function within that particular socio-political, cultural-historical unity (Giddens, 1987). Once this is achieved, teacher and students then move on to develop historical hermeneutics (Habermas, 1972; Gadamer 1989), that is, achieve a deeper understanding of the epistemic worldview of the theorist/ author or research discussed (Lisle, 2000, pp. 123-125).

One limitation to this study is that it involves a group of students who agreed to take part in the study and they just happened to be on the course at that particular point in time—accidental? The objectives of action research or reflexive practice are usually 'situational and specific' and the samples 'restricted and unrepresentative with little or no control over the independent variables' (Cohen & Manion, 1994, p. 35). Thus, the findings of action research or reflexive studies are thought not to have general application. In this study, I cannot claim for example that introducing dialectical reflexive practice into my teaching practice will result in autonomous learning for students because many students are autonomous learners to begin with. What I can say however is that dialectical reflexivity is more likely to facilitate the development of deep learning and autonomous learning in comparison to formal monologic teaching for example because the very nature of practising reflection—thinking, causes changes in brain activity and structure (Ratey, 2001) equated with deep learning/semantic learning. That is unless one is daydreaming, but such reflections are not the desired intentions of reflexive practice aimed at learning. Dialectical reflexivity is meant to prevent any misunderstanding. For example, dialectical reflexivity overcomes the biases of perception thus eliminates the possibility of illusion (Winter, 1987), in that, student understanding is achieved and evaluated as part of the ongoing process of dialectical reflection: If you want to know if the students understand a concept you can ask them or engage them in debate that will reveal their understanding. This is not always easy but I will attempt it!

Literature review and theoretical framework: Activity theory

The main theoretical framework for this study is activity theory. Karl Marx was one of the main advocates of activity theory; his main premise was that ideas for social change come from alienated material practice and the critique of such practice. In his early writings (1837-1844) he said:

> 'It can be seen how the history of industry and its previous objective existence is an open book of man's faculties and his psychology available to view. It was previously not conceived of in its connection with man's essence but only under the exterior aspect of utility, because man, moving inside the sphere of alienation, could only apprehend religion as the generalised existence of man, or history in its abstract and universal form of politics, art, literature, etc., as the reality of human faculties and

the human species-act. In everyday material industry . . . we have the objectified faculties of man before us in the form of sensuous, alien utilitarian objects, in the form of alienation. A psychology for which this book, and therewith the most tangible and accessible part of history, remains closed cannot become a genuine science with real content [if it is ignored].' (McLellan, 1977, p 93 *Karl Marx: Selected Writings*).

What Marx is referring to here is that the human species engages in activity as part of the ongoing cycle of needs in a material world. At times when human creative experience becomes alienated such as now and at the onset of the industrial revolution, the psychological experience of alienation emanating from the problematic material practice leads to thoughts of and about changes in that material practice. Through change, i.e. acting on solutions to problematic material existence, material existence becomes less alienated and the psychic tension reduced because the problem is confronted. Both individual 'needs' and 'common needs' are met through putting into practice the ideas developed from the alienated material practice and human psyche is objectified through this process which is the dialectic movement of Marx's historical materialism: the historical development of human essence (including his faculties) and society. The reflexive practice of action research because it involves the deliberative process of reflection to solve problems associated with alienated material practice, is a distilled, modern manifestation of Marx's practical-critical activity—dialectical historical materialism.

The course of action Marx decided on to eliminate the alienating social relations and social practices of capitalism was a working class revolution. Whilst a social class revolutionary did not take place as Marx envisaged it transformations have and are occurring via practical-critical activity throughout many social institutions and with many social relations. Through reflexive practice and action research in the educational context, the transformations include changes in individual's psyche unit, thoughts and intellect of students and staff, and changes to the social relations and/or practices that make up the historical unit: the teaching and learning process as a spatial and temporal movement of historical unity. Acquiring reflexive thinking: critical evaluative thinking should be emancipatory for the student because critical dialogue with a situation leads to changes towards improvement (Schön, 1983). However, students' control over the teaching and learning process is still limited because of the very nature of the power relations within education and the context variables.

Part of my reflexive practice is to develop student reflexive practice: sensing, reflecting and evaluating in cycles to improve learning and teaching practice. In doing this—reflexive practice—we are combining Locke's ideas of sensation, succession and reflection (Chappell, 1994). We are sensing/perceiving the situation, reflecting on it/analysing it and succession/evaluating it in cycles of reflection, evaluation and action. During in the process, idea formation moves from the simple mode of operation to the complex, thus we are developing intellectual skills and bringing about changes in the patterning of social relations/social structures (Lisle, 2000, p 113).

When using the terms simple and complex cognitive operations, they represent a synthesis between Locke's ideas of sensation (simple ideas of sensual material experience), reflection and succession (complex ideas) (Chappell, 1994) and Bloom's (1956) use of simple and complex classes of behaviour to represent cognition in the learning objective taxonomy he and his associates developed. It is an hierarchical taxonomy and reflexive practice would be placed at the top, most complex end of the cognitive scale but would also include the lower classes in it: 'i, knowledge, ii, comprehension, iii, application, iv, analysis, v, synthesis, vi, evaluation' (Bloom, 1956, p. 15) and one I add—vii, reflexivity. Classes within the taxonomy relate to the cognitive behaviours that make up the linguistic compound structure: dialectically reflexively radical practical-critical evaluative activity. It is a clumsy equation but I think it encompasses the activity I aim to investigate, as something that is valid and consistent made up as it is of elements from Bloom's taxonomy. The cognitive behaviours that make up the linguistic compound structure have been incorporated into this study, mainly because they are the cognitive behaviours to be tested as part of the learning objective taxonomy (result), and partly because they represent the methodology—the process of acquiring the cognitive behaviours (tool).

Adoption of Marxian methodology: Vygotsky

Vygotsky, a Russian psychologist, was one of the first psychologists to use Marxian methodology—practical-critical activity—as the practice of method. According to Newman & Holzman, Vygotsky saw the methodology of Marx and the result as the same thing, 'it is the productive activity which defines both—the tool (method) and the product (result)' (Newman & Holzman, 1993, p. 38). In other words, practical-critical activity is the methodology of understanding human activity and the activity by which we develop understanding. This for Vygotsky meant a tool for understanding learning and development, and a tool to produce learning and development in others, the development of higher modes of thought.

The distance between the actual level of development of the child/learner and his/her potential level of development through instruction, Vygotsky termed the zone of proximal development (ZPD). Vygotsky's ZPD consists of the intrapsychology of the child/learner, and the interpsychology between learner and instructor in Marx's methodology—practical-critical evaluative activity as a psychological unity. The ZPD as a psychological unity is a sociocultural, historical unity, the unit in which psyche is changed and the unity of social relations, which are changed through the process of interaction (Newman & Holzman 1993, p. 65). The unity may also be viewed as socio-political, cultural-historical unity. Interests, motives and values are part of the interactions between students and teachers. Teacher's interests, values and motives affect the teaching and learning process. Reflexive practitioners aim to improve learning via reflexivity. Thus, the context of dialectical reflexivity here (i.e. the dialectical reflexive practice of communicating participants—teacher and students) is the moving force for change—improving the teaching and learning situation and student learning.

Vygotsky believed that if we could determine the exact level of a child's/ learner's development then their development could be improved. This for Vygotsky meant distinguishing between, 'that which has already matured' i.e. mattered or formed, and the 'maturing' mattering/forming process. What a child/learner can accomplish independently shows that which has matured/ mattered, development. And what a child/learner can do in collaboration with others shows the maturing/mattering process, learning. We imitate and take instruction on what we are in the process of learning because 'it comes within the developmental level' (Vygotsky, 1962 p. 50). Vygotsky believed therefore, that learning and development were linked. Instruction facilitates learning that converts into development. The results of learning led development in the ZPD are that the child/learner acquires scientific concepts or the knowledge the child/ learner is expected to learn.

Spontaneous and nonspontaneous concept development

Vygotsky distinguishes between spontaneous concepts, which he regarded as the learning of things in a taken-for-granted way, unconsciously, like the learning of everyday concepts, such as how to address a neighbour or ride a bike; and scientific concepts such as relations of generality and empirical connections.

While the child/adult learns spontaneously everyday concepts, scientific concept learning is harder it requires concentration, i.e. deliberative conscious awareness. Learning led development in the ZPD however, motivates the child/adult. It is similar to behaviourist lineal programme of learning. Finding the exact level of development and then applying instruction at that level, is the motivating force. Once this is achieved, then the child/adult will be able to learn scientific concepts in the same way s/he learns spontaneous concepts: 'Learning led development in the ZPD is the growing ability to engage in activity volitionally and with conscious awareness' (Newman & Holzman, 1993, p. 61).

In other words, the greater the level of conscious awareness of scientific concept learning (due to systematic co-operation between teacher and pupil) leads to voluntary control in scientific thinking. Vygotsky's instructional learning in the ZPD is to develop the conscious awareness of scientific concept learning and development so that the learner becomes to learn and form scientific concepts spontaneously, just like everyday concepts are learned spontaneously. The experience with spontaneous and nonspontaneous concepts however, is different but related and instruction can alter the child's and/or adult's intellectual development:

> '[T]he two processes—the development of spontaneous and of nonspontaneous concepts—are related and constantly influence each other. They are parts of a single process: the development of concept formation, which is affected by varying external and internal conditions but is essentially a unitary process. Instruction is one of the principal sources of concepts and is also a powerful force in directing their

evolution; it determines the fate of the child's total mental development', (Vygotsky, 1962, p. 85).

Because of the child's/adult's different experiences of spontaneous and nonspontaneous concepts, they have different developmental paths, spontaneous concepts, such as the concept family or male and female are learned by students in a routine automatic fashion from everyday life experiences. In social theory, the concepts family, male and female are used scientifically and without any direct encounter with real objects. Through instruction, the teacher mediates the relationship between the spontaneous concept family as immediate relatives, blood kin, and the nonspontaneous concept, scientific concept, family as a social institution, the social structure of interdependent relationships, which socialises individuals into particular gendered roles.

The spontaneous conception of male and female, the biological differences between the two is linked to the scientific concept, the social construction of gender roles. Students have understanding of spontaneous concepts from the lower level, from the simple mode of idea formation, the taken-for-granted socially constructed reality of everyday life. This connects to a higher level of understanding of these concepts, the scientific understanding from above, the social construction of gender and family, the complex mode of idea formation, through instruction. Newman and Holzman suggests: 'Their relationship through development transforms not only each of their separate paths, but the totality of the child's [and adult's] mental processes' (Newman & Holzman, 1993, p. 64).

In the example I have discussed here, the students' mental processes change from spontaneous concept formation to scientific concept formation. The medium of this process is language: 'Word meaning is an active process—"the basic and decisive process in the development of the child's thinking and speech"' (Vygotsky, 1987, p. 24). Thus, Vygotsky's 'tool' is the shared meaning of language in the ZPD and the 'result' is scientific conceptual understanding and formation, the development of higher modes of thought. The tool (method) and result are the same, the practical-critical activity of instruction led learning, in a climate of shared understanding and meaning. The ZPD being the point at which this tool—the shared meaning of language and result—the development of higher modes of thought—takes place. In this study, dialectical reflexive practice forms part of the 'tool' used to raise conscious awareness of concept formation, and the 'result', reflexive thinking, thinking in the complex mode rather than the simple.

Relationship between language and thought: Word-meaning

When Vygotsky searched for the relationship between language and thought, for example, how does the shared meaning of language induce learning and development, thought, he broke language, more precisely, words, into two parts—the phonetic and the semantic. According to Vygotsky (1962), to learn words does not mean the child has fully grasped the scientific concept. Learning a word only reveals the phonetic acquisition, 'parrot talk'. For development to take place, the semantic aspect, meaning acquisition must take place. Therefore, I suggest that to learn words is similar to surface learning, when words are learned and repeated and not fully understood and that to acquire word-meaning is deep learning, learning that leads to intrapsychological activity, thought and development, because acquiring word-meaning is an active process—a process that begins through interpersonal communication and then becomes intrapersonal within the child/learner. '[M] emorising words and connecting them with objects does not in itself lead to concept formation; for the process to begin, a problem must arise that cannot be solved otherwise than through the formation of new concepts', (Vygotsky, 1962, p. 55).

For Vygotsky, concept formation was goal-directed activity. The acquisition of a concept is a means to an end, a way of solving a problem. The problem is the determining tendency, in that, it directs attention, activates inferences, imagery and associations, which are influenced by context. The word however 'is the means by which we direct our mental operations, control their course, and channel them toward the solution of the problem confronting us', (Vygotsky, 1962, p. 58). In Vygotsky's research, the formation of concepts was not the cause of the process itself, although in higher education and adulthood it is quite often the case that the process of concept formation is the cause. In many instances, advanced conceptual thinking in adult learners involves directing mental processes (i.e. concentrating, critically analysing and evaluating/being reflexive) with the aid of words to form scientific concepts, i.e. the relationship between language and thought. It involves complex thinking in which inferences; experience and imagery are created and combined as a basis for generalisations.

From the conglomeration of objects that form the generalisation, abstraction occurs in which a single element is chosen that represents all the objects and symbolises the maximum similarity. The single attribute is a potential concept. But 'A concept emerges only when the abstracted traits are synthesised anew and the resulting abstract synthesis becomes the main instrument of thought', (Vygotsky, 1962, p. 78). In this way, the process of concept formation goes through the stage of syncretic thinking, where groups of objects are created at random; through complex forms of thinking, in which objects are grouped for maximum similarity; to potential concepts in which a single trait is abstracted, and finally, to true concept formation in which thought is concentrated on the synthesised abstracted trait or traits.

Active approach to learning

A newly acquired concept can be difficult to describe or use outside the context in which it is acquired. The child or student may have difficulty describing the concept in their own words or on a 'purely abstract plane' without reference to personal impressions or experiences or without reference to concrete personal material situations. Analysis of concepts with reference to everyday materially situated experiences and reality therefore, according to Vygotsky, precedes analysis of the concepts themselves for spontaneous concepts, but for nonspontaneous concepts, the process is in reverse, from the abstract to the concrete. In my experience, during interactive lectures and discussion groups, the two go hand in hand, the abstract/theory and concrete/materially situated experience come together through discussion, the 'discursive turn'.

Using interactive lectures (instructional led learning) and active seminar participation, the student builds on, and brings together, personal materially situated experiences and lay language with scientific research and technical vocabulary (i.e. scientific concepts). This then represents the individual's worldview. The student moves through the stages of concept formation, from the simple mode of thought, thoughts based on materially situated, empirically sensed experience to the complex mode, in which the abstract and concrete are united. From instruction led learning of scientific concepts to active learning and spontaneous use in discussion. Then, by introducing students to self-reflexive learning, autonomous spontaneous scientific concept formation will develop whereby the student is able to use scientific concepts spontaneously. And through self-reflexivity and self-directed study, learn autonomously scientific concepts and use them spontaneously. This is illustrated in diagram 1 starting with the left hand box and moving to the right. 'Beyond the Pale', a learning-led development play written by Newman & Holzman, (1997), is another learning strategy—role play—which involves instruction-led learning and active learning leading to concept formation.

The concept matrix

'The higher levels in the development of word meanings are governed by the law of equivalence of concepts, according to which any concept can be formulated in terms of other concepts in a countless number of ways. We shall illustrate the schema underlying this law by an analogy not ideally accurate but close enough to serve the purpose . . . the location of every concepts may be defined by means of a system of co-ordinates, corresponding to longitude and latitude in geography. One of the co-ordinates will indicate the location of a concept between abstract conceptualisation and the immediate sensory grasp of an object—i.e., its degree of concreteness and abstraction. The second co-ordinate will represent the objective reference of the concept, the locus within reality to which it applies. Their intersection determines all the relationships of a given concept to others—its co-ordinate, superordinate and subordinate concepts. This position of a concept within the total system of concepts may be called its measure of generality', (Vygotsky, 1962, p. 112).

When teacher and students engage in group discussion, both bring to the conceptual arena personal materially situated experiences and antidotes to explain ideas and concepts. What happens is that students and teacher move up and down concept hierarchies within the conceptual matrices, oscillating between everyday spontaneous concepts and scientific concepts until scientific concept formation/ word-meaning is achieved. As Vygotsky states:

> 'When the process of concept formation is seen in all its complexity, it appears as a *movement* of thought within the pyramid of concepts, constantly alternating between two directions, from the particular to the general and from the general to the particular', (Vygotsky, 1962, p. 80).

Students acquire new concepts, scientific concepts that they can relate to personal experiences and everyday reality. In this study, scientific concept formation will not only be achieved because of the shared meaning of language in the zone of proximal development, but also because of the reflexive practice incorporated into the learning context, which initiates higher consciousness awareness. Students are introduced to reflexive practice and expected to monitor their learning to achieve greater results. In this way, students are given meaning to their actions, that is, to achieve deep learning rather than surface learning, to learn independently scientific concepts and use them spontaneously in discussion group exercises.

Action and meaning

When Vygotsky studied development, he was interested in the meaning of actions. In his discussion of the role, play has in development he suggests that the child is initially interested in the action. The child mimics the behaviour of others much like the behaviourist social learning theory—modelling behaviour. As Cole et al (1978) suggest, in this activity, action is dominant to meaning. But as the child develops, meaning dominates activity until in adulthood all activity is subordinate to the meaning behind it.

This latter statement however is questionable because even adults engage in activities without fully realising the meaning behind those activities. Many actions are habitual typifications or 'normal ways' of acting in accordance with the mores of a particular society that are learned during the process of socialisation: Thus, even as adults there are times when we need to be made aware of the meanings behind our actions. Many students, who come to university for example, are simply doing what is regarded as normal practice in their social community. It is a means to end in that they will obtain a degree, which in turn will improve their employment prospects. Only a few are interested in learning a subject because they want a deeper understanding and knowledge of the subject. The former thus engage in university learning without understanding the meaning behind the activity whereas the latter type of students are interested in the meaning and not just the activity. The same can be said for the processes involved in the teaching/learning situation.

For example, at the start of a module with first year undergraduates, for many students, the response to information or questions is reactive. Question and answer sessions however, are not a form of interrogation to elicit surface information, but are there to develop understanding and meaning. The question-answer process therefore elicits the development of deep learning. By introducing reflexive practice into the teaching and learning process, and encouraging the students to monitor their learning, asking questions if they do not understand, and think critically about the information they acquire, the main determinant of behaviour for the students moves from the initial stage of action, surface learning, to meaning, the meaning to the process question-answer session, which is the development of deep learning. They become to engage in question and answer sessions not because of the action itself, but because of its meaning, the development of deep learning. Students move to the second stage of development.

This is similar to Vygotsky's role of play in development. The child/adult first acts out the role of student for example, and the action itself determines the behaviour. But through acting out this role, the agent comes to understanding the meaning behind the action/role, to acquire knowledge. Acquiring knowledge, the meaning behind the action becomes the reason for performing the action. Meaning thus becomes the determining factor for playing the role of student. The action becomes contingent to meaning.

Once the meaning behind the action is established, the action can be changed. For example, students who want to acquire deep learning will engage in other activity which facilitate deep learning such as self-directed learning, which is Cole says 'the appearance of voluntary operations with meanings' (1978, p. 101).

Activity systems and context

'Contexts are activity systems. An activity system integrates the subject, the object, and the instruments (material tools as well as signs and symbols) into a unified whole . . . [From which] Production and communication are inseparable', (Engestrom, 1996, p. 67).

The activity system of higher education involves the subjects/students and teachers, who are the objects; the instrument is dialectical reflexive communication, discussing consciously disciplinary knowledge to acquire word-meaning—the production is knowledgeable people. In addition, there are implicit and explicit rules governing the activity system that can constrain actions. By incorporating reflexive practice into the activity system as an explicit rule governing action, the interests, motives and values of agents should increase the productive potential of the activity system. Thus, the unit of analysis—dialectical reflexive communication/ conscious acquisition of word-meaning, 'result', is assessed through dialectical reflexive communication 'tool'. We can assess this acquisition through analysing the students' verbal responses in the ongoing cycle of reflexive action.

Allan (1997) discusses modular design features that influence students' perceptions of learning. One, the clarity of module expectations, two, congruence between learning outcomes, taught sessions and the assessment regime, three, the learning activities and four, the teaching context—she defines as taught sessions and seminars and encompasses one to three. She suggests learning outcome-led modular design features influence students' perceptions of learning in a positive way. If there is congruency between approaches to learning (i.e. surface, deep and achieving, active/passive), assessment, and learning outcomes/objectives: '[I]t constitutes appropriate action in terms of "the how" of learning . . . giving greater prominence to meta-cognitive skills by raising their importance to a higher level of consciousness in both learning and teaching action', (Allan, 1997, p. 217).

Documentation given to students at the onset of the module consisted of a module guide, outlining all the learning outcomes/objectives, teaching and learning strategies (i.e. approaches to teaching and learning including reflexive practice) and the assessment criteria. Thus, the study focuses not only on the teaching and learning process in individual taught sessions, it addresses design features in the planning stage of the research. Thus, it is not just 'reflection-in-action', as it involves pre-planning, as in action research. The contexts of the activity system here then are illustrated in figure 1.

Method/Approach to learning	Assessment	Outcome/Learning objectives/ Skills
(1) Dialectical reflexivity and instruction led learning	(1) Evidence of knowledge and understanding of the subject discipline i.e. word-meaning of concepts and theories shown through active student participation in seminars and taught sessions and the ability to present the knowledge learned is essays and exam in an organised and personal way showing evidence of spontaneous scientific concept formation	(1) Deep learning, organisational skills, creative skills (such as writing coherently in different styles) communication skills, interpersonal skills, spontaneous scientific concept formation

(2) Reflexive practice/active student participation in seminars i.e. critical analysis and evaluation of the teaching-learning process and the subject discipline, self-reflexive, self-directed study	(2)Reflexive practice in seminars, complex thinking strategies—critical analysis and evaluation of the teaching and learning process and subject discipline, evidence of critical, analytic and evaluative skills and autonomous spontaneous scientific concept formation in essay and exam showing synthesis of ideas/perspectives and ease of use in a personal way	(2) Reflexive Practitioner, organisational skills, creative skills (such as writing styles), communication skills, interpersonal skills, critical analytic and evaluative skills, self-assessment and self-evaluation, autonomous spontaneous scientific concept formation
(3) Reflexive practice/active student participation in seminars i.e. critical analysis and evaluation of the teaching and learning process and the subject discipline leading to self-reflexive, self-directed study, autonomous learning and development	(3) Autonomous spontaneous scientific concept development, evidenced via input in seminars, critical analysis, evaluation and synthesis of ideas showing ease of use and evidence of independent thought and originality in a personalised way	(3) Reflexive Practitioner, organisational skills, creative skills (as above), communication skills, critical analytic and evaluative skills, self-assessment and self-evaluation, autonomous scientific concept formation and development i.e. original and personalised conceptual thinking

Figure 1

To summarise, the activity system involves imparting word-meaning in the zone of proximal development including critical analysis and evaluation of theory, the author's worldview and research—the reflexive practice of critical psychology and the reflexive practice of learning. The tool thus becomes critical evaluation of the shared meaning of language through dialectical reflexive communication. The results, the development of student reflexive practice i.e. the meaning behind the activity, deep learning (i.e. scientific concept formation), autonomous scientific concept formation, and/or autonomous scientific concept formation and development (the ability to critically evaluate, hermeneutically, theories and concepts in an original personalised way).

For the purpose of this study, and because it includes adult learners who have completed Vygotsky's childhood stages of development and are mainly in the process of acquiring word-meaning; the zone of proximal development will be defined as the interface of development: the point at which integer (word-meanings as units of information) are exchanged and understanding takes place. Thus, the ZPD here is the unity of students' actual level of development and their potential development as both are juxtaposed during dialectical reflexive communication. So that, acquiring word-meaning, learning, almost simultaneously converts into development. An analogy is a roadway that connects two cities. The cities represent the information already stored in memory; the newly built road way represents the acquisition of word-meaning, which brings new meaning to the information already stored in memory: the cities. However, it could be that there is a third element in the equation, such as consolidation leading to retention, because often even though we acquire work-meaning, we can often forget, thus the distinction between maturing (learning) and matured (development) could be one of degree in which the latter is like a well established sheet of ice on a pond and the former, thin ice awaiting consolidation for it to be retained: Hebb's theory of trace path development, 1949, in the brain in which with every use of the concept/information the path becomes firmly established and if not used decays.

Through dialectical reflexive communication, the ZPD becomes the fusion point for the individual's psyche unit in Marx's dialectical historical materialism. The psychological unit, learning-and-development, intra-psychology, where shared meaning of language and higher modes of thought fuse in the 'socio-political, cultural-historical unity' in the activity of inter-psychology: Gadamer's fusion of horizons. In this instance however, dialectic historical materialism rather than being an external societal thesis, antithesis and synthesis, is the dialectic of mind and brain as learning converts into development: The dialectic unity of opposites in the spacio-temporal movement of change—dialectical historical materialism. Learning is the process and development the result. The creation of ideas from material practice as cognition unites materially situated personal practical concrete experiences and abstract theoretical concepts. The dialectic of theory and practice in reflexive practice is simultaneously the dialectic psychophysics of mind-brain. Hebb's trace path formation as synaptic activity in the brain/matter, leads to the development of synaptic connects/the mattering process, mind, and vice versa (Lisle, 2005). Ratey (2001) suggests that neural tissues in the brain develop through use. Indeed I suggest (Lisle, 2005) electrochemical signals pass through the brain when thinking—mind—forming conceptual connections and developing concepts, which I am suggesting is equivalent to the synaptic neural networks that develop linking existing brain cells. Therefore, development would be representative of existing brain cells and existing synaptic neural connects, learning would be representative of using the existing brain matter, which initiates the sending of electrochemical signals—mind/thought—that then converts into brain matter through use, through active learning, reflexive practice. The reverse of course is Hebb's trace path decay, when neuronal trace paths fade through non-use: fissure.

Research design and methodology

The research design for this study is dialectical reflexive practice as a form of Marxian methodology—dialectical historical materialism as the production of ideas through practical-critical activity. It is both positivistic and interpretive in that through the reflexive activity cycle, i.e. planning, acting, observing, reflecting and revised planning, materially situated experience, perceptions and interpretations of the social encounter are united, critically analysed and evaluated in an ongoing cycle of action in light of dialectical reflexivity. In other words, the empiricism of positivism: obtaining data through the senses is linked with interpretivism: theory and thought through the dialectic reflexive cycle (Lisle, 2000). The interactant reflexive practice of teacher and students—validates the research because it cuts out the 'guess work'. If you want to know whether the students have learned the material for example, you ask them.

Ontologically, this study unites realism and constructivism. Action research unites these two perspectives because it involves the dialectics of material and ideological ontologies through practical-critical activity, the oscillation between theory/idealism and practice/materialism. Through situated material practice, patternings of social relations can be discovered, i.e. situated social encounters, which can be recorded and used to build iconic models, plans of action, for future episodes of social encounter, which can be built into a matrix, a catalogue of social encounters in the classroom for example, similar to the model building involved in retroduction, realist methodology. It is constructivist because social encounters in the classroom are constructed, deconstructed and reconstructed through dialectical reflection in a cyclical process. However, it is through the constructivity that patternings of social relations are replicated and recognised as the patternings and mechanisms that underpin the singular reality of realism.

The causal relationship sought is that between dialectical reflexive practice and learning-and-development. The Newman and Holzman's adaptation of Vygotsky's 'tool' and 'result' methodology. Does dialectical reflexive practice, a heightening of conscious awareness of the exchange of word-meaning in the zone of proximal development, spur development on? To be more precise, does dialectically reflexively radical practical-critical evaluative activity (DRRP-CEA) of dialectically reflexively hermeneutically-critical emancipatory interpretive activity (DRHC-EIA) lead to doubly double hermeneutics (Lisle, 2000, pp. 123-126)? Through DRRP-CEA of DRHC-EIA, teacher-student interaction is maintained in the zone of proximal development and hermeneutics is achieved between teacher, students and the theorist: doubly double hermeneutics.

The method of continuously monitoring the teaching and learning process is in the same instance, continuously working in the zone of proximal development. New information continually builds on existing knowledge. In other words, the aim is to achieve DRRP-CEA of DRHC-EIA equal to doubly double hermeneutics which should lead to the heightening of consciousness and the development in students of autonomous spontaneous scientific concept formation, thus deep learning. This is the plan of action in each individual session, and the planning of consecutive sessions will be based on group reflection of the session: the teacher and students' assessment of learning achieved. Weeks one and eleven were further reflected on by me, recorded and make up the bulk of my study. Figure 2 illustrates the dialectical reflexive cycles used.

Figure 2 Dialectical reflexive cycles in the classroom

The overall plan for this research is continuous monitoring of the teaching and learning process, which involves:

Stage One
Plan for the whole module from week 1 to week 12

Stage Two
Several cycles of reflecting, acting/interacting, observing per week depending on number of learning objectives, one cycle for each learning objective:

Cycle one: learning objective one:
Plan (Session topic, aims and learning objectives, teaching-learning strategies developed at Stage One)

↓

    Act (Communicative Interaction between teacher & learners of content of
                            learning objective 1)

↑

Dialectical Reflection
Ask students for their understanding
Think of ways to achieve understanding
Get the students involved in the process
Move onto learning objective two when understanding reached/Observe
(Have we achieved fusion of horizons, have students learned objective 1)

Cycle two: learning objective two:
        Act (Communicative Interaction between teacher and students of the
                      contents of learning objective two)

↕

                           The oscillation between action/ interaction and dialectical reflection is the continuous monitoring of the teaching and learning process: DRRP-CEA of DRHC-EIA

Dialectical Reflection/Observe

Critical analysis and evaluation week one

The learning objectives: What social psychology is, it's roots in sociology and psychology, the different perspectives drawn from psychology, their models of man, research techniques and social constructionism were presented to the students using the methodology in figure 2.

Examining the student responses revealed that they were use to being taught the traditional way via didactic lectures and surprised when asked to engage in self-directed study, 'If that's the case then what's the point in coming here then (.) we might as well stay at home and read books.' The students were interested in the module content because it 'sounded different and novel' (extract 1 line 6) but were perturbed by the content because they thought it was 'complicated' (extract 1 line 5).

Extract 1
Lines:

1. STUDENT 1: We got the outline sent to us when we enquired about the module
2. (2) it is social psychology we're doing isn't it?
3. ME: Yes (.) yes (2) what makes you ask that question?
4. WHOLE GROUP: Laughter
5. STUDENT 1: // Well it's this reflexivity bit (.) it sounds complicated //
6. STUDENT 2: // It seems a bit different (.) novel (.) not at all like the psychology I remember//
7. STUDENT 1: What's it got to do with social psychology? I mean (.)
8. Psychology is about studying individuals in relation to groups isn't it?
9. ME: Yes
10. STUDENT 1: So where does reflexivity come into it?

From the discussion I could assess they were a mixed ability group. Some had background knowledge of social psychology (extract 1 lines 7 to 8) and some had none for example one student said 'Well can you just tell us this week what it's all about and then we can learn for ourselves later on?' It is evident that student 5 had limited understanding of what reflexive practice is; both as the reflexive practice of critical psychology and the reflexive practice involved in teaching and learning, self-development. I decided to ask other members of the group what they thought reflexive practice was because I needed to further assess students' knowledge of social psychology including the reflexivity of it, and whether they knew what self-reflexive development was. This would give me an idea of the existing level of develop of the group overall. I got the following response:

Extract 2
Lines:

1. STUDENT 3: I've read the module outline and I get the impression that reflexivity
2. is similar to analysing things you've done (.) like reminiscence?
3. ME: Well sort of (h) can you expand on what you mean by reminiscence?
4. STUDENT 3: Well it's like memoirs (1) thinking about things that have happened in the past and
5. analysing it (.) wondering why you did something in a particular way and what you'd do to change things
6. ME: Yes (.) yes (.) can you give me an example?
7. STUDENT 3: (h) (2) Well (.) well (.) I once (.) I used to tune pianos (.) and one day I was tuning a piano
8. and a child asked me how I did it (.) I'm deaf you see (.) the child knew this of course (.) and so I started
9. to tell the child about the vibrations the piano makes (.) well looking back now (.) I think I could have mad
10. myself understood more clearly if I'd demonstrated the vibrations

All the students needed coaching in the art of reflexive practice and the reflexivity of social psychology. One student had given the example of reminiscence (extract 2 lines 1 to 10), as a form of reflection, which showed personal understanding of reflexive practice. Student 3 had analysed past experience and decided, in light of reflection, how to change his actions to improve his communication skills (extract 2 lines 7 to 10). The student had united the concept 'reminiscence' with the concept 'reflexivity' and was able to describe in his/her own words what reminiscence was and in so doing described reflexive practice. For example, through reflecting on the conversation the student had had with the child, s/he had learned in light of reflection that 'I could have made myself understood more clearly if I'd demonstrated the vibrations' (Extract 2, lines 9 to 10). The student had developed spontaneous use of the scientific concept 'reflexivity' by bringing together personal observation from the concrete level and using it to explain the abstract and thus acquired deep learning. It supports Vygotsky's theory of language and thought in that the acquisition of word-meaning activates thought processes.

To illustrate the social constructionist perspective, we discussed the social construction of gender identity using a personality inventive, which was followed by group work of theory construction to illustrate the social construction of social psychology. The class was divided into two groups. One group had to construct an argument to support the biological view of gender divisions; the other had to construct a theory to support the social constructionist view of gender divisions. Members of the groups were told to individually write on a piece of paper that was passed from one member of the group to another, views or explanations of gender divisions in line with their allocated theoretical stance: A bit like Chinese whispers.

The two groups were told to build a social psychological discourse in this way, containing single concepts or experiences, which were united by the perspective, i.e. either biological or social constructionist. Afterwards, the groups presented their concepts and theories to one another and were then instructed to critically evaluate their opposing group's theories.

Extract 3
Lines:

1. ME: Right then (.) can you please tell the other group how social constructionists suggest gender
2. identity develops?
3. STUDENT 7: Well it's to do with socialisation isn't it (.) you learn from your parents whether
4. You're a boy or a girl (2)
5. ME: Yes go on (.)
6. STUDENT 5: I can remember when I was at school (.) all the girls did house craft and all the
7. boys did woodwork (1)
8. ME: Yes (.)
9. STUDENT 5: Well that's how it works isn't it (.) you learn things that correspond to your gender
10. you learn the stereotypes (.) you learn a stereotyped image which becomes you
11. STUDENT 13: Yes (.) stereotypes (h) stereotypes are everywhere (.) you see them on T. V. (.) mags
12. people in the street are stereotypes (.) they're either typically male or female
13. STUDENT 2: Laughter (h) what's a typical male?
14. STUDENT 13: You know what I mean (.) a man or boy who wears typical male clothing and does
15. typical male things (h) like driving the family car
16. STUDENT 2: Ah ah ah women drive cars as well these days
17. STUDENT 7: Yeah but driving is classed as a man's thing (.) men are always criticising female
18. drivers (.) men think they're cut out to drive but females aren't
19. STUDENT 14: It becomes ingrained in yeah as you grow up
20. STUDENT 10: Yeah role models we copy role models (.) it's usually dad who drives the family car

Those students, who had background knowledge of social psychology or related disciplines, used knowledge of existing theories to explain gender divisions (extract 3 line 3 'socialisation', line 10 'stereotypes', line 20 'role models'). But, students with no background knowledge of social psychology learned or understood the process of social constructionism equally well. For example, one student commented after further discussion of social constructionism 'Is that it then (.) I thought it was going to be really complicated'.

What is evident from extract 3 is that the students were analysing the social construction of gender and through the analytical process acquired deep learning. For example, line 3 'Well it's to do with socialisation isn't it (.) you learn from your parents', and line 6 'I can remember when I was at school (.) all the girls did house craft and the boys woodwork'. It was a mutual learning experience whereby the students combined technical language with lay language and each benefited from the others' contributions. They were able to bring together everyday concepts and experiences, such as school life and family experiences i.e. lines 14 to 15 'does typical male things (h) like driving the family car' and concepts such as stereotypes, socialisation and modelling to form scientific concepts. In addition, through the constructive exercise, they had acquired the concept of a socially constructed identity and a socially constructed discourse. They were learning through instruction and doing, they were given the concept 'socially constructed gender', as a problem they had to solve, i.e. find the meaning of and through the process of doing, i.e. discussing the concept they acquired the meaning behind the concept.

Likewise, because the students had acquired deep learning, in the same instance, double hermeneutics was achieved. During group discussion, students gained insight into the other groups' worldview through discussing personal experiences and observations. For example, on line 12 'people in the street are stereotypes (.) they're either typically male or female'; student 13 gained insight from the worldview of student 5, lines 9 to 10 'you learn a stereotyped image which becomes you'. In this way, the students achieved double hermeneutics as Giddens describes it. It involved a two-way interchange of meaning. And because the students had brought together spontaneous meanings of everyday experiences and observations with nonspontaneous meanings of a socially constructed and socially acquired identity (the new concepts), at the same time they achieved historical hermeneutics (Habermas, 1972 and Gadamer, 1989). The students had gained understanding of the concept stereotypes as the theorist who coined the term had defined it and used it to discuss how stereotyping affects identity construction.

Furthermore, the practical-critical evaluative activity of the group discussion became the methodology of understanding human activity 'stereotypes' and the activity by which the students developed understanding of it, acquired the concept. For example, critical analysis line 16 'women drive cars as well', critical analysis, line 17 to 18 in response 'Yeah but driving is classed as a man's thing (.) men always criticise female drivers', further analysis and evaluation line 19 'It becomes ingrained in yeah as you grow up'. Here the students are discussing human activity (discussion being the tool for learning and development) and through this discussion are developing understanding of that human activity (the result), the Marxian-Vygotskian 'tool' and 'result' methodology for initiating learning and development. In this case, instruction-led active learning and group discussion as forms of practice-critical activity induce the dialectic movement of Marx's historical materialism: the dialectic interchange of brain and thought/mind in the maturing/ mattering process of learning that converts to development.

The group discussion exercises were planned to get students actively engaged with social psychological discourse. This approach to learning thus determines the learning outcome, autonomous spontaneous scientific concept formation, and use, which the students would be assessed on. Much of the social psychology discourse the *students* were using came from their existing conceptual schemes. However, through getting the students involved in group discussion, the students were able to practice using the discourse, thereby tuning the spontaneous application of the discourse in readiness for essay writing and written examinations. This therefore represents a way of achieving congruency between approaches to learning, learning outcome and assessment (Allan, 1997).

Week eleven

In week eleven, the topic was Berger and Luckmann's 'Social Construction of Reality'. By this point in the course, most if not all of the students had received grades for assessed essays and were actively engaged in the learning process through self-directed study and participation in discussions. The students were conversant with the processes of social construction and deconstruction, the notion of worldviews and/or perspectives and reflexivity that had been introduced in relation to the various topics throughout the module. In some respects, this topic, the social construction of reality, was the crescendo. We examined the social construction of knowledge and reality and the social construction of social psychology itself. All that remained was to assess whether or not social psychology was a worthwhile discipline: assess whether or not the discipline addressed social issues such as gender, race and class inequalities.

The evidence for hypothesis 3 was interesting. Some of the students had read the book by Berger and Luckmann and had made notes. What follows is the classroom discussion of Berger and Luckmann's book 'The Social construction of Reality' and its application by the students and me, to personal experiences and understanding of the social construction of reality. The learning objectives were the historical context to Berger and Luckmann's book, the social construction of reality described by the authors in the book and social constructionism as a reflexive perspective.

Extract 1
Lines:

1. STUDENT 1: I read it but I didn't get that understanding from it (.) I thought the social construction of
2. everyday life meant the social structures (.) you know (.) institutions (2) like the social roles in the

3. family ways of acting that have been passed down through the generations?

4. ME: Well yes it does (.) reciprocal typifications of habitualised actions that have become

5. Institutionalised the family being one of those institutions (h) an institution being social arrangements

6. or patternings of social interaction (.) that have become adopted by the majority of people (h) so that they

7. have become the normal way of behaving in those social arrangements (h.) be it in the family or education

8. or work or at the local pub that's a part of the socially constructed reality (1) but you need to look at it in a

9. wider context and over time the way science has affected everyday life Freudian psychoanalysis

10. STUDENT 2: You mean the way the American's spend a fortune on visiting a shrink?

11. ME: Yes (.) yes (1) and what does that say of Freudian psychoanalysis?

12. STUDENT 2: Well a lot of people believe in it (.) otherwise they wouldn't spend all that money

13. STUDENT 3: That doesn't make it right though does it? (.) I wouldn't spend money on psycho-therapy

14. anyway (.) I'd rather talk to a friend if I have problems

15. ME: Why do people believe in Freudian theory (.) or should I say (.) psychiatry as a form of therapy? (1)

16. STUDENT 4: It's well established (.) it's been about since the turn of the century (.)

17. STUDENT 3: Yeah but just as many people go to behaviour therapists these days (.)

18. ME: And which body of knowledge has influenced the development of behaviour therapy?

19. STUDENT 2: Laughter (.) behaviourism of course

20. ME: Yes (.) so here we have two bodies of knowledge that have had an immense impact (.) on society (.)

21. knowledge that started out as science and is now part of everyday reality (1) who constructed that reality?

22. STUDENT 1: Scientists (.) you mean scientists don't yeah?

23. ME: Yes (.) and what does this tell us about other forms of knowledge that we take for granted

24. as everyday common knowledge or everyday social reality?

25. STUDENT 2: Some (.) one (.) constructed it (laughter) oh I see what you mean now (.)

26. the social construction of reality

27. STUDENT 5: Oh my God it's frightening (.) you don't know what to believe now

At this point in the discussion, doubly double hermeneutics was achieved (hypothesis 3). By dialectically reflecting on Berger and Luckmann's theory of everyday reality (Extract 1 lines 1 to 12) and critically evaluating it (Extract 1 lines 13 to 22), the students had acquired understanding of the theory. From their understanding of the theory—the social construction of reality, students linked their understanding to personal observations and experiences, critically evaluating and analysing Freudian psychoanalysis as an example of theory construction that has influenced everyday reality. During the process, the students achieved doubly double hermeneutics, fusion of horizons between them and me, and fusion of horizons between class members as a group and the theorists Berger and Luckmann. It appeared, in some respects, to be a great awakening for student 5, extract 1 line 27, 'Oh my God it's frightening (.) you don't know what to believe now'.

Gadamer and Habermas historical hermeneutics was achieved through dialectical reflection at two levels. One level of understanding was that between the group members concerning the social construction of reality using personal experiences and observations to illustrate points such as line 12 'Well a lot of people believe in it (.) otherwise they wouldn't spend all that money', and line 16 'It's well established (.) it's been about since the turn of the century', making reference to the influence of Freudian theory within society. And through critical evaluative dialectical reflection, the second level of understanding was achieved between students and me about the nature of this socially constructed Freudian reality as an example of the social construction of everyday reality the way the authors (Berger and Luckmann) had described it (for example lines 10 to 26) but not particularly in relation to just Freudian theory.

In the same instance, the students experienced deep learning. They were not just remembering facts, they had acquired word-meaning: the meaning behind the social construction of reality, concept formation. Locating student's zone of proximal development was achieved by exploring different pieces of knowledge, spontaneous and nonspontaneous concepts, for example the theories of psychoanalysis and behaviourism (extract 1 lines 10 to 25), they were familiar with until it connected with information that they could apply it to, such as psycho-therapy in America, and then connecting it to the present knowledge to be learnt, the social construction of reality. This extract demonstrates the oscillation between concrete everyday concepts and scientific abstract concepts in the conceptual matrix until the new concept has meaning, the new concept of the social construction of reality and scientific discourses. In this way, abstract concepts presented to the students acted as cues to their existing acquired knowledge i.e. concept matrix, which is syncretic thought. Once existing information was cued and recalled and discussed it formed part of the critically analysed (lines 10 to 27) and synthesised, complex thought. Then once the students found that there was maximal similarity between the pre-established concepts and the new ones, the students acquired the concept social construction of everyday reality.

On reflection, the process involves expanding memory by cueing already established memory stores (conceptual schemes) with which to categorise and encode new information, the new concept. Locating the zone of proximal development is a search for memory-cues, which will unlock conceptual schemes especially those that have relevance to the concept you want the students to learn. 'What information/ concepts do the students already hold so I can make a connection?' you might reflect.

Deep learning can be achieved by making as many connections as possible to pre-existing conceptual systems, such as personal experiences and observations the student holds. The greater the number of connections made the greater the number of memory trace paths developed connecting the short-term memory to the long-term memory, and the more likely the student is to acquire word-meaning, concept formation. This is achieved through discussion because each conceptual scheme brought into the conceptual arena acts as a cue. The learning is less likely to fade because the information held in the multiple memory stores such as personal experiences and observations is well established and used, thus preventing trace path decay as often occurs during surface learning in which facts are remembered but not connected to existing well-established pieces of knowledge. The students' own personal experiences make up some of these trace paths along with information already taught on the module and other complementary modules, and concept formation in which word-meaning is achieved. The greater the number of trace paths and existing concepts the student has on a topic the more likely the student will go on to develop autonomous spontaneous scientific concept formation because they are forming connections more and have the knowledge to form more connections. Thus enabling the student to further develop/acquire scientific concepts—they have a more holistic picture of the knowledge system and how it works. In extract 2 for example, student 6 took the concept 'God' and used it to illustrate Berger and Luckmann's social construction of reality. The student made connections between existing conceptual schemes held and the new concept to be learned, thereby acquiring the new concept.

The process of forming trace paths I suggest is the mattering process in Marx's dialectical historical materialism. If a trace path is successfully formed, i.e. if the word-meaning is acquired it will activate another area of brain matter. This using of the additional brain area is part of the revolutionary development of the individual and evolutionary development of the human species.

Extract 2
Lines:

1. STUDENT 6: Talking of God (.) you can say the same of religion can't you? (1)
2. ME: Yes (.) would you like to expand on that idea?
3. STUDENT 6: We (.) believe (.) Well we believe in God in a matter of fact way (.) don't we?
4. ME: Go on (.)
5. STUDENT 6: (.) Well it's not as if we can see God (.) but we believe in his existence don't we?

6. STUDENT 2: Laughter (.) well some of us might do
7. ME: No but look at the idea more seriously (.) in what ways can we talk of God as socially constructed?
8. STUDENT 7: Well he's depicted as a man isn't he?
9. STUDENT 2: Or (.) he might not be a man (.)
10. STUDENT 8: All priests were male up until recently
11. STUDENT 9: That's right (.) we now have female clergy (.)
12. STUDENT 10: There's a play on in London which has a female God (.) or God is depicted as a female

In can be seen in extra 2 extract that the students have understanding of the meaning of a socially constructed reality and are applying it to other forms of knowledge or believe systems (extract 2 lines 1 to 12). At this point therefore, the students achieve autonomous scientific concept formation and development. They had taken the concept of a socially constructed reality and used it to analysis other forms of knowledge on an abstract as well as a concrete plan. In extract 2, the students acquired understanding of the overall picture of a socially constructed reality and subject (extract 2 lines 1 to 13 and extract 3 lines 37 to 55), including a socially constructed social science reality and methodology of analysing reality and the subject. In addition, the students acquired an understanding of the reflexivity of social constructionism as a critique to social science theory and methods 'It's like a tool isn't it . . . we've got to see if it does the job' (extract 3 line 55). At this point therefore, we had achieved the learning objectives for that session.

Extract 3
Lines:

1. ME: So you can see then that these bodies of knowledge// /(.) or
2. STUDENT 2: //(Laughter) bodies of knowledge//
3. ME: belief systems (.) knowledge systems
4. STUDENT 2: belief systems
5. ME: A belief system is a collection of related ideas which people believe to be true (.) like the
6. concept God and the related religious ideals (1) we can see then that belief systems
7. are socially constructed what does this tells us about social psychology as a discipline?
8. STUDENT 2: That it's socially constructed of course
9. ME: So does that make it a worthwhile body of knowledge?
10. STUDENT 2: Well that depends doesn't it?
11. STUDENT 11: It depends on whether or not the knowledge is based on fact (.)
12. ME: But how do we know if social psychology is based on fact? (1)
13. STUDENT 11: Research (.) research supports theory doesn't it?

14. ME: Well so they say (.) but if the theory has already become part of that taken for granted
15. everyday reality then really (.) theory precedes fact (.)
16. STUDENT 11: I don't know what you mean (1)
17. ME: Well let's look at mental disorders (.) the notion of mental illness is a Western ideology
18. (.) if someone suffers from severe depression then they might end up according to
19. Western medicine being treated with Electro Convulsion Therapy
20. STUDENT 2: What's that?
21. STUDENT 12: ECT (.)
22. STUDENT 2: What the alien?
23. STUDENT 5: No! Electric shock treatment
24. ME: Yet (.) in other societies (.) non-western (.) the patient might receive a different treatment
25. depression might not be classed as a mental disorder at all (h.) it's like the disorder schizophrenia
26. in Western societies it's classed as a mental disorder but in other cultures it's not (.) some cultures
27. regard the symptoms as a sign of giftedness (2) take Shaman for example//
28. STUDENT 4: //Yeah (.) they think they're blessed
29. STUDENT 11: //Oh I get it know (.) culture (.)
30. knowledge is culture (.) and theory is influenced by culture
31. ME: Yes (.) that's right (.) and culture is a belief system just like any other body of knowledge
32. STUDENT 2: I don't think I get what you mean? (1) what's that got to do with research and facts?
33. STUDENT 13: Ideology comes into everyday reality and becomes that reality (1) so when
34. sociologists do research the facts they get are of theories that have already influenced society
35. ME: Excellent (.)
36. STUDENT 14: It's like Charles Husband's top-down bottom-up theory
37. STUDENT 2: Oh I get it now (.) but I can't explain it (.)
38. STUDENT 14: You explain it for her I don't think I can put it into words either
39. STUDENT 2: Oh I get it (.) I get it now (1) it's like psychosomatic health problems (.) because
40. you know the symptoms you can go on to develop the disease (.) well in your own head anyway then the researcher classifies you has having that disease
41. STUDENTS: Yes!
42. ME: To get back to the point (.) is social psychology a worthwhile body of knowledge give that

43. knowledge is social constructed and two (.) social facts are also socially constructed?
44. STUDENT 2: Arrrh (.) you've just given me an head-ache
45. STUDENT 15: Well I can understand it (.) that's where post-modern reflexivity comes into it (.) it's like what we did the first week choosing from different points of view which one best fits reality
46. STUDENT 2: Yeah (.) but reality is a social construct
47. ME: Right (.) so (.) we've got this body of social constructed knowledge (.) social psychology
48. And now that we've found it to be socially constructed in a reality that is also socially constructed
49. we have to decide whether or not it is of value (.)
50. STUDENT 2: (.) you could ask that about any body of knowledge
51. ME: does it help us to resolve social problems (1) such as bystander apathy and so on? (.)
52. STUDENT 1: Well it seems to (.)
53. STUDENT 7: It's like a tool isn't it? social psychology is like a tool we've got to see if it does the job

The students were also monitoring their learning in the classroom at the same time I was monitoring their learning—dialectical reflexivity. The students had developed reflexive practice toward their learning in the classroom situation. On line 16, student 11 was monitoring his/her own learning 'I don't know what you mean' s/he wanted to understand so asked for further clarification. S/he wanted a deeper understanding, and she acquired it line 29 'or I get now (.) culture (.) knowledge is culture (.) and theory is influenced by culture'. Self-monitoring is evident all through the extract, for example line 32 'I don't think I get what you mean', line 37 'Or I get it now' lines 39 to 41 'it's like psychosomatic health problems (.) because you know the symptoms you can develop the disease'. This student really laboured to achieve understanding of this particular concept but s/he learned it through monitoring his/her own learning and revealing to the rest of the group that s/he needed further clarification. It is also interesting the way student 5 line 27 extract 1, reacted to the concept of the social construction of reality (i.e. 'Oh my God it's frightening (.) you don't know what to believe now (1)'). The technical language and understanding of it triggered thought and the development that occurred was evident in the response.

In extract 3, there is much evidence to suggest that the students had acquired the meaning behind the action of dialectical reflexivity and interactive learning. The first week some of the students were perturbed by this method of teaching expecting me to read through handouts like a script, but by the eleventh week the students were familiar with interactive teaching methods and were fully engrossed in discussions wanting to engage the topics rather than just sit and listen. On reflection, I think this was due to the dialectical reflexive process and encouraging the students to acquiring deep learning. They achieved understanding; the understanding was dialectically reflexively hermeneutically-critical emancipatory interpretive activity, extract 3. In addition self-monitoring in the classroom situation led to autonomous learning and autonomous spontaneous scientific concept formation for some students. By monitoring their learning, some students were searching for understanding and in some respects were searching for information that would connect to information they already held. Once the connection had been made, the new concept could be applied to other forms of knowledge such as culture, psychosomatic health problems, and ideology in the interactive teaching session. The connections made, I suggest, are mirrored by synaptic connects in the brain.

I gathered information from students during the feedback session that followed the taught session that revealed they had acquired the learning objectives. Some of the students had acquired a deep understanding of the whole module and both main themes. One had learned the fundamentals of the different topics covered but had not mastered the skill of critical analysis. Many of the students had learned a great deal from the module and were reflexive in that they offered evaluations of the module that could lead to improvements. The students thought that I had laboured the point about being reflexive and monitoring learning. The main principles of self-reflexive study were taken on board but offset by constraints such as family commitments and paid employment. The students had become self-reflexive in the classroom situation but I had not seen any written evidence to suggest that they engaged in self-reflexive study outside the classroom situation such as recorded reflexive practice I could only go on what was said.

Reflections and conclusions

After evaluating the evidence, the conclusions reached are that reflexive practice as the continuous monitoring of the teaching and learning process in this study led to the pin pointing of and maintenance of student-teacher interaction in zone of proximal development. Not all students however were at the same stage of development, but through class discussions and group work, those students who had the least understanding gained greater understanding so that by the end of each class all students achieved the learning objectives.

To build on the learning of those student who had a greater level of understanding, technical language/scientific concepts were used which the students connected to existing knowledge and personal experiences and thus in the process all the students experienced learning and development. This supports Vygotsky's theory of language and thought and was demonstrated in class discussions. Class participants discussed the problematic concepts until the word-meaning was learned, then the concepts were assimilated into existing conceptual schemes and the concepts were used spontaneously during discussion, development. Through dialectical reflexive discussion, those students who had the least understanding had time to increase their understanding and those students who had a higher level of understanding were given the opportunity to consolidate and demonstrate their learning. The latter students were given the time to think about the instructional information, link it to existing conceptual systems and personal observations then discuss their ideas with the other students and me. It also allowed them to clarify their ideas.

Thus, the reflexive practice of action research is a distilled form of the Marxian-Vygotskian 'tool' and 'result' methodology works. Through my reflexive practice, I could local students' actual level of development and linked it to their potential developmental level; remaining in the ZPD long enough to allow all students to acquire learning which was converted into development through discussion.

Reflexive action defined here as: dialectically reflexively radical practical-critical evaluative activity leads to double hermeneutics. At the start of the module my reflexive practice: continuous monitoring of the teaching and learning process with the aim of achieving shared meanings was modelled by students who monitored their own learning in the classroom situation and developed reflexive skills, so double hermeneutics was achieved. The students were able to listen to instructional information and relate it to their personal experiences, observations and conceptual schemes. This gives support to Vygotsky's notion of instruction led learning and language as the media of learning and development in social interaction. It was an empathic interchange of language and meanings, which Giddens suggests is the essence of double hermeneutics.

When introducing a third element, the author, researcher or theorist, and dialectically reflexively hermeneutically analysing, criticising and evaluating the theorist, author or research to reach an understanding of them or it, which is closer to reality, doubly double hermeneutics was achievable. Students had acquired word-meaning of 'the social construction of reality', and as a group analysed and critically evaluated the concept using personal experiences and existing knowledge schemes.

All students acquired deep learning: they could discuss theories and research and apply that research to personal experiences. Students had hermeneutic understanding and critically evaluated authors, theory and research. Some students could develop theories further some students did all this, and applied theory to personal observations, critically evaluated them and put forward their own ideas.

To acquire deep learning/new concepts and be able to use them spontaneously in class discussion and apply the concepts outside the class situation in other context may be related to students' existing conceptual schemes. For example, on reflection, I noticed that during class discussions, students achieved a deep understanding of the social construction of reality, and some students went on to link the concept to other knowledge systems such as religion, culture and psychosomatic disorders. Once a link is made between existing conceptual schemes and the new concept to be acquired, it could be that trace paths develop in the brain (Marx's dialectical historical materialism as the mattering/maturing developmental process). Trace paths grow stronger if linked to established conceptual schemes like concrete personal experiences and existing abstract conceptual schemes. Those students who had to learn not only the concept of the social construction of reality for example, but also the examples, given that the examples may not have come from their memory store, may have been able to remember the concept of social constructionism and perhaps one or two examples but not all that was discussed. Whatever the case, these students still acquired deep learning but did not demonstrate that learning as much as students with greater conceptual systems to link the knowledge to in other context.

At the onset of the module, the students did not know what reflexive practice was. Some students liken it to being 'astute', because they were already conscientious about their learning. However, through taking part in the feedback sessions at the end of each class, and being instructed to monitor their learning throughout the teaching sessions and on a general level, many of the students developed reflexive practice skills, particularly in the classroom situation. The amount of self-directed study students engaged in depended on other commitments such as family responsibilities and full and part time work. Whether or not the students continue to engage in reflexive practice will depend on the learning contexts they find themselves in and whether or not they found it of value. Again, this will be down to the individual. Perhaps the next time I incorporate reflexive practice into a module I will ask students to write a reflexive log as part of the assessment criteria, so that they can log their learning on a weekly basis.

Several students during in class discussions, written essays and exams demonstrated autonomous scientific concept formation. Again, autonomous learning appears to be influenced by individual circumstance as well as instruction. In the classroom situation, it is clear that some students who acquired new concepts from self-directed study demonstrated this autonomous learning in discussions. The students were instructed to monitor their learning and read further on topics they were unsure of or to read up on topics in advance and so on. But many students engage in self-directed study anyway, usually for written course work or class papers or out of interest so how much of the autonomous learning was due to the learning context and how much was due to individual circumstances is hard to say.

On reflection, some students can understand reflexivity, can take on board knowledge of critical psychology, but cannot apply it outside the class situation. Autonomous spontaneous scientific concept formation and development appears to be context dependent for those students who have recently acquired the knowledge and also appears to be influenced by individual circumstances. In the class situation, when discussing the social construction of reality most students understood what it was by the end of the session. Most students, whether relating the concept to personal experience or other knowledge systems, achieved spontaneous scientific concept formation. But not all students could apply this knowledge in situations outside the class context such as in written work or examinations. It could be because students have different levels of understanding, i.e. different conceptual schemes and whether or not the new knowledge learned is preserved may be dependent on the students' existing conceptual systems. If the student can connect incoming information to a higher number of existing concept systems then they are more likely to be able to apply the new information outside the class situation and use it to go on to develop autonomous spontaneous scientific concept formation and development.

Thus, dialectical reflexive practice and instruction-led learning can lead to spontaneous scientific concept formation and autonomous spontaneous scientific concept formation but not always outside the context in which the concepts are acquired. Those students who were already ardent learners and autonomous learners continued to be so, and all students acquired the skills of reflexive practice in the classroom situation. Some of the barriers to reflexive practice outside the classroom situation are presages factors discussed by Biggs (1990) and Allan (1997). For example, family commitments, work commitments and socio-economic status, all of which some students suggested prevented them from engaging in the amount of self-reflexive study they wanted to.

The outcome-led curriculum design model is a good model to use as it gives the students a clear indication of what is expected of them and the skills to be demonstrated are learned and practised as part of the approach to learning. Reflexive practice as an approach to learning and the outcome, reflexive practitioner in this study was related to the reflexive practice of critical psychology and the reflexive practice of learning. Although the students acquire reflexive skills in the classroom situation, I think a reflexive journal would ensure the learning was not context dependent. The major downfall of using the learning-outcome-led modular design is that it can be prohibiting for students and not truly emancipatory. To counter this, second and third year students might find it more emancipating if they were allowed to choose the curricula content of certain modules. Then, if learning was recorded in a reflexive log, much like a personal development progress file, student learning would be more autonomous, self-referential and individually customised. An independent study is a good example.

Were double hermeneutics achieved and doubly double hermeneutics? I would like to think so but then like most researchers my opinion may be biased. After reading this study several times and realising that I developed the module including the indicative content—the social construction of reality (pun intended) it is therefore very difficult to decide.

If there is a drawback to this study, it must be that it is difficult to assess the amount students learned in the class situation as opposed to through self-directed study. In addition, it is difficult to assess whether or not taking part in dialectical reflexivity motivates students to become self-reflexive or autonomous learners. For example, some students were already autonomous learners and they may have already been self-reflexive but were unconscious of their self-reflexiveness.

Through conducting this study, I have gained much insight into the learning and developmental process most of which is revealed in the critical analysis and evaluation section. For example, I have found that a mixture of instruction-led learning and active learning i.e. reflexive practice in the classroom situation initiates the developmental process. In addition, I have found that it is worthwhile continuing the discussion of a concept through introducing as many examples as possible, regardless of who introduces the information, because this way all students are more likely to gain understanding, deep learning, through making connections between existing knowledge systems held by students and the incoming information. This is, I suggest, what Marx regarded as the production of ideas through practical-critical activity and in the process trace paths develop in the brain, which is what I suggest is involved in the maturing/mattering process: development—the ontogenetic dialectic movement of the psychophysics of brain-mind.

Chapter Four

God said let there be light:
The psychophysics of brain-mind

Abstract

Marxian psychology has gone through a number of changes and various interpretations have developed relating Marx's theoretical work to present positions in the social sciences, and natural sciences such as biology (i.e. Lynsenko). For a number of years, the Marxian dialectical approach to psychophysics lay dormant. To my knowledge, no one has investigated the relationship between the Marxian dialectic and psychophysics. Marx's theory of dialectical historical material was built on by Vygotsky and theorised as a 'tool' and 'result' methodology for understanding cognitive development and producing cognitive development through instruction led learning at the zone of proximal development. The methodology—dialectical historical materialism—practical-critical activity, unites theory (cognition) and practice (action) and is a dialectical self-movement perspective: Psychophysics as the ontogenetic dialectic process of cognition: the dialectic of brain and mind (that is, mind as consciousness and processor of information) producing ideas and development (perhaps even top-down, bottom-up processing) it is a dual dialectic. This paper outlines my ideas about the Marxian perspective and psychophysics.

Keywords Dialectic, Brain-mind, Historical Materialism, Reflexive Practice

Clarifying Marx's dialectical historical materialism

Marx was a materialist. He made his position quite clear when he wrote 'The Materialist Conception of History' 1844-1847. Under a side heading in the manuscript

'French Materialism and Origins of Socialism', Marx delineated his theoretical position. Starting with French Enlightenment, Marx discusses what he sees as the weaknesses and strengths of their philosophy. Marx suggests that French Enlightenment marked the beginnings of socialism and communism and represented a form of humanism. The French Enlightenment Philosophers emphasised either rationalism or empiricism, or a mixture of both as opposed to secular authority or religion as dictates for human existence. The whole philosophical movement stood for *progress*; improvements in the natural and social conditions of human beings; *fraternity*—the unity of all people; *equality and freedom*—it stood in opposition to the absolute state and religion; and *science*—it advocated the accumulation of knowledge based either on rationalism: reason and rationality (influenced by Descartes metaphysics, 1596-1650) or empiricism: knowledge based on experiential information (Locke, 1632-1704), or both. Marx saw science as a more advanced form of knowledge because it generated 'truths', facts, about existence that are seen as the basis for progress and emancipation. Thus, Marx dismissed religion and the state as established bearers of knowledge and aligned himself with the principles of enlightenment thinkers: that scientific knowledge, which leads to progressive (or Marx, revolutionary) changes and emancipation through to socialism should be the bedrock of social life. This philosophy was complementary to Marx's notions of communism and influenced his methodology, that of rational empiricism.

Secondly, Marx dismissed those philosophers who aligned French Enlightenment Materialism with Romanticism, manifest in French everyday life as over indulgence of the pleasures of the material world. The only good point that flowed from this form of materialism for Marx was that it questioned seventeenth century metaphysics. 'It's anti-theological, anti-metaphysical, and material practices demanded corresponding anti-theological, anti-metaphysical, and material theories' (McLellan, *'Karl Marx: Selected Writings,* 1977, p. 150).

Thirdly, Marx dismisses metaphysicians such as Descartes, Spinoza (1632-1677) and Leibnitz (1646-1716), which he suggested philosophy stood in opposition to—particularly enlightenment materialist philosophy—because metaphysics as a concept was taken as a form of theology and used to give substance to religious doctrines and the divine rule of kings. Materialist philosophy was regarded by Marx as more realistic because it was based on material experience and not some pre-established order. Leibnitz's monads for example, were metaphysical atoms, synchronised by a pre-established hierarchical harmony of which God was the prime monad. It may be correct that the world is made up of atoms and that the whole universe is composed of the same physical elements but this does not prove the existence of a divine creator, only a universal organisation of matter, atoms, which appear to be metaphysical because they are not visible to the naked eye. This is precisely what Marx wanted to reveal. Marx wanted to show that man's self-consciousness was the highest divinity and that all Gods were manmade. In *'Towards a Critique of Hegel's Philosophy of Right'* Marx wrote:

'Man has found in the imaginary reality of heaven where he looked for a superman only a reflection of his own self . . . man makes religion,

religion does not make man . . . God is no abstract being squatting outside the world' (McLellan, *Marx: Selected Writings,* 1977, p. 63).

In addition, given that man's consciousness is the nurturer of religion and gods, Marx wanted to show that consciousness emanates from material/physical substances and metaphysical ones such as atoms and atomic elements when he states 'One cannot separate the thought from the matter which thinks. Matter is the subject of all changes. The word infinite is meaningless unless it means the capacity of our mind to go on adding without end' (McLellan, *Karl Marx: Selected Writings,* 1977, p. 152). In this statement then, Marx shows his materialist point of view to the full, giving in fact, a monistic interpretation of human psyche, one that is purely materialistic and one that places matter first in the universal order and one that conflates the metaphysical level to the physical. Without the physical level therefore, Marx is suggesting there would be no metaphysical level because they are both the same.

Meikle (1991) suggests Marx to be an Aristotelian. Marx used Aristotelian formulas for explaining capacity and Meikle suggests many of Marx's followers rejected his theory of value because it was based on Aristotle's (384-322 BCE) metaphysics and not Hume's (1711-1776) metaphysics more common in Europe. Is Meikle suggesting that Marx advocated metaphysics or just some of the more basic concepts? From reading Marx's materialist concept of history one gets the impression Marx was opposed to forms of metaphysics which confuse the view of reality. Plato's (428-348 BCE) and Kant's (1724-1804) metaphysics for example, do this because knowledge that is *priori*, meaning, that humans are endowed with the power to distinguish forms (i.e. forms such as tree and animal), is taken out of context to suggest a metaphysical reality which exists alongside the physical and in some way manipulates it in some pre-ordinance through the possession of a consciousness superior to humans. Each living human cell may in fact contain in its neuron DNA, genetic information for the blueprint of human biological physique; as well as information for the atomic elements that make up the human form i.e., proteins and ions such as sodium, with corresponding electro-chemical particles.

However, this is material and does not in itself evidence the existence of a divine creator, only material existence on an elementary level that was pre-human form but is now part of that human form. Aristotle's metaphysics may be concerned with studying the whole of being, therefore 'phantasma' but he does this using empirical analysis 'how do you learn the elements of all things and at the same time have *a priori* knowledge of them . . . we need to use our physics, senses because we have no other way of deducing' (Rev. John H. M'Mohon, 1879, *'Aristotle's Metaphysics'*). It appears to me that Marx's critique of metaphysics is aimed at branches of it such as Descartes' dualism because it separates the physical reality from the metaphysical one and at Liebnitz's monadism because it was use to perpetuate social inequality particularly at the time of the Reformation and the rise of the Protestant Ethic. Marx criticises interpretations of metaphysics that bring into being a realm of reality that is based purely on supposition and abstractions. This appears to me to be the main reason for Marx's prejudice of the concept.

Fourthly, Marx discusses two forms of French Enlightenment Materialism: Descartes, which influenced Newtonian physics and gives a mechanical view of motion. Marx skips over the Descartes-Newtonian theory of motion because of human potential volition. Indeed, Marx was a dialectician and wrote a joint paper on the topic with Engels (1949) *'The Dialectics of Nature'*, (Engel doing most of the work). I will come back to this point later. The second form of French Enlightenment Materialism came from Locke, a British born empiricist.

Marx particularly liked Locke's materialism because knowledge was seen as coming directly from the senses—empiricism—as a basis for human reason, not *a priori* knowledge from the metaphysical level, or religion. Locke opposed the 'divine rights of kings', an oppressive doctrine of which Marx wanted to ride society. Being the radical revolutionary he was, Marx took on the notion of empiricism but not the religious undertones to Locke's sensuousness, (Locke saw as a manifestation of theistic essence in man), and incorporated it into his own way of thinking because 'Condillac, an advocate of Locke, provided foundations for Locke's principle anyway by suggesting the soul and senses are matters of experience and habit', not *a priori* 'metaphysical fancy'.

Thus Marx incorporated materialism, rationalism and empiricism into his theoretic work. Materialism was most important to Marx because it placed reality in the 'here' and 'now', the present material world and not some imperceptible predetermined world of metaphysics (the atomic kind accepted), which bore fruit to such notions of a parallel world, a transcendental world—heaven or ultimate reality which only the gods have privy to. The massage appears to be one suggestive that we should live in a material world that is in our range of possibility. In relation to methodology, in 'Theses on Feuerbach', Marx uses Locke's empiricism and the concept of sensuousness to highlight faults in existing materialism, particularly that of the German variety: Hegel and Feuerbach, and links empiricism/practice with rationalism/theory.

For example, Marx states: 'The Chief defect of all hitherto existing materialism is that the thing, reality, *sensuousness*, is conceived only in the form of the object or of contemplation, but not as *sensuous* human activity, practice, not subjectively' (McLellan, *Karl Marx: Selected Writings*, 1977, p. 156). What I think Marx means by this is that reality is sensuousness, a derivative of the senses and 'sensible' capable of being apprehended by the senses in everyday practical activities. Feuerbach places reality correctly in the external object—outside human consciousness but when referring to inside human consciousness—thought Feuerbach reiterates in part the post-Kantian Hegelian idealism by placing thought above practice as a means to true knowledge. Marx is a rational empiricist and unites theory with practice; for Marx, practice is sensuous and reality sensuousness. 'Man must prove the truth, i.e. the reality and power, the this-sideness of his thinking in practice' (McLellan, *Karl Marx: Selected Writings*, 1977, p. 156), the practice of empirical science and rational thought—'mysticism find their rational solution in human practice and in the comprehension of this practice', (McLellan, *Karl Marx: Selected Writings*, 1977, p. 157). Thus, unless we have practical experience of things in some form then we will not understand it as a concept.

The 'Theses on Feuerbach' then outline Marx's methodology, that the process of solving theoretical problems is practical-critical activity: the unity of theory and practice (Gumbrell, 1983). In addition, Marx did not dismiss rational philosophy, he gave it a political edge, changing passive interpretation into revolutionary practice, which he states in the XI and final these on Feuerbach.

Marx first came across the materialist concept in the writings of Ludwig Feuerbach's (1841) *'The Essence of Christianity'*, in which Feuerbach suggests religious beliefs came from 'alienated human desires' (Gumbrell: 1983, p. 32), thus God was just an outer projection of human's inner self. Marx admired Feuerbach's 'inverse ratio' of Hegel's dialectic but felt Feuerbach did not go far enough i.e. was lacking in political will and thus regarded his materialism as ineffective. However in comparison to the Young Hegelians:

'Feuerbach is the only person to have a serious and critical relationship to Hegelian dialectic and to have made real discoveries in this field; in short, he has overcome the old philosophy. The greatness of his achievement and the unpretentious simplicity with which Feuerbach presents it to the world are strikingly opposite inverse ratio' (McLellan, *Karl Marx: Selected Writings, 'Critique of Hegel's Dialectic and General Philosophy'*, 1977, p. 97).

Feuerbach then, turned Hegel's idealist conception of reality into a materialist conception of reality and this had an enormous impact on Marx's writing. Marx did however retain many of Hegel's concepts in his writings which led some to suggest Marx's historical materialism 'has to be understood through reading Hegel's logical dialectic (Swingewood, 1975). Whilst Wilde (1991, p. 288) suggests that Marx was not a post-Kantian Hegelian rationalist because Marx 'conceived the movement of modern society as a dialectical process, but his total was the mode of production rather than the "idea"'.

Ameriks (2000, p. 272) outlines several notions that suggest Marx's materialism 'can be understood as a direct "economic" application of Hegel's account of the "pathway of consciousness" . . . i.e. superstructure, dialectic, stages of development' and so forth. Thus concludes 'Marx's philosophy can be read as taking over the most fundamental philosophical project of German Idealism: the glorification of human history as having a thoroughly dialectical shape in its development as the complete and immanent fulfilment of self-consciousness'. Nevertheless, this self-consciousness for Marx now manifests itself in the material realm of human self-consciousness and not the pre-ordered self-consciousness of the absolute spirit (Have you read the book 'The 12 angry men?'). So, what was Hegel's idealist dialectic?

According to Taylor (1975, p. 127) Hegel's 'idea' system was based on a theological reality in which the absolute spirit/idea (one element of the universal dialectic triad: thesis, antithesis and synthesis) is the governing principle of the universe. In human beings, the absolute spirit is manifest through consciousness of reality, but because humans are only partial reality in relation to the infinite spirit of the triadic absolute his consciousness is limited and unaware of the existence of total spirit/mind/idea. Hegel suggested that the idea unfolds itself and manifests itself as all things material and non-material, once manifest achieves self-consciousness and through self-consciousness realises true circumstances. When this occurs in imperfection, i.e., working class suffering, then the spirit/idea, recoils itself, i.e., redeems itself by bring back into itself that imperfect existence through the double negation and the dialectic process of thesis, anti-thesis and synthesis.

For example, thesis is capitalist accumulation, with the negation of master dominant to slave relationship. The anti-thesis is the negation of slave dominant to master and the synthesis; resultant positive (taken that negative plus negative equals a positive) is equality between master and slave. Hegel saw human consciousness as partial but he viewed it as the highest expression of the absolute spirit through which it can experience itself. In this way, Hegel sought to rationalise religion and give it prominence free from dogma and historical prejudices. Hegel's *'Phenomenology of Spirit,'* was thus a way of putting rationalist theology into the realms of science and at the same time, like the Protestant Ethic of German origin, turning the aims of humans into spiritual values (Lichtheim, 1961).

Marx's historical materialism, following in the footsteps of Feuerbach, stands in direct contrast ('inverse ratio') to post-Kantian Hegelian rationalism (Cornforth, 1949; Lichtheim, 1961; Swingewood, 1975; Gumbrell 1983; Wilde, 1991 and Carver, 1991). Marx's critique of Hegel's 'idea' system is twofold. Firstly, his system is abstract sophism (that is, clever argument without visual materialist reasoning). Hegel, although acknowledged the materialist conception of history or material being-process, what he called the process of becoming, was idealist. The procession of the 'idea' was for Hegel, the dialectic process of the absolute spirit manifesting and struggling through contradictions in material existences to one where only the idea would exist and one in which the dialectic of the idea was paramount: Hegel's dialectic was in the idea. As Marx stated:

> 'Since the abstract consciousness that the object is regarded as being, is only in itself a phase in the differentiation of self-consciousness, the result of the process is the identity of consciousness and self-consciousness, absolute knowledge, the process of abstract thought that is no longer outward looking but only takes place inside itself. In other words, the result is the dialectic of pure thought' (McLellan, *Karl Marx: Selected Writings,* 1977, p101).

The dialectic for Marx was a material dialectic and not the dialectic of thought. Marx reversed Hegel's 'Phenomenology of Spirit', i.e. the becoming of 'ultimate reality', spirit-idea into material existence, to, the unfolding of the material world in history by the process of ideas that come from sensuous material practice. The dialectic hence, was between humans and the human condition: between man and his social and environmental conditions. Thus, Marx put the material/physical world before the 'idea' world, not as Hegel did, putting the 'idea' world before the material. In addition, whilst Hegel's rationalism resides in the idea as some 'mysterious' phenomenal ether outside the material world and beyond perception,

Marx's rationalism resides in the physical realm precisely because he conflates the meta-physical to the physical. Rather than Marx not understanding Hegel's 'idea' dialectic correctly, as some suggest, Hegel contorts metaphysical rationalism into an illusory non-existent apparition, as Marx states of all German idealists:

> 'The phantoms of their brain have got out of their hands. They, the creators, have bowed down before their creations. Let us liberate them from the chimeras, the idea, dogmas, imaginary beings under the yoke of which they are pining away. Let us revolt against the rule of thoughts . . . Once upon a time a valiant fellow had the idea that men were drowned in water only because they were possessed with the idea of gravity . . . his whole life long he fought against the illusion of gravity, of whose harmful results all statistics brought him new and manifold evidence', (McLellan, *Karl Marx: Selected Writings 'The German Ideology'*, 1977, p. 159-160).

Without doubt, Marx was a rational empiricist, this passage from *'The German Ideology'* speaks volumes concerning his ontological, and epistemological believes. His ontology is firstly materialist, secondly, dialectical materialism and epistemology rational empiricism (together his ontology and epistemology is the dialectic unity of rationalism/logical thought and empiricism/sensory perception as practical action) not the rational idealism of Kant and Hegel which places the dialectic in abstract thought. As humans this has to be the case. Hegel's dialectic for example may well be within DNA and thus is made up of all the elements within the universe as unfolding ideas-DNA. However, we live in a material world that is not all to our form and if it is not functional to our needs we either adapt to the environment or change. In Hegel's idea world we adapt; that is we undergo genetic mutation. In Marx's material world we change the world to suit our needs. In actual fact under the principle of dialectic both occur.

Marxian dialectics

Was Marx a dialectician? He did not writing on the topic of dialectics, he merely refers to the dialectics in Hegel's works and took from Hegel those concepts he thought were correct but through 'inverse ratio', presented material dialectics and not idealist. He left it to Engel to write on the topic of dialectics and once again writers such as Thomas (1991) suggest not only that Marx never intended to write on the topic, that he was more concerned with political economy, but also that Engel's dialectic when applied to nature amounted to nothing but complete confusion. I can see Thomas's point of view here. Marx's political and materialist beliefs prevented him from writing on the topic of dialectics in the way that Engel did because above all else he was concerned with freeing human potential—freeing the labouring classes from an estranged position. He thus applied the dialectic to the mode of production—the relation of production, bourgeois dominant to proletariat, and the means of production, the process by which one means of production—proletariat, work on the other means—raw materials and machinery, to produce a saleable commodity of which the bourgeois had the power of appropriating the surplus valve produced.

The proletariat can only sell their labour power in a labour market in which the supply of labour is greater than demand, due to the migrant reserve army of labour. Thus the proletariat become poorer and poorer, the bourgeois richer and richer, resulting in a situation in which the mode of production is no longer feasible because it cannot sustain the relations of production—bourgeois dominant to proletariat. The proletariat as it were 'languishing in poverty'. Herein therefore, is a situation ripe for revolutionary change due the dialectic contradiction inherent in the capitalist system? The bourgeois are committed to accumulating profits to survive in a free market economy, thus continue to exploit the working classes, who as a result of this exploitation 'sink deeper into pauperism' thus have to revolt in order to survive. The pending revolutionary change therefore emergent from the contradictory dialectic of capitalist social relations is meant to be one where human relations to the mode of production change. Marx thought the change to be to socialist relations but this remains to be seen.

Engel's *'The Dialectics of Nature'* is confusing because most of the discussion centres on physics and chemistry as it is applied to nature—the physical environment, and the analogy he makes between the physical dialectic and human activity remains a little foggy. He likens the way atomic particles in motion produce change—energy, a dialectic process, to the way energy is a product of human activity. The underlying theme of the paper only becomes apparent toward the end when Engel's supplants 'work' for theory of motion (i.e. motion/work is the cause changes):

> ' . . . in all these processes the form of motion that initiates the process, and which is converted by it into another form, performs work, and indeed an amount of work corresponding to its own amount. Work, therefore, is change of form of motion regarded in its quantitative aspect', (Engel, 1934, p. 99).

Thus suggesting work/labour causes change. If this is what Engel is implying, then the dialectic he sees is between humans as active agents working on and thus changing nature. In contrast, Marx dealt with the topic in a slightly different way in *'The Materialist Conception of History'* when discussing the dialectical contradiction of the mode of production (outlined above) and *'The Economics'* when he wrote the theory of surplus value and the rate of surplus value. Marx's dialectic is societal, Engel's between humans and nature. Merely reiterating the reversal of Hegel's dialectic as given then discussing dialectics in physical and chemical terms analogous to the production of energy from physical human activity, Engel discussion does not go far enough.

In *'Dialectical Materialism and Science'*, Cornforth (1949), advances the Marxian dialectic perspective. Mechanical materialism holds the view that the universe consists of interacting particles, whose motion in space and time is the result of external forces. A comparable theory in biology is Darwin's theory of evolution, whereby evolutionary motion works via the process of natural selection in which the external environment works on the biological organism eliciting the characteristic which is the 'fittest', most adaptive in a given ecological niche. Dialectical materialism on the other hand offers a self-movement perspective—the dialectical contradiction of opposite forces as the theory of movement at various levels (from physics to biology) that can be demonstrated as arising from the previous form of movement. Cornforth (1949, p. 61) refers to Engel's notion that 'in order to gain an exhaustive knowledge of what [the dialectic of] life is, we should have to go through all forms in which it appears, from the lowest to the highest'. To understand human nature and the human condition, therefore, one needs to study it through the dialectics in the disciplines of physics through chemistry and biology to human psychosocial ecology.

The Marxian dialectician, Lysenko cited in Cornforth, discovered the dialectics of biological organisms and presented a substantial critique to Darwin's theory of evolution. For Darwin, the evolutionary process of random environmental natural selection led to mutant variation of inherited characteristics. Lysenko suggested that mutation occur in the adapting organism through the assimilation of environmental conditions, whereas Darwinian evolutionary theory dealt with the evolution of species—phylogeny, Lysenko's evolutionary theory dealt with the evolution within the individual—ontogeny. The organism is in this respect forced to evolve to survive to pass the adapted gene onto the next generation. For example, at some point in human evolution our ancestors needed to communicate with one another via language. Those humans who managed to achieve language survived to carry forward the genetic trait of language: our ancestor Homo Sapiens. This then became the starting point for the new generation constituting the characteristic difference between it and preceding generations.

According to Darwin's theory however, language use would have occurred completely randomly also implying that the organism had a potential for language—an untapped recessive gene that is brought out by random selection, inbreeding or cross breeding. Lysenko does not disagree with this he develops the notion that evolution is active within the individual as adaptive changes take place and not just between generations. Taking this notion further, Vygotsky enhanced the social interaction between child and instructor through instruction led learning at the zone of proximal development to increase the child's intellectual capacity because Vygotsky suggested, mind is enhanced through social relations—he was in fact encouraging adaptation at the individual level. Thus, this then is one branch of the Marxian perspective that examines the dialectic process within the biological organism. In addition to this, advances of kind that are relative to the materialism dialectic have come from neurophysics and quantum physics.

Working with this as a starting point, I will build on Marx's, Engel's, Lysenko's and Vygotsky's work by clarifying how dialectic historical materialism, or at least what I view as the genesis of Marx's dialectical historical materialism, the creation of ideas from material practice in the human biological organism unfolds, regarding as done, Marx's application of the materialist dialectic to society, the critique of it and the numerous counter-arguments that unfolded in relation to it.

I intend to start from the Marxian perspective firstly, because from Marx came the notion that ideas are the product of practical-critical activity (Theses on Feuerbach), the materialist dialectic of theory and practice, what I call dialectical psychophysics. This has two important implications; a, mind is a direct product of brain matter, and further brain matter develops through the dialectic of brain and mind, b, because of this and because we are in constant flux (the dialectic)—sensation and perception are active processes. The mind is ever increasing producing brain matter and brain matter mind—the dialectic of mind and brain matter is the dialectic of human consciousness in relation to their social and natural conditions—the ontogenetic evolutionary process of consciousness (this is the source for change Vygotsky tapped into with his theory of the zone of proximal development). Secondly, I start from the Marxian perspective because I believe by applying dialectical historical materialism to brain processes focusing on the genesis, the derivation of ideas from material practice and critique of such practice it will open up an area of Marx's theory that has not, to my knowledge, been united before with the natural physical dialectic. In addition, by analysing the material dialectic, it might enable understanding of dialectic processes in other disciplines.

Dialectical historical materialism: The natural dialectic at the dawn of time

The natural dialectic in physics is a good starting point. It could be argued that dialectical historical materialism started at the onset of the universe. If you conceive dialectical historical materialism to be the creation of physical matter in the universe, then the Big Bang theory describes the process of dialectical historical material from the onset of creation. Starting with physics we can examine the dialectic contradiction of opposite forces as a theory of movement at various levels from physics through chemistry, biology, to human psychosocial ecology and perhaps demonstrate how one level arises from another like Engel suggested.

Dialectics as applied to the nature of the universe was first discussed by the Greek philosopher Heraclitus (535-475 BCE) who suggested that changes in the universe where caused by oppositions in which things pass over into their opposite (Guthrie, 1967). Nevertheless, it was Sir Isaac Newton (1614-1727), one of the first classical physicists who formulated laws that governed nature presenting a mechanical theory of the world. Laws of gravity and motion governed a world in which matter, including small-scale light particles what Newton called 'corpuscles', existed in a fixed or absolute system of space and time. All motion having a cause and effect relationship and Newton suggested that if a state of motion was known in the present then the state of motion could be discovered in the future or the past. Newton's laws of gravity in fact, have been used to predict planetary motion with considerable accuracy (Akrill, Bennet & Millar, 1979; Novikov, 1990; McEvoy & Zarate, 1996). Material particles interact eternally within the absolute system so that mass (matter) and its gravitational pull or push is in constant motion. Newton suggested that all phenomena including biological could be explained using his theories of gravity and motion and this is why it is called a mechanical theory and a very deterministic one.

In the universe, these laws apply. The solar system is made up of suns and planets (matter), and the large gravitational fields of suns, hold plants in orbit around them. In addition, vacuums—gravitating black holes exist in the universe—the aftermath of exploding stars, which following the explosion firstly have a gravitational force in the direction of the explosion which dissipates or flattens and then goes in reverse, attracting matter into its vacuous abyss. Newton did not discover black holes, the first black hole was observed by John Michell in 1784 (Novikov, 1990): As more observations have been made then so the theories of the interactions between material bodies with gravitational forces have built up. Another major theory in classical physics came from James Clerk Maxwell (1864), who found through experimentation that magnetism and electricity were the same. Electric conductors generate magnetic fields and a moving magnetic can generate an electric field. Maxwell's theories of electromagnetism and Newton's mechanics are two of the most renowned theories in classical physics (Akrill, Bennet & Millar, 1979; McEvoy & Zarate, 1999).

Max Planck 1900, through applying mathematics to the phenomena linked the gravitational force of mass (matter) from Newton to Maxwell's electromagnetic fields. Planck found that in order to solve the problem of why energy produced by the movement of particles can be averaged as in the entropy of a system and yet the electromagnetic vibrations of light energy could not; was that light energy had specific wavelengths and if they were averaged then it would result in the ultraviolet catastrophe. For example, if the number of particles was 6, n6, and each had a velocity between 1 and 8 one could predict that 6 particles with an average velocity of 2.5 would produce 100 kilowatts of energy. But because light energy has specific wavelengths, you cannot state that 6 electromagnetic vibrations would produce a specific amount of energy. Different wavelengths of light have different colours making up the light spectra (Balmer, 1885). Red light has a wavelength of 656.210, green 486.074, blue 434.01 and violet 410.12. Each wavelength has a different light energy frequency, ultraviolet being the most intense—the hottest—because it has a very short wavelength but an extremely high frequency.

Thus, the electromagnetic vibrations of ultraviolet light energy cannot be averaged with the light energy of red light for example, because light energy does not only have an electromagnetic vibration, it comes in small packages, quanta, and thus Planck was able to resolve the mystery of the ultraviolet catastrophe through this discovery. The quanta of light did not come from the light wave but from the internal properties of atoms, which emit and absorb radiation in discrete quantities. With Planck's discovery of light quanta came a new branch of physics—the study of quantum mechanics—study to discover the laws that govern small particles.

At the quantum level, physicists have found that atoms Newton's 'corpuscles' have sub-atomic particles—nuclei containing neutrons, neutral or charge-less particles and protons with a positive charge (gravitational force) orbited by electrons that have a negative charge (gravitational force)(see figure 1).

At the sub-particle level, the gravitational positive charge of the proton interacts with the negative charge of the electron holding the electron in orbit around the nuclei. Opposites attract, thus at the quantum level some of the theories and laws of classical physics (laws of gravity and motion) apply as they do to the solar system. According to the classical and quantum physical world, proton atoms have existed since the Big Bang. They have an eternal quality to them. Throughout their lives sub-atomic particles decay or transform by emitting light rays; nuclei (neutron and proton atomic centre) emit alpha rays (daughter nuclei), protons emit beta rays (electrons) and electrons emit gamma rays. Different chemical compounds, Hydrogen, Helium and Sodium and all matter is composed of elements whose chemical interaction depends on the number of electrons orbiting the nuclei of atoms, and atoms form elements by sharing electrons. Light is absorbed and emitted in the form of photons when atomic electrons jump between orbits (see figure 2).

What turned this nice simple picture on its head was the discovery of an anti-particle—anti-electron in 1932 by Dirac. Neutrons can emit electrons and change to protons, but also, protons can emit anti-electrons and change to neutrons. Anti-electrons are anti-matter. After Dirac's discovery of the anti-electron, complementary sub-atomic particles: neutron/anti-neutron, proton/anti-proton electrons/anti-electrons were discovered by various physicists (Gamow, 1966; Akrill, Bennet & Millar, 1979; McEvoy & Zarate, 1999; Fraser, 2000). With the discovery of anti-particles, the picture became complex. Is the physical dialectic between matter plus charge and matter plus charge or matter and anti-matter?

The onset of the universe was proposed to have started according to the Big Bang theory (the most popular theory in physics) from a mass of gas, which was spread across space in patches thicker is some places than others. In parts where the gas cloud was dense, gravitational fields emerged which caused the gaseous whirlpool to collapse in on itself causing the fusion of atoms resulting in the emergence of a sun. Nuclear fusion releases enormous amounts of energy, so does fission—the splitting of atoms. The amount of energy generated at the Big Bang explosion caused the universe to go expanding 15 billion years after the event. The Big Bang theory is the most popular theory in physics because 'cosmic background radiation' which was predicted to be an aftermath of the Big Bang was discovered in 1965 by Penzias and Wilson (Fraser, 2000, p. 200). However, as Fraser suggests if this theory is correct, there should be equal amounts of matter and anti-matter in the universe when in actual fact matter dominates the universe. Thus, the natural dialectic cannot be between matter and anti-matter as some physicists presently conceive it. Sakharov (1965), a Russian scientist began his study of matter and anti-matter in the universe. He found that on average, 'one cubic metre of universe contains one billion quanta of radiation, one proton and no anti-protons' (cited in Fraser, 2000, p. 123). There were no anti-particles or so few that under no circumstances could they balance matter. In fact, anti-particles live for approximately one billionth of a second, where as matter, particularly protons, have been around since the dawn of time. In 1998, NASA sent the Space Shuttle discovery on a mission to look for evidence of anti-particles in space. And according to Fraser, if none is found then theories of the universe and physics need re-examining (2000, p. 207).

This is a precarious base from which to start my analysis of the dialectic levels. However, on a much happier note I have come to the conclusion that anti-particles are not particles at all but the incomplete expulsion of the emitting particle's gravitational charge due to the instability of the emitting particle. For example, nuclei with surplus protons P+ (more protons than neutrons) tend to decay by anti-electron emission. That is, by emitting an electron with a positive charge E+ (an anti-electron also called a positron) that is immediately annihilated by an electron with a normal negative charge E-. An E+ (anti-electron) has a life span of a billionth of a second. Thus, the emission of an E+ by a P+ will automatically result in the atom gaining an E—from its surroundings to maintain the balance between the attraction of P+ particles in the nuclei and the orbiting E—particles.

Or following my idea through, an atom containing a surplus P+ particle is so unstable that it emits a mass-less charge E+, which is almost instantaneously annihilated by its complementary opposite E-. This would suggest that the surplus P+ atom does not possess the negative charge energy to make a complete emission of E—to maintain stability so emits a mass-less charge E+ that then has the effect of attracting an E—particle rather than emitting them to restore balance. When E—annihilated E+, two mass-less gamma rays are emitted, again suggesting that anti-particles are charges without mass just like gamma rays are radiation without mass.

Quarks discovered in the 1950s by various physicists are particles found inside the sub-atomic particles, neutrons, protons and electrons that constitute an atom. When a new particle is formed, it has an electric charge that remains stable and a 'hyper-charge' that is unstable and lives for the duration of its birth time (probably one billionth of a second). The electric charge remains with the sub-atomic particle through its birth, all through its life, until it decays. Quarks are like magnets, no matter how many times a magnet is fragmented, it will always retain a positive charge at one end and a negative charge at the other but instead of positive and negative charges quarks are either left-handed or right-handed. These quark-anti-quark particles were found in experiments at PETRA in the 1970s (Fraser, 2000). The two ends, left and right are held together by gluons(see figure 3). Gluons stick quarks and anti-quarks together and can stick three quarks together to make a proton, which has two right up spinning, or clockwise rotating quarks and one left down or anti-clockwise rotating quark.

If these quark left and right spins were equivalent to charge, it would form part of the dialectic symmetry of opposites missing from present physics theory. In addition, if quarks are charges, then perhaps in the beginning the universe was a three-dimensional void, collapsing in on itself generating opposite forces: The collision 'gluing' left-force and right-force together, forming quarks. In turn quarks forming protons; protons atoms that make up the constituents of cosmic dust which went on to form the gaseous whirlpool that collapsed in on itself culminating in the Big Bang. Therefore, the dialectic would be between matter plus charge and matter plus charge, on a material and a sub-atomic particle level; and the original dialectic of opposite forces of gravitating energy fields culminating into quarks—the charge and gamma rays—the radiating energy. Like Heraclitus, my theory would also suggest a universe in which opposites change into their complementary or dichotomy whichever way you want to view it, or are gamma-radiation the same as quark-gravitation?

This would make gamma rays the mutually in-exclusive opposite of quarks. Gamma rays are emitted during nuclear reactions and they are the cosmic rays that form background radiation in out space. Like quarks (emitted through experimentally induced annihilation of E+ by E-) when an E—and an E+ collide normally, the E+ is annihilated by the E—producing two gamma rays emitted back-to-back that go off in opposite directions. Gamma rays are electric radiation with no mass, no charge and are unaffected by magnets. They are so small they pass through substances and only occasionally, cause ionisation by giving some energy to an E—putting it out of its orbit. So quarks form the charge of sub-atomic particles and gamma rays are absorbed and emitted by them in the form of radiation energy. Both are essential to matter, they form the bedrock of matter in the universe: The natural dialectic of quark-gravitation, gamma radiation. Substituting gamma-radiation (waves) for anti-matter and quark-gravitation for matter-particles would explain the lack of anti-matter in the universe. Given however quarks maybe absorbed within the atom, the dialectic would be between gamma-radiation and quark-gravitation. The gluon is a mini vacuum that may be the anti-matter in billionth seconds.

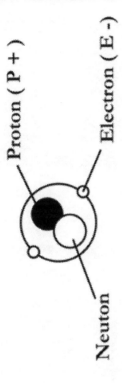

Figure 1 Atom

Figure 2 Electron Jumping Orbits Emitting Gamma Rays

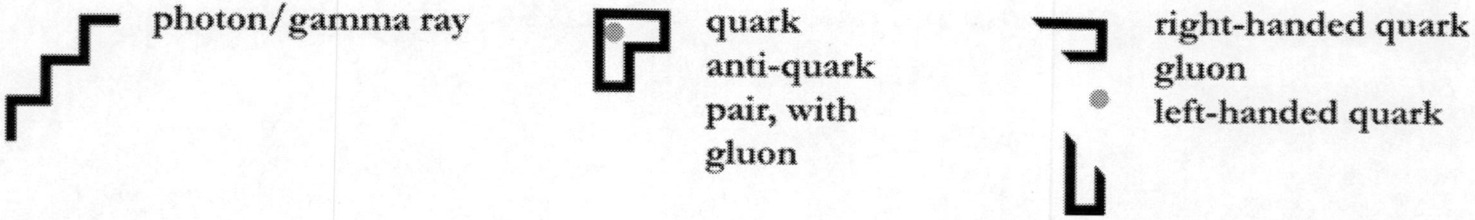

photon/gamma ray

quark
anti-quark
pair, with
gluon

right-handed quark
gluon
left-handed quark

Figure 3 Gamma Rays and Quarks

Dialectical historical materialism: Physical matter into biological

The quark of physics plays a similar role to deoxyribonucleic acid (DNA) on the biological level. Quarks determine the negative or positive charge of a sub-atomic particle. DNA is self-replicating and responsible for the reproduction of inherited characteristics of organic and biological matter. However, the biological organism is that bit more complex, it is a bounded system that has insulated itself from the pre-established laws of classical and quantum physics thus its hereditary characteristics are not so deterministic. Marx criticised Newtonian physics as fixed, because Marx's is a dynamic theory: the process of dialectical historical materialism is evolutionary and revolutionary. Biological organisms, especially those high on the phylogenetic hierarchy, have consciousness and can choose how to act depending on the stable or unstable internal and external environmental conditions. Inherited characteristics are programmed by DNA just as the charge of a sub-atomic particle is determined by quarks; because the biological system has evolved from the organic system, which in turn evolved from the chemical system that evolved from the physical system. Thus, the biological organism contains within it, the properties of the physical system but in a much more elaborate fashion owing to the dynamism of the evolutionary dialectic process. Therefore the existing laws of classical and quantum physics do not completely govern the biological organism, but remnants of them remain in an adapted more complex form.

Dialectical historical materialism: Psychophysics of brain-mind (Top-down bottom-up processing)

How did consciousness develop? Is consciousness a facet that has evolved due to its survival potential or is it an incidental product of the nervous system? The brain evolves one way via the dialectic of the human central nervous system and the physical world. Like muscle development in other parts of the body, brain cells take in neuropeptides, proteins (Thompson, 1993). Neurotransmitters have an organising function in relation to neuropeptides and what we eat can have a direct effect on our brain functioning. Nerve cells however do not increase in number through the intake of nutrients. We are born with approximately one billion brain cells, but synaptic connections continue to develop until we die. Each neuron has somewhere between one thousand to ten thousand connections with other neurons and it appears to me that the development of synaptic connections is the result of the evolutionary dialectic between the central nervous system as a whole and the mind: consciousness: and other brain processes.

Hobson (1999) discusses two level of consciousness, the secondary, which involves 'elaborate processes: memory, thought, language, intention and volition, orientation and learning', thought processes that an individual develops through experience and the primary level, 'sensation, perception, attention, emotion, movement and instinct' are characteristic of consciousness that babies are born with. If consciousness develops the secondary processes through experience, then consciousness must be necessary for these processes and have the ability to control their development. Primary states of consciousness such as perception, sensation, emotion and movement are all facets of the old mammalian brain (Short Term Memory (STM) is too, involving the hippocampus so therefore so is thought ('be' without 'ing') that would imply that the nervous system is an incidental product of consciousness. It appears to me that there is a dialectical process between brain and mind, between matter, and mind as an electrochemical field of consciousness. Just like quarks and radiation, one is inseparable from the other and as opposites form an inseparable harmonic tension of the dialectical process they constitute.

Because the nervous system contains electrical synapses, you would think that the brain was a by-product of the nervous system because biological organisms low down on the phylogenetic hierarchy have electrical synapses and those high up on the phylogenetic hierarchy have a mixture of chemical and electrical synapses. The human brain contains both electrical and chemical synapses but electrical pre-synaptic elements are so large it limits the number of synapses to only a few per neuron. Learning and memory are limited in a nervous system with only electrical synapses. Chemical synapses on the other hand are much smaller so there are thousands of synapses on each neuron (see figure 4) allowing associated learning for example, to occur much more rapidly (Thomas, 1993).

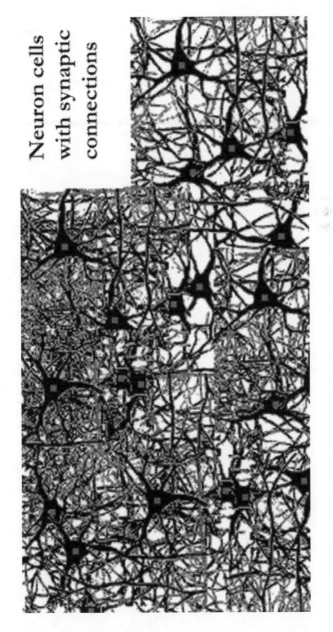

Neuron cells with synaptic connections

Figure 4 Neuron network: Site of electronchemical field of consciousness

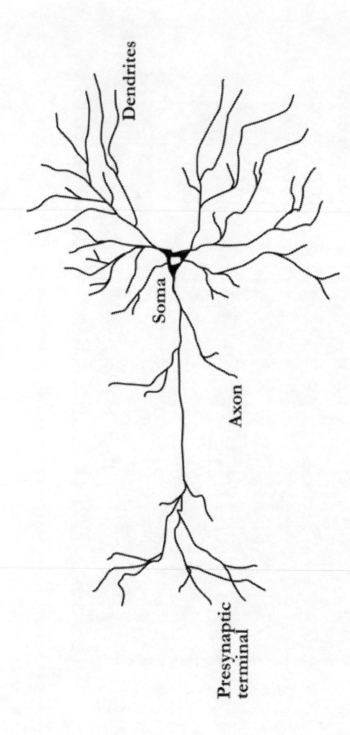

Figure 5 A single neuron

The Dopaminergic Modulatory System

The 3 dopamine pathways

Cortex

Thalamas

Substantia nigra

Cerebellum

Site of Pineal gland

Hypothalamus

Ventral tegmental area

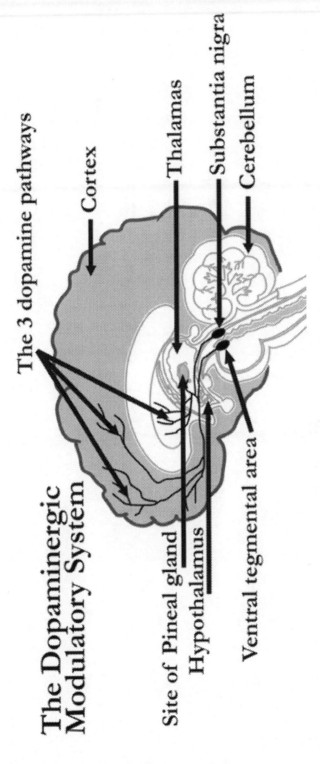

Figure 6 Dopaminergic modulatory system

Locating the Rehearsal Loop in STM

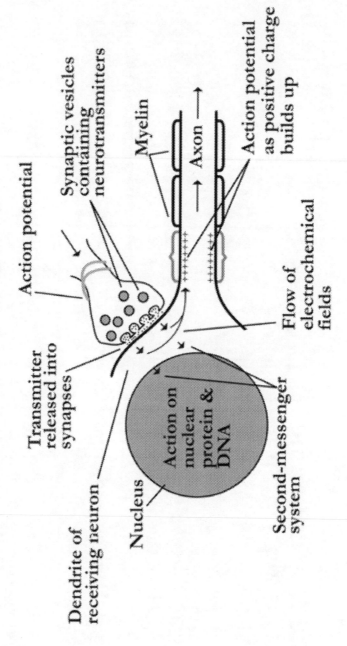

Figure 7 First and second-order messenger system (Rehearsal Loop in STM begins when first messenger as action potential fires and triggers others close increasing first release of neurotransmitter into synapse)

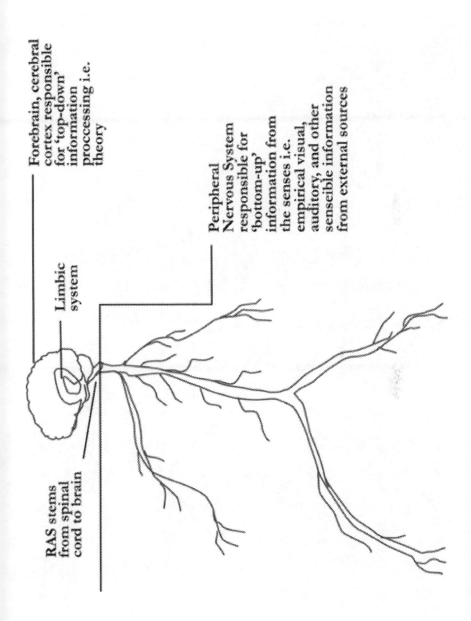

Figure 8 Central nervous system

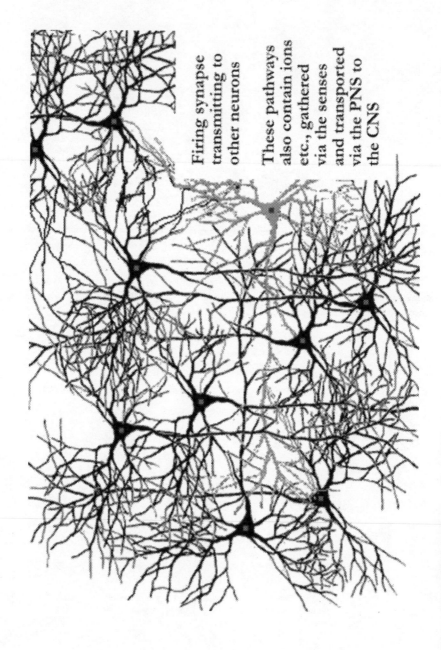

Firing synapse transmitting to other neurons

These pathways also contain ions etc., gathered via the senses and transported via the PNS to the CNS

Figure 9 Synchronised synaptic excitation

This has importance for the way physics has been united with psychology by others. If the laws of classical and quantum physics govern biological matter, then it would be best if neuron synapses were electrical because electrical neurotransmitters would probably travelled as the speed of light rather than at one to two milliseconds as chemical neurotransmitters do. Notwithstanding, both are present so perhaps each have different functions within the brain—one transmitting through the nervous system the other into organs and the endocrine system for example.

Penrose (1997) a quantum physicist, was perplexed as to how biological brain matter achieves global binding causing a unified state of consciousness. He suggests that to apply classical and quantum theories to consciousness you would need to use three constants: Planck's quantum constant h, which is the smallest divisible unit of quantum matter (mass); the second is the gravitational constant G, which governs the attraction between bodies of matter, and the third is the Dirac-Einstein's constant C-1, which incorporates the equivalence principle and represents either speed of light or the speed at which either radiation or neuron activity achieves global binding. How does the brain produce and change states of consciousness? One minute you might be writing a book, then all of a sudden, you remember that you put the kettle on and it may have boiled dry. The change in thought from writing to remembering is accompanied by a different state of consciousness, from deep concentration to an alert state that demands immediate action. Penrose suggests that the mechanism that synchronises a unified experience of consciousness may be in the microtubules or axons. Axons are strands of tissue fibre that branch from neurons and form synaptic connections through the dendrites with other neurons.

Neurotransmitters travel through the network of axons and dendrites (figure 5) and cross the synaptic gap between neurons carrying chemical messages: electrochemical communication (also see figure 4). According to Penrose, within the neural network there must be some sort of 'large-scale, quantum coherent activity, somewhat like a superconductor . . . coherent quantum oscillation taking place throughout the brain . . . producing . . . the globalisation of consciousness' (1997, p. 132-33). This would make the brain a quantum system in which all the synapses fire in unison causing global binding—a unified field of consciousness. Changes in states of consciousness would resemble Bohr's objective reduction in physics, when electrons jump from one orbit to another around the nuclei emitting gamma radiation, in the brain the radiation emitted representing mind/consciousness.

However, although the neuron network in the brain might be the site of global consciousness—a unified emission of electrochemical radiation—the global organisers are not in the axons/microtubules. Neurotransmitters are the electrochemicals of global binding because they fill the synaptic gap causing fusion between synapses and neurons but neurotransmitters are regulated by chemical modulatory systems (Thomas, 1993) of which there are four: the noradrenergic, the serotonergic, the dopaminergic and cholinergic (Hobson, 1999). Serotonin, noradrenaline, epinephrine (adrenaline), acetylcholine, dopamine, GABA (gamma aminobutyric) and peptides, glycine, glutamate and aspartate are all neurotransmitters that have different effects on the brain.

The dopaminergic modulator system has three dopamine circuits connect by one neuronal pathway(see figure 6). One of the dopamine systems is located in the hypothalamus one pathway goes from the substantia nigra to the basal ganaglia and the third run from the midbrain and penetrates deeply into the cerebral cortex and forebrain limbic system (Thomas, 1993). The dopamine modulatory system is interesting; it is responsible for global binding associated with higher states of consciousness: thought, memory and positive emotions. In addition, the dopaminergic is the only modulatory system active during REM sleep when vivid and lucid dreams occur, and in animals that are alert, brain cells oscillate in synchrony producing gamma rays.

First-messenger neurotransmitters such as dopamine travel through the modulator system exciting or inhibiting synapses. There are thousands of synapses on each neuron. Synaptic potential can be generated anywhere on the cell body or dendrites. Neural activity is both spontaneous and continuous causing only a small depolarisation in the cell membranes. But the sum of these brief depolarisations—called excitatory postsynaptic potential—if cause synapses to activity simultaneously, will cross the action potential-generating threshold, influencing states of consciousness: the electrochemical field of consciousness.

Once the transmitter attaches to the postsynaptic receptor, it activates the second-messenger system causing a chemical reaction: 'A biochemical process within the cell which alters its excitability and can change the pattern of gene expression in the DNA of the cell' (Thompson, 1993, p. 151; Hobson, 1999, p. 148). See figure 7.

But what activates modulatory systems? The serotonergic modulatory system is governed by the pineal gland, a tiny structure at the top of the brain stem, which secretes melatonin, a hormone that activates serotonin production, a neurotransmitter that in turn regulates sleep, temperature and is also involved in the activity of the female gonads. Thus when it excites synapses is can induces a global state of consciousness, sleep. During wakened states of consciousness, serotonin excitation of synapses has a calming effect and can produce states of euphoria. Too much serotonin in the brain leads to depression and it inhibits thought processes because when it inhibits synapses, in blocks the uptake of dopamine. Too little serotonin can lead to schizophrenia because dopamine is allowed to build up in the brain cells. Hobson (1999) suggests serotonin is involved in associative learning in sea slugs. So it appears that serotonin and dopamine regulatory systems counteract each other, because when dopamine causes excitation of synapses it blocks the uptake of serotonin, and vice versa.

Hobson suggests that the modulatory systems are more involved in brain states than the reticular activating system (RAS) but I think that both play a part. The RAS runs from the spinal cord to the forebrain carrying sensory information and motor information, it also synchronises visual and auditory reflexes based on information from the hindbrain. The forebrain contains the cerebral cortex where the development of the brain continues after birth, such as cognitive development and sensory motor development (Gross, 2000). The RAS is responsible for alertness and selective attention so that we only respond to changes in stimuli if it is necessary.

The limbic system in the brain serves as a meeting place between the cortex and older parts of the brain, hypothalamus and thalamus. From the cortex the limbic system receives interpreted information about the external environment, and from the hypothalamus and thalamus it receives interpreted information about the body's internal environment, homeostasis: motivation and emotion. This information is integrated in the limbic system and sent back to the cortex, the cortex being responsible for the analysis and evaluation of the combined information.

I have a hunch therefore that the RAS and the limbic system, from which the dopaminergic pathways stem, play a vital role in regulating not only dopamine modulation but also cortical activity and development which depends not only on higher brain function but also on the other parts of the body involving movement, homeostasis, and sensory information. These in turn can be controlled by the working memory situated in the neuronal network as short term memory and the frontal cortex. Therefore, the limbic system and RAS supply the cortex with all the information it needs for adaptive development because together are responsible for alertness and selective attention and also supply the electrochemical transmitter needed to maintain a state of consciousness that affords secondary states of consciousness. Lastly, the RAS carries sensory information from the spinal cord to the cortex. Peptide neuronal modulators are thought to be involved in encoding memories, and they are also involved in sensory transmission, thus the sensory data that memories are composed of, could contain sensible qualities of the external environment as well as the internal one.

What I am suggesting here, is that memories encoded in peptides could have a one to one correspondence with reality. Sensory information: visual, auditory, taste etc., which consists of atomic particles, could be transported and encoded in peptides that form the basis of memory. More importantly, what this analysis shows is that secondary states of consciousness: thought, memory, intention and volition are the product of information that is a unity of sensory data from the internal (homeostasis: drives and emotions etc) and external environment (visual, auditory, touch taste etc) that is analysed and evaluated in the cortex. Thus, secondary states of consciousness are the product of the dialectic of cortical and empirical data, Marx's dialectic of theory and practice: practical-critical activity.

A second proposition is that dopamine, appears to be a modulatory system that alerts the work memory where reflexive practice and higher mental processes occur. The working memory situated in the frontal cortex also coordinates incoming information from the senses and would therefore be an ideal candidate for changes in global consciousness. If we regard sensory information representative of Planck's quantum constant h, the existing neuronal matter would represent G, and the working memory Dirac-Einstein's constant $C-1$. Although any of brain modulators would be representative of Dirac-Einstein's constant $C-1$, for example GABA (gamma aminobutyric) that can enter the brain matter directly. The working memory is also thought to be mainly short term memory (STM) and STM is situated in the axons and dendrites when action potentials release electrochemical neurotransmitters into synapses causing global binding when the synaptic clefts are bridged.

Dialectical historical materialism: theory and practice

Marx did not discuss the physical nature of human beings but regards activity emanating for human physical nature—both practical and theoretical—as a starting point for dialectical historical materialism (McLellan, Karl Marx: *Selected Writings*, 1977, p. 160). The interaction between theory and practice: practice as active sensuousness—as a material reality informing consciousness, through the senses; and active perception whereby active sensuousness and active perception lead to theory production i.e. the formulation of ideas. Reflexive practice is a more intense form of practical-critical activity, the oscillation of theory and practice. Reflexive practice involves 'a reflective conversation with a situation in which we reflect on practice in the midst of it' (Schön, 1983), in cycles of planning, acting, observing, reflecting, re-planning and acting. We deliberately direct consciousness, trying to maintain a higher level of awareness so that understanding and meaning occur. Reflexive practice incorporates both retroductive and abductive strategies of investigation (Lisle, 2000), strategies that have lead to some of the most important discoveries ever made. By maintaining heighten consciousness, reflexivity acts like a modulatory system. A brain state that was once induced in situations demanding alertness, can now be deliberately brought on by focusing consciousness on a problem until you find a solution, ideas that come from the 'reflexive conversation with the situation'. Therefore, I am suggesting that 'mind challenges genes' inducing states of consciousness the process which in turn affects the DNA! Schizophrenia according to neurobiologists is a brain disorder that an individual can become predisposed to because the neurotransmitter dopamine can build up in brain cells and affect DNA (Thompson, 1993; Hobson, 1999) so I cannot see any reason why neurotransmitters are not equally able to affect DNA in the same way but to the benefit of the individual!

God said let there be light: Consciousness

When Reflexive practice focuses consciousness, it represents an intense stimulus to the neuron, enough to produce an action potential that exceeds the threshold of response. An intense stimulus will increase the frequency of firing thereby affecting a greater number of other neurons which in turn release neurotransmitters into synaptic clefts (probably dopamine) which increases the binding of neurons radiating an electrochemical filed of consciousness that is sustained for longer periods due to the increased amount of neuron firing and neurotransmitter release. The neurotransmitter in turn activates the second message system causing a chemical reaction in neuron cells, where protein-encode memories can affect the DNA. The global binding of the neurons corresponds to the development of trace paths in the brain (connections between short term and long term memory, Hebb, 1949) that are responsible for associative learning, the first step in Vygotsky's stages of cognitive development that leads to scientific concept formation. The global binding process links areas of the brain forming a lattice, and given that memories are encode in protein molecules in brain cells, the global binding lattice weaves the protein-encoded memories together like a concept matrix(see figure 9).

For example, during class discussion exercises using active learning techniques, you can direct class discussions so that the conversation moves up and down the concept matrix (Vygotsky's concept matrix, 1962, p. 112) from technical vocabulary to concrete personal experiences and antidotes. The more links a student makes between the information presented, and information (memories) they already hold, the more likely they are to achieve concept formation. Word meaning is achieved through connections—trace paths connected via the electromagnetic field of consciousness. What I am suggesting is that each piece of information acts as stimuli to cue memories that are cocooned in the globalised field of consciousness. Information coming in from the senses, auditory, visual etc., that is encoded in peptides and ions, travels through the axons between synapses and when the dopaminergic modulatory system is activated i.e. alerted by the stimuli—problem (what does this word mean), if a neuron (which may possess as many as 10,000 synapses) receives enough synapses excitations it will fire. And the dopaminergic modulatory system will cause synchronised firing of synapses and neurons that in turn if they too contain enough synaptic excitations will fire.

The electrochemical neuron transmitter that is released in turn will sustain the field of consciousness alerted by the stimulus-problem until the problem is solved—until an idea is formed or synaptic connections are made that join together existing memories. What I am suggesting occurs is that the synapse that fires is the one which is connected to a neuron that contains protein encoded memories that are associated to the incoming data, peptides and ions from the senses. If the concept is similar it will come to mind.

The fusion between the protein encoded memories in the neuron cells and the ions and peptides which are allowed in due to synaptic firing is the production of a new idea in the electrochemical field of consciousness—mind-light. And at the same time it constitutes the creation of brain matter—new synaptic connections—trace paths. Through bringing as many personal experiences as possible into the conceptual arena to illustrate a concept you are more likely to cue stored memories in students' consciousness that will connect thereby eliciting the creation of a new idea through association in the synaptic relay system: the acquisition of a concept the learner did not know the meaning of prior to the discussion. Eureka!

Interactive teaching techniques produce better results than didactic ones because students are actively involved in the process their minds are more active therefore forming synaptic connections. Directing consciousness through student reflexive practice in this way spurs learning and development on because reflexive practice heightens consciousness awareness increasing the dialectic interchange between mind and brain; between the enveloping electrochemical lattice of global consciousness and cell protein encoded memories.

Conclusion

Thus, we arrive at a definition of Marx's dialectical historical materialism that relates directly to practical-critical activity, or the present day ubiquitous reflexive practice as the fusion point between matter, brain and mind. The oscillation of theory and practice in cycles of reflection and action intensifies global states of consciousness meshing together cell protein encoded memories leading to concept formation—transcendental knowledge—light, truth. It is a reflection of reality, truth, because through reflexive practice, information from the senses—empirical information is linked to cognitive rationality. This occurs because on the psychophysical level, the dialectic of the nervous system (internal and external sensory information) is brought together in the limbic system and the reticular activating system combining information from the internal biological system, and external information via the senses; and central nervous system (brain-mind) which is working memory as a short term memory store of information it directs consciousness to information to such as that from the above sources.

Through sensing and perceiving therefore, external reality is brought into the biological system, combines with the internal system through consciousness and produces ideas leading to material developments in brain-mind: Ontogenetic development. I am suggesting a one to one correspondence with external reality and symbolic systems if the concepts are processed through the oscillation of practice and theory. The dialectic of mind and brain mimics the dialectic of quantum physics in which quark-gravitation-direction (a gluon to quark gravitation may be a mini vacuum/black hole thus anti-matter) and gamma radiation are in an inseparable struggle causing one to change into the other, the process involved in Marxian psychophysics creating ideas and development. This interpretation of Marx's dialectical historical materialism offers some neuro-electrochemical foundation to concept formation from material practice, the dialectic ontogenetic process of evolution: learning and development, but much of what I have suggested as yet remains theoretical.

My theorising runs congruent with that of Newman and Holzman (1997). Their concept of activity-theoretic if taken literally, suggests a situation in which developmental community members engage in activity—group reflexive practice—producing ideas—definitions of the situation based on their immediate spacio-temporal situatedness in order to further the development of the community: Marx's methodology of producing ideas from material practice. My analysis describes the fundamental ontogenetic dialectic process in psychophysical terms, the psychophysics of activity-theoretic. The community develops precisely because of the psychophysical dialectic: the incorporation of external reality into the psychophysical system through mutual reflexive practice of their spacio-temporal situatedness. In other words, the ideas the community develop are based on sensations and perceptions of the immediate reality and not some pre-given theoretical system. Having said this, unlike Newman and Holzman who prefer to see an end to knowing, I would suggest that group reflexive practice facilitates the beginning of knowing and is more likely to lead to valid knowledge production.

Chapter Five

Assessing learning styles of adults with intellectual difficulties

Abstract

The development of an electronic inventory to assess learning styles of adults with intellectual difficulties was seen as an inclusion strategy to aid learning and achievement. Forman, Nyatanga and Rich (2002) argue for the 'centrality of E-learning to educational diversity' for example. The use of VAK inventories (whether electronic or paper based) however, has been derogated as leading to theory-practice pedagogy that is misinterpreted and ill-informed (Geake, 2005). The focus of this paper therefore is dual in that the vigour and 'user friendliness' of the tool developed is analysed in the midst of a critical appraisal of its use. Assessments conducted using the inventor developed showed 34% of the participants have visual preferences, 34% have auditory, 23% have kinaesthetic, and 9% have multi-modal learning preferences. Thus, this participant group require a varied and diverse learning programme. The inventory was found to be user friendly but in need of further development, and would best be used as part of a self-reflective learning package.

Keywords, *Learning Difficulties, Learning Style Inventory, Adult Learners*

Background and context

It has been well research that each individual has a preferred style of learning, and understanding of it can influence students' learning in a positive way. Knowledge of one's learning style can lead to enhanced learning and helps the learner focus on improving weaker points. Learning styles analysis is also useful for informing the teaching and learning process and can be used as a tool to enhance achievement and inclusion (DfES, 2004; Rose & Nicholl, 1997; Smith, 1996). The DfES (2004) for example, produce guidance materials centred on the use of learning styles information to develop teaching practice and they are recommended for use by teachers studying for Master Degrees or if they want to gain membership of the General Teaching Council of England (DfES, 2004). Much educational pedagogy however, usually involves teachers learning the practice side of education but without understanding the theory behind it including that of learning styles assessment; this is not always supportive of learning. The DfES (2004) guidance is a move away from this style of teaching and learning so that a thorough understanding of learning styles and the application of differentiated teaching based on them make up the guidance product.

The use of learning styles assessment and consequential synchrony with learning opportunity can help to remove obstacles to learning generally and can be beneficial to and supportive for adult learners with intellectual difficulties. A learning style inventory was thus developed for adults with intellectual difficulties because it was thought that such an inventory would enhance achievement and inclusion. In addition, because there is a move toward E-learning generally as a way of achieving an inclusive education system with a flexible learning environment, an electronic learning styles assessment tool was seen as the way forward, as Forman et al (2002) suggest 'it is the new wave strategy that sits comfortably with other strategies developed for the 21st century'. The Visual, Auditory and Kinaesthetic (VAK) learning styles inventory was chosen as a model to build on; initially developed by Rose (1985, Rose & Nichol, 1997) and then Smith (1996). The VAK assessment tool was seen as fit for purpose due to its simplicity and affinity with sensory modalities i.e. seeing, hearing and doing (touch).

It is noted here however, that advances in the field of neuropsychology have influenced teaching practice including ideas associated with the VAK learning styles assessment, and it is suggested, such advancements have had a counterproductive effect on student achievement manifest as they have become: theory-practice educational pedagogy based on over fervent conclusions of behavioural representation in specific brain areas. Geake (2005) for example, is unhappy about the way neuropsychology is incorporated into teaching practice:

'... reports estimate a 1000 UK schools are using brain gym exercises. Unfortunately much of this well-intentioned interest is predicated on an over-simplification of brain research e.g. lateralisation biases mis-interpreted as left—and right-brain thinking . . . from results of experiments that have been mis-interpreted and not environmentally validated outside the experimental lab' (Geake, in 'Researchintelligence: BERA', 2005, p11-12).

Are VAK modality assessments valid given Professor John Geake's comments? It was felt that not only should the inventory developed here be analysed and evaluated for validity of purpose but through taking on board what Geake (2005) had said, further analysis of the VAK modality inventory was essential in light of his critique. For instance, developments in neuropsychology have unintentionally misled teaching practice, not just brain gym work but also the way VAK has been used as a system for labelling learners one style or the other without thought for the consequences or development of multi-sensory learning.

The rationale for conducting this study therefore, is to understand the teaching and learning process fully, particularly the modalities of the cognate process. As learners, individuals can influence their learning by firstly understanding it, secondly taking control of it and thirdly improving their weaknesses once understanding of their learning preference is assessed using the VAK modality inventory developed. In this way, it is hoped participants will be empowered. Although auditory learners prefer to listen to instruction, visual learners prefer to use diagrams and pictorial information, and kinaesthetic learners like to do practical tasks (Barbe, 1985; Gardner, 1993; Rose & Nicholl, 1997; Smith, 1996), each individual learner will use elements of all three learning styles whilst learning but will operate in one modality more than the others. In addition, learners may use different modalities for different information learning tasks. Hence, through assessment and instruction learners can be shown how to lead with their preferred primary modality to begin with whilst developing their lesser-used secondary modality/modalities (Bouldin & Myers, 2002) leading to multi-sensory enhanced learning.

Literature review

VAK, neuro-linguistic programming and accelerated learning

Gardner's theory of Multiple Intelligence (1993) was one of the first to focus in on the learning process to discover how people process information such as learning styles. Gardner suggested that intelligence was not a single unitary entity but made up of several systems of ability that are independent yet interrelated. He for example, suggested that we each have multiple intelligences and in 'Frames of Mind', Gardner outlined several different intelligences: Logical/Mathematical, Visual and Spatial, Musical, Bodily and Kinaesthetic, Interpersonal, Intrapersonal, Naturalistic and Experiential. This system of abilities allows the individual to solve problems. Three of these intelligences are relative to the modalities of VAK: visual, linguistic/auditory, and kinaesthetic. His theory is widely used in schools today to enhance the teaching and learning process, for example, Sears et al (2001) links multiple intelligences with Rose & Goll's (1992) six stage of learning.

Theories that aim to support and scaffold learning in this way have in fact become known as accelerated learning theories. The aim as the name suggests is to spur on learning and development through the understanding of the learners' learning style or information processing modality within a given social context. From this the Neuro Linguistic Programming Approach was formed, an approach that highlights the use of VAK inventories to assess learning styles and assist learning.

Using learning style assessments to empower learners is extensive amongst all manner of learner from pharmacy and biology students to primary, secondary and FE students (Rose & Goll, 1992; Briggs, 2000; Sears, 2001; Bouldin & Myers, 2002; Sprenger, 2003; Perry & Ball, 2004; Cassidy, 2004). Perry and Ball (2004) for example, examined various learning style programmes such as the Myers-Briggs' Type Indicator (1962) and Kolb's Learning Style Inventory (1984) as well as Gardner's Intelligences (1993) and concluded how useful learning style assessments were for course development and teaching practice generally. Therefore, students with intellectual difficulties can benefit from learning modality assessments and VAK teaching strategies equally as well.

Neuro-Linguistics is about the way the nervous system (the central nervous system being equated with cognition) receives information through the senses; including language and nonverbal communication and the mapping of this information reception to neural matter in the brain. The programming of neuro-linguistics can be essentially that, enhancing learners' ability to organise the nervous and linguistic system for learning and achievement, in this instance, tuning VAK modalities for learning, in other words, tuning the senses: hearing seeing and doing for learning.

Why the VAK system for assessing learning styles?

The VAK system is used for assessing learning styles here rather than one of the other systems such as Honey & Mumford (1982) Learning Styles, or Kolb (1984) Experiential Learning because it is reflective of the sensory information reception and processing modalities. Sprenger (2003) for example outlines the sensory pathway approach to learning styles assessment and how incoming information links to memory by way of the sensory pathway used. Thus, the learning modalities determine the sifting, assimilation, and retrieval of all information produced (also Rose & Goll, 1992: Tileston, 2004). The VAK system is partly supported by the experimental work of Riding & Douglas (1993), cognitive psychologists who discovered a relationship between the presentation of information and recall in that those subjects with 'Verbal-Imagery' cognitive style preferences respond better if information is presented 'text-plus-picture' i.e. visual stimuli rather than 'text-plus-text' without a picture. In other words, the experiment showed a relationship between visual learning style preference and the presentation of information. Again, emphasizing the relationship between sensory input and learning style.

Is there such a thing as the kinaesthetic learning style?

It is suggested that the kinaesthetic learning style (doing or active learning and touch) is unfounded. Coffield (2005) suggests that the kinaesthetic learning style is 'kinaesthetic nonsense'. Yet, until a child learners to read and write it will rely greatly on visual, auditory and kinaesthetic information about the environment. Story bags for example enhance kinaesthetic learning because the child has to feel inside a bag it cannot see into and decide whether the object felt is of a particular kind. The blind also learn through touch and sound. This is the onset of kinaesthetic learning and a valuable asset and compliment to visual and auditory information. As a child journeys through the education system they will learn through seeing (visual), hearing (auditory) and doing (kinaesthetic) means. The latter in particular, learning by doing, active learning or kinaesthetic learning—is extremely important for learners who have not developed reading and/or writing skills. The problem is not whether it exists it is more to do with whether the child is encouraged to develop the visual and auditory modalities to compliment the kinaesthetic. Therefore, the VAK assessment should be used to highlight not only the primary modality, but also the underused modalities so their development can be encouraged.

A case for individualised learning plans

Coffield et al (2004) further suggests there is widespread 'conceptual confusion' in Post-16 education surround learning styles. Which learning style system should be used for example? What do you do with the information once you have it? If VAK inventories are used widely, how can we tackle the 'mis-use-culture and ethos?' I think that because of its multi-sensory modal nature, VAK is extremely useful for primary and secondary education as well as for adults with intellectual difficulties because of its simplicity but particularly its affinity with the sensory pathways to memory. Tileston (2004) for example advocates the use of multi-sensory approaches to teaching and learning linking it to information processing models of memory, as does Sprenger (2003) and Rose & Goll (1992). If VAK is used together with personal development planning and the encouragement of reflective learning, weaker points/modalities can be strengthened leading to multi-faceted learning. If multi-faceting learning is encouraged, then this will help tackle the 'mis-use-culture and ethos'.

Sears et al (2001) investigated the use of learning styles information as a non-judgemental tool for differentiated teaching with SEN and non-SEN learners based on the work of Rose & Goll (1992) but Sears et al applied it to secondary education, rather than further education. Sears et al found that by making pupils' learning more explicit in terms of learning styles and the six stages of learning, pupils' understanding of the learning process led to enhanced learning. The six stages of learning being: the reception of information and state of mind, the intake of information (VAK) and perception, the exploration of the subject and the processing of it (mind mapping, flash cards, poem writing/rhyme, writing notes, highlighting text); the memorising of information and encoding, recalling and showing what you know, and lastly, the metacognitive process of reflecting on how you learn such as VAK learning styles and the 6 stages of learning outlined.

In California, Shelton et al (2002) developed a multi-sensory instruction programme incorporative of the VAK assessment tool to be used with students who have learning difficulties (LD) that firstly determines learning style, which is then built into a learning plan to enhance language acquisition and reading ability. Research that supports the effectiveness of learning programmes based on multi-sensory approaches to learning is numerous (Rose & Goll, 1992; Joshi et al, 2002; Shaywitz, 2004). A very recent experimental approach to learning styles use, Shaywitz (2004) using functional magnetic resonance imaging (fMRI), found increases in activation in left hemisphere regions of the brain after intensive multi-sensory phonologically-based reading intervention programmes, whereby the LD brain patterns resembling those of the control group. However, this type of research is still in the process of development and is the kind of experimental research Geake (2005) suggests we should look critically at until we know for sure what the fMRI actually measures.

Empowerment and inclusion

Practitioners such as Lacey (2000) think that 'learning disability is a multi-professional, multidisciplinary topic and therefore educationalists should get involved with the care of adults with intellectual difficulties because their care is dominated by the medical profession and therefore this group of people do not get the access to education they deserve' (2000, pp. 100-2). Lacey suggests that 'people with learning difficulties find learning difficult by definition' (2000, p. 100) so their need for help is greater. Perhaps this inventory will help. It will in the least represent one of the preconditions of person centred planning (Iles, 2003) or personal development planning already active in higher education.

No one learning style modality is regarded as better than another, although it has been suggested that Western Education favours auditory, then visual, then kinaesthetic (Gardner, 1993). Kinaesthetic learners are to some extent discriminated against in education because auditory and visual delivery styles of teaching are more predominant particularly beyond primary education. Learning styles assessments can help change this because the information obtained from them can be used to inform teaching, specifically, the planning of it so that teachers can plan taught sessions for different styles of learning. Sprenger (2003) for example, assesses students' learning styles and constructs individual learning plans. In the UK, independent education plans (IEPs) are used for students with special educational needs in primary and secondary education. We can learn from this practice by using planned learning methods in further and higher as part of students' personal development planning on a general level. Indeed, Gollwitzer (1999) suggests that planning learning actually increases success—we are more likely to achieve our goals if we plan.

The disabled individuals this assessment tool is aimed at are mainly mature and have a variety of learning difficulties. Some learning style inventories were too complex for use; Honey & Mumford's (1986) model for example had little meaning to this student group, and whilst the Visual, Auditory and Kinaesthetic (VAK) modality type indicator was pitched at the correct level, the VAK tests that were available were either aimed at children or did not have the correct ingredients. Some learners who cannot read or write cannot do VAK tests without assistance so a VAK paper test seemed limiting as is the VARK: Visual, Aural/Auditory, Read/Write, and Kinaesthetic inventory. It was decided therefore, an electronic VAK inventory would be beneficial in this context as it would allow the use of pictures and sounds which this specialist group would find more enabling. The use of information technology as a form of scaffolding to enhance learning has been greatly documented and acknowledge because of its interactive quality (Ager, 2000).

The VAK assessment and predicted outcomes

The questionnaire for the test was modelled on several Accelerated Learning varieties of VAK, such as Barbe (1985) Rose & Nicholl (1997) and that of Smith (1996) endorsed by the DfES for use in primary and secondary education (2004). A paper copy of the VAK questionnaire can be found in the Appendix at the end of this chapter.

The VAK inventory used here consists of presenting the participants with a computer based multiple-choice questionnaire that is pictorial (images are used), auditory (a voice-over is used) and visual-structural; the questionnaire has a series of individually presented questions as text with picture and voiceover on the computer screen. The questions test the learning preferences/modalities with which individual learners receive information for processing in the brain, the processing of it and then the recalling of it.

The VAK modalities are briefly outline here: Visual learners prefer images, diagrams, charts and other visual information as aids to learning, such as colour, texture, maps and pictures. Auditory learners use aural communication, sounds, dialogue, discussion, rhythmic patterns and reading materials. They are usually the talkative ones in a group, more likely to ask questions. The Marxian-Vygotskian methodology of practical-critical activity is partly kinaesthetic learning, it involves bringing together the abstract and concrete through role-play, poster making and learning games (Lisle, 2000; 2006). Kinaesthetic learners are active learners who prefer to do practical tasks and activities. Linking theoretical and practical task together this way actually mirrors the action of scientists when involved in abductive and retroductive reasoning (Lisle, 2000).

It is suggested that the usual outcome from the VAK modality indicator is 25-30% visual, 25-30% auditory, 15% tactile/kinaesthetic and 25-30% mixed modalities (Rose, 1997). Briggs (2000) found from research in FE, an even distribution across the modalities, but in terms of gender, females showed stronger visual preferences and weaker kinaesthetic. Groups of students on paper based courses tended to favour visual learning styles, but results were distributed across the three modalities. Bouldin & Myers (2002) found from research using pharmacy students (176 in total) and the VARK inventory, 79% of participants were multi-modal; and of the 21% who were uni-modal, the majority were primary kinaesthetic. It appears that pharmacy students like to do experiments as well as learning theoretical based knowledge. This I suggest represents the synthesis of abstract and concrete thinking during the process of concept formation (Lisle, 2000; 2006).

Aims and objectives

The main aim of this research is to discover whether the assessment tool is fit for purpose and to evaluate this, there are several objectives. The questions posed then are: Is the inventory valid, does it have test validity i.e.—can it actually differentiate learning styles accurately? Some of the questions have face validity for example, the 'Best Way to Learn' question, 'What is the best way for you to learn? Choice of answers being: 'By watching how it is done (V), by listening to an explanation (A), or by trying to do it yourself (K)?' The tool also has content validity as each modality is equally tested. The type of validity that is difficult to discern, is construct validity: do the questions measure the VAK modalities as they are defined as the learning style modalities? Reliability is not tested for because learning style preference can and does change over time. In addition, the electronic assessment tool developed has additional features such as voiceover and pictures to assist delivery, thus whilst some questions appear to have face validity others are harder to evaluate. A further questionnaire relating to the user-friendliness of the assessment tool was developed to discover for instance, what the participants think about the pictures, the voiceover, the use of computer software and whether the participants understand the questions and whether they found the assessment useful and enjoyable to do.

Research design and methodology

It was thought that because the initial group of adults had been collaborative agents in the development of the inventory; some of them appear in the photographs for example, or had done a similar test, that the inventory should be tested on a separate group who were 'naïve' having no prior knowledge of the test to prevent the results being confounded. It addition, for ethical reason it was agreed that the participants remain anonymous; therefore using a secondary group in the testing of the tool allowed greater anonymity.

The assessment for learning style became part of the induction to the programme of study participants were to undertake. Answers to the 16 multiple-choice questions of the inventory will generate quantitative data (Leach, 1991: Gorard & Taylor, 2004). The 16 questions are not identical to those of other VAK tests but they do resemble the questions of inventories such as Barbe (1985) Smith (1996) and Rose & Nicholl (1997). The questions have been simplified for this client group. If clustering appears in the data for individual questions it may be suggestive that some questions do not lead participants to differentiate because of learning style preference but because of tastes and/or customs within the populace: cultural influences, or one of the participant characteristics such as age, gender and/or disability. It is suggested for example, that younger learners prefer kinaesthetic learning tasks (Briggs, 2000). Therefore, culturally sensitive questions are examined and discussed as part of the overall aim to ascertain construct validity.

Using mixed methods—questionnaires containing quantifiable data from the VAK assessments and details from the participants including an interview with the tutor who will administer the assessments—will lead hopefully to the generation of qualitative data as well as quantitative. Data obtained that firstly assesses the construct validity of the VAK questionnaire, and secondly assesses its usefulness because through asking participants and staff questions, the meaning of the test and its value to then can be ascertained (Leach, 1991: Gorard & Taylor, 2004).

As almost all existing research suggests a mixture of modality preferences within a given populace, then this will partly inform my guide. However, things to consider include type of disability. This is because someone who is blind for example will not have this modality preference and someone who is deaf will not have auditory preferences. A secondary questionnaire detailing individual differences of participants is used as well as the assessment questionnaire to inform such biases.

The sample is accidental, in that the participants are all learner-volunteers: elements of attribution nonetheless, include learning difficulties, educational entry level, reading skill, gender and age. Sixty participants volunteered for the study. The majority of the participants did not reveal the precise details of their learning difficulty yet all the participants regarded themselves as having learning difficulties. The majority of the participants (86%) had mild learning difficulties, 12 percent had moderate learning difficulties and 2 percent had severe learning difficulties. One participant was severely deaf. The level of learning difficulty was mainly mild or moderate, see Figure 1.

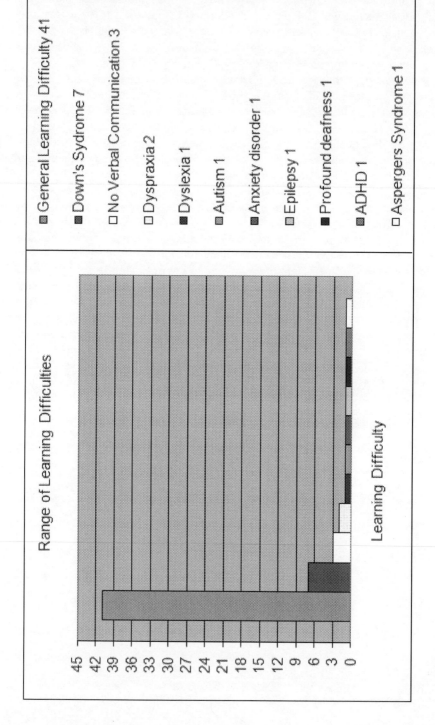

Figure 1

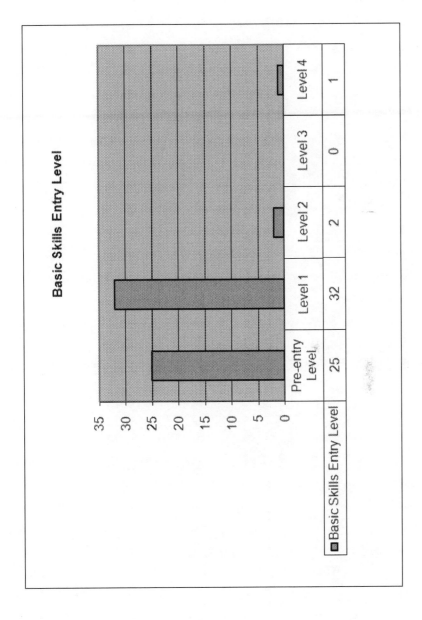

Figure 2

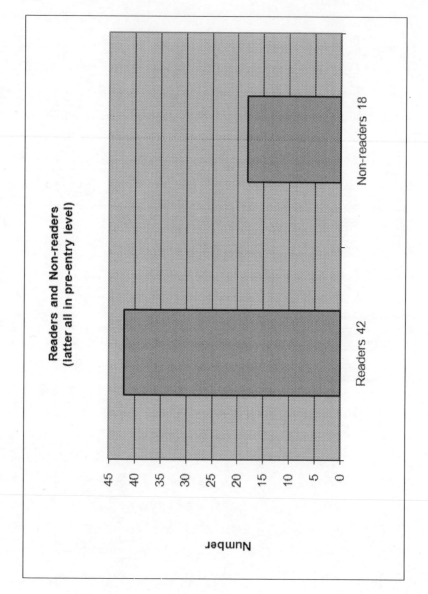

Figure 3

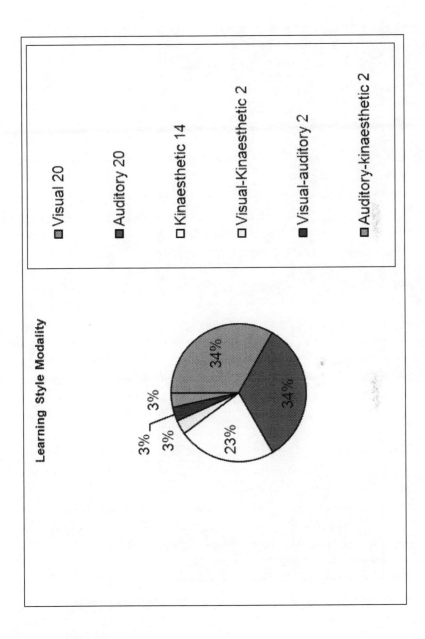

Figure 4

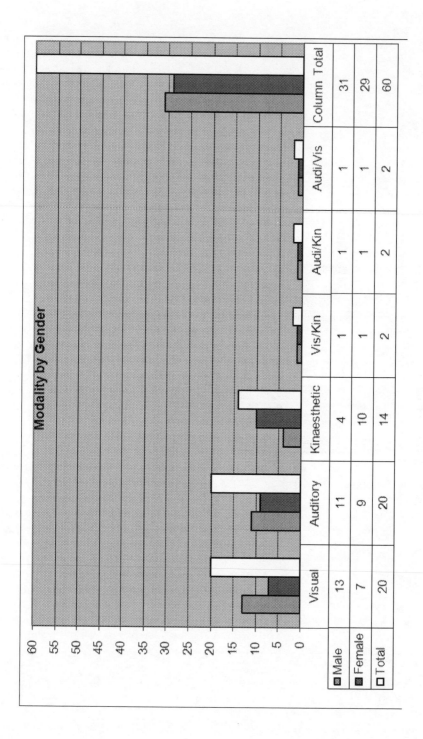

	Visual	Auditory	Kinaesthetic	Vis/Kin	Audi/Kin	Audi/Vis	Column Total
Male	13	11	4	1	1	1	31
Female	7	9	10	1	1	1	29
Total	20	20	14	2	2	2	60

Modality by Gender

- Male
- Female
- Total

Figure 5

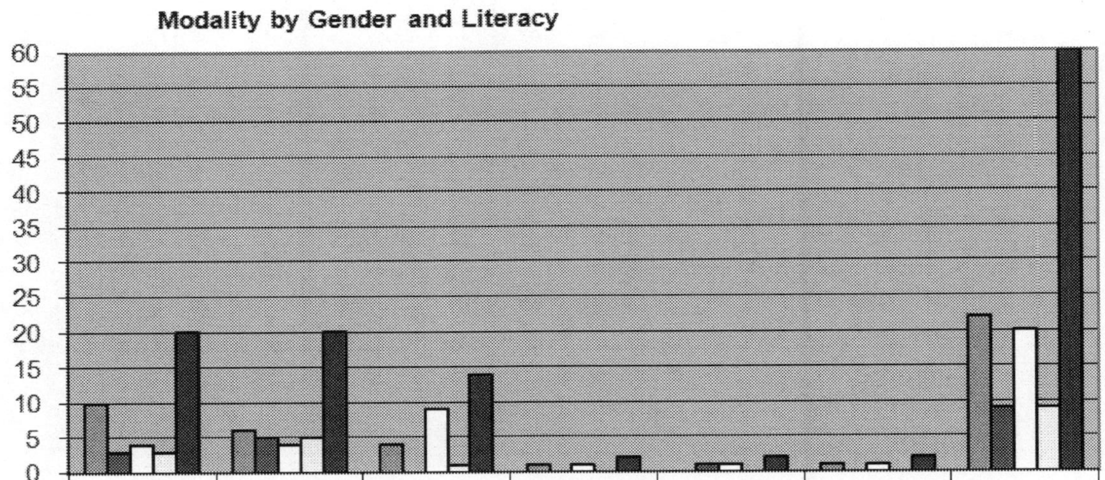
Modality by Gender and Literacy
60
55
50
45
40
35
30
25
20
15
10
5
0

	Visual	Auditory	Kinaesthetic	AudioVis	AudioKin	VisKin	Column Total
Male Reader	10	6	4	1	0	1	22
Male Non-reader	3	5	0	0	1	0	9
Female Reader	4	4	9	1	1	1	20
Female Non-reader	3	5	1	0	0	0	9
Column Total	20	20	14	2	2	2	60

Figure 6

Participant age range was from 16 to 61; 13 were under 20, the remainder over 20. Twenty-five of the participants were pre-entry level, which means below the basic skills level of education. Of these, eighteen were non-readers and seven were readers. Thirty-two of the participants were level one and readers; two were level two and readers, and one level four reader (see Figures 2 & 3).

The information in Figures 2 and 3 is used when assessing the validity of the individual questions. For example, are readers more visual then non-readers or are non-readers predominantly kinaesthetic?

Aggregate results

Sixty assessments have been completed using the Inventory. Of the 60 assessments conducted, the results showed that there is a mixture of learning styles amongst the participants. Twenty of the participants had visual learning preferences, twenty auditory and fourteen were kinaesthetic. Six participants assessed are multi-modal: Two auditory-visual learners, two auditory-kinaesthetic and two visual-kinaesthetic (see Figure 4).

At face value the results appear to follow the normal pattern suggested by Rose (1997), Briggs & Nicholl (2000) and Bouldin & Myers (2002), in that, participants are distributed across the three learning styles in similar numbers. The majority are visual learners 34%, and auditory, 34% with 23% kinaesthetic, similar to the findings of Briggs (2000) for male participants. When gender differences were examined, it was found that in this study males were mainly visual learners and auditory learners. For females the pattern was, K10 >A9 >V7 >VK1, AK1, AV1. Briggs found the opposite from her participants, V>A>K for both males and females but more evenly distributed for males. Figure 5 illustrates how gender and learning style preference interact.

Females in this study tend to have greater kinaesthetic preferences than males; i.e. for females, K10 > A9 > V7 preferences and males V13 > A11 > K4 which runs concurrent to neuro-linguistic information on right and left-brain functioning for males and females outlined by Head in Murphy & Gipps, (1996). An examination of learning style modality, gender and reader, non-reader nonetheless, suggests reading ability to be almost equal, 22 male readers to 20 female (see Figure 6).

Because this client group is atypical further examination was needed to assess the relationship between reading skills and disability. For example, if a client has hearing impairment or visual problems would this influence the results? It was found that related difficulties such as Dyspraxia, Dyslexia, Asperser's Syndrome, Autism and ADHA have visual and kinaesthetic learning modality preferences. Down's syndrome individuals and the hearing impaired have auditory and visual modality preferences. Down's syndrome individuals are known to have physical difficulties at birth that affect their physical development so this may interact with preferences

When examining the relationships between literacy and learning style, it appears, this group's characteristics tend to be that non-readers prefer visual and auditory learning styles and readers have a mixture of learning style preferences. So readers share this similarity with the wider populace and non-readers are atypical. In this particular sample, five of the non-readers have Down's syndrome and three of them do not communicate verbally, one suffers from anxiety disorder. Nine of the non-readers did not declare their difficulty, which makes analysis problematic. But, Down's syndrome individuals and the hearing impaired tend to lip-read which requires visual focusing on lips and facial expressions. In addition, Down's syndrome individuals have a general preference for visual stimuli that is thought relative to the syndrome.

In the younger age group, 60 percent of the participants have kinaesthetic preferences. Briggs (2000) had similar findings. In addition, all of the clients with kinaesthetic preferences are readers. It would be expected clients with visual and auditory preferences to be readers more so than those with kinaesthetic preferences. The mature clients aged 22 and over tend to be a mixture of readers and non-readers with learning preferences predominantly auditory, 20, then 13 visual then kinaesthetic at 6. Mature individuals nationally do tend to predominate in further education colleges rather than sixth form colleges where individuals tend to do 'A' levels and NVQs. The age group of the participants then accounts for learning preferences here in line with findings from Briggs (2000). Disability has an influence on the results here, in that Down's syndrome participants are concentrated in the older age range i.e. 21 and above. Therefore, there are more non-readers in the older age range; Down's syndrome participants use sign language. Participants with kinaesthetic learning preferences tend to be readers in this older age group as well as in the young, with the exception of one female of 47 years of age. Kinaesthetic preferences are more predominant in the lower age range. Briggs (2000) found those NVQ students who were expected to be kinaesthetic did in fact have preferences for observing and listening before doing.

Result and evaluations for the individual assessment questions

All 16 questions were analysed for construct validity using gender, learning style preference and reader or non-reader characteristics to assess clustering around modalities influenced by variables other than actual learning style preference. It was found that indeed there was further work needed on the wording and construction of the questions. In answer to the directions question one for example, almost half of the participants chose to be led to another place (kinaesthetic modality) rather than read a map or listen to directions, suggesting the kinaesthetic modality is predominant: K28 > A17 > V15. Given the level of achievement perhaps something instead of a map might be better used as an example of visual information and aid to understanding for this question, because it may have influenced the results.

The response to the greetings question (two) is K27 > V24 > A9; females in particular responded with a 'hug' majority and males 'see them' response, followed by 'hug'. It is part of British culture and language to refer to seeing someone whether you like to hear their voice or hug them. In addition, females are thought of as the nurturing sex/gender that may account for their preference majority 'hug them'.

It could be that these cultural influences have affected the responses here: The males influenced by language and females by gender identity constructs (Berger and Luckmann, 1966: Qakes et al 1994).

In answer to the teaching methods question (three) both male and female participants predominantly chose the auditory modality: A25 > V18 > K17. Given that females were predominantly kinaesthetic across the 16 questions combined; one would expect it to be evident here. Similarly, given that males are predominantly auditory and visual learners one would expect them to choose those methods of teaching but the kinaesthetic preference was also high for males.

The majority answer to the enjoyment question (four) is the auditory modality: A41 > K10 > V9. Forty-one of the sixty participants (68%) chose to listen to music in their spare time. It appears that non-readers like to listen to music and the next preferred modality for the males is the kinaesthetic. Because music is such a favourite pastime, perhaps another form of auditory relaxation/task might be better used here to prevent possible bias and skewed results.

Ekman and Friesen (1975) suggest that new born babies are equipped to read facial expressions: it is innate. It is not surprising therefore that the majority response to the emotions question (five) is in the visual modality: V28 > K21 > A11. Notwithstanding, babies and indeed adults do equally respond to voice cues such as shouting etc that signal emotions and behaviour is probably one of the most valid indicators of feelings. The feelings question/answer alone would not be a valid indicator of learning modality since it is influenced by our innate capacities to interpret emotions and emotional behaviours we may or may not have been exposed to during our lives.

For pastimes with friends question nine, the male preference was: V14 > A9 > K8. When the questions for this test were constructed, simplicity was the aim but perhaps the results show that some of the questions are too simple making the responses vague with connotations that deter participants from choosing them. 'Doing things with friends' is suggestive, sociable and intimate. Once again, the language here may influence the participants' perceptions, constructs and identification with one answer rather than another. The female participants' responses: V11 = A11 > K0 show none chose the kinaesthetic preference here yet females were more likely than males to have kinaesthetic preferences.

Analysis and evaluation

The aggregate results produced from this study are not too dissimilar to those of other studies. Rose (1997) for example, found that the percentages across the three modalities were: visual learners within the range of 25-30%, auditory learners within the range of 25-30%, and kinaesthetic learners within the range of 15% with 25-30% multi-modal preferences. In this study 34% of participants were visual learners, 34% were auditory learners and 23% kinaesthetic learners, whilst only 6% came out as multi-modal. The inventory assesses multi-modality (percentages appear at the top of individual test results stored on the computer data base) but the card printout and the final assessment given on paper is uni-modal and is based on the ranking of the percentages thus it appears there are fewer multi-modal preferences than there actually are. This element of the inventory needs refining.

Similarly, to Rose & Nicholl (1997) and Briggs (2000), there are more visual and auditory learning style preferences than kinaesthetic learning style preferences. Do learners prefer to be passive rather than active learners? In this study, there were more females with kinaesthetic preferences in comparison to males of other studies where male preferences are more evenly distributed (Briggs for example, 2000). This information does not support left-brain, right-brain neuropsychological theory that would predict there being more male kinaesthetic preferences than female. The number of adult participants may have influenced these findings.

Because the participant group is atypical, learning difficulty was analysed in relation to VAK preferences. Participants with learning difficulties such as ADHD, Dyspraxia, Dyslexia, Autism and Asperser's Syndrome, tend to be readers and mainly kinaesthetic, then visual, then auditory and Down's syndrome participants were predominantly non-readers, yet had auditory and visual learning preferences. Down's Syndrome individuals tend to learn signing because of their associated hearing impairments, so visual and kinaesthetic learning preferences would have been the most probable when in actuality it was A>V>K. There were only nine Down's syndrome participants however, in this group so they are not truly representative of the group as a whole, and Down's syndrome individuals are said to have visual preferences anyway. When examining age and leaning style preferences, kinaesthetic preferences are concentrated in the younger age range, this Briggs (2000) suggests is typical.

A rigorous analysis of the individual questions would suggest a number of problems with the wording of the questions. Some of the questions are too vague 'see things, hear things or do things' for example, is overuse of the word 'things'. When the questionnaire was written the authors wanted the assessment to be self-administered E-learning to enhance access for a diverse group, so the vocabulary was deliberately made simple and accessible but this has resulted in lost meaning and possibly biased results for some of the questions. These problems however are not surmountable and whilst I have been critical of the questionnaire, I still think with modifications it will make a useful teaching and learning tool, particularly in relation to language development, such as reading and as part of a self-reflective learning plan.

Some of the participants found it difficult to choose one answer above the others. For example, they would have preferred to choose all three options i.e. auditory, visual and kinaesthetic sometimes rather than just one of the three. This seems to be predominant among the pre-entry level students rather than level one upwards. The tutor thought it might be a case of indecision as a characteristic of the younger participants' age and learning difficulties. Nonetheless, if the participants were muli-modal rather than uni-modal then this information is important. Likewise found, the participants could not change their minds if an answer was clicked by mistake, making results invalid. If an inventory that does not give the full information of multi-modal preferences of participants is use; then this is bad practice, suggesting the use of instruments that are poorly developed and a poor indication of participants' learning modalities. Rather than the instrument aiding inclusion, it may in fact perpetuate less than optimal learning and bad practice.

On a more positive note, 'the learners so far have really enjoyed completing the questionnaire, the same comments keep being made' the inventory administrator reported. As an ICT exercise then, the test came out on tops because it is multi-modal interactive: with visual stimuli, pictures and images, auditory voiceovers and kinaesthetic key board work. ICT therefore works as an excellent scaffold for learning, it is user friend and extremely interactive—it's VAK!

If used as part of a reflective learning log, or self-reflective learning plan, the VAK assessment will help prevent social constructs such as left—and right-brain theory becoming the taken-for-granted-reality (Berger & Luckmann, 1966: Geake, 2005, Coffield, 2005), because learners can plan their learning using the information from the inventory as a starting point for personal development planning (PDP). They can plan to build on their primary modality and develop their secondary modalities, similar to target setting or learning objective planning. Rose & Goll (1992) recommend the use of learning style assessment to be built into a learning package that is inclusive of and reflective of their six stages of learning, for example, self-reflective learning plan, and this is the way forward as far as learning style assessment is concerned, especially when it is configured with learning outcomes that are goal directed and set in the context of personal development planning.

Conclusion and recommendations

The results are promising showing that the inventory can distinguish between learning styles but the product is by no means full functional, it is in its infancy and further trials and modifications are essential before it can be stated positively that it produces valid and reliable results. In use with informed Personal Development Planning, it can greatly influence learning in a positive way. In fact, personal development planning is a form of reflective learning style that incorporates all three modalities of VAK, and is another learning style that individuals can benefit from. An integration of both learning styles: VAK and reflective practice would be something to consider for future research and would help make intellectual difficulties more multi-disciplinary as Lacey (2000) suggested we should work toward. What Iles (1999) suggests person centred planning involves thereby moving towards recommendations in the White Paper (2001) for valuing people; in this case, learners with intellectual difficulties. Indeed, this is what Rose & Goll (1992) intended when they developed the six stages of learning.

The VAK assessment therefore becoming part of a learning package incorporative of self-reflective learning as a meta-cognitive strategy of understanding one's learning including learning style so the information can be used to enhance learning and make it a more individual and a more self-motivated endeavour. Developing the E-learning assessment tool to determine learning styles for adults as part of literacy programme also merits further investigation, to see if such a development package does in fact promote literacy skills in this populace.

Appendix

A paper copy of the electronic assessment questionnaire

This is a Visual, Auditory and Kinaesthetic learning styles assessment. Answer the questions in the left hand column by choosing one of the answers along the same row under Visual, V, Auditory, A, and Kinaesthetic, K. The three preferences, V, A, and K, represent different learning styles and by choosing one above the other responses, you will obtain a guide to your learning style. The questions test whether the individual prefers to learn by visual means, auditory means or by physically doing things, kinaesthetic means. If you wrote mainly V in the response column, you like to learn through visual means. If you wrote mainly A, then you prefer to learn by auditory means, and if you wrote mainly K, then you like to learn by physically doing things; being active. Many people are multi-modal and will learning through a combination of seeing (V), hearing (A) and doing (K).

VAK Learning Style Assessment (a paper copy of the electronic assessment questions and answers)					
	Question	**Visual (V)**	**Auditory (A)**	**Kinaesthetic (K)**	**Respond by writing V, A, K in the spaces below**
Type of Directions	If you need to get somewhere nearby, what help would you like?	To see a map	For someone to tell you the directions	For someone to walk you there	
Greetings	When you meet an old friend, is it good to . . .	See them?	Hear them?	Hug them?	
Teaching methods	Which of these do you like a teacher to use?	Drawings and pictures	Talking and discussion	Practical activities	
Enjoyment	What do you enjoy doing the most?	Reading and looking at books	Listening to music	Doing things	
Feelings	How can you tell how another personal is feeling?	By looking at their face	By the sound of their voice	By how they act	
Aids to memory	What helps you to remember?	Someone showing you pictures	Listening to instructions	Trying things yourself	

Best way to learn	What is the best way for you to learn?	By watching how it is done	By listening to an explanation	By try to do it yourself	
Favourite pastimes	Do you like to . . .	Look at pictures?	Listen to stories?	Play games with friends?	
Pastimes with friends	Which of these do you like doing best?	Meeting friends face to face	Talking to friends on the telephone	Doing something with friends	
What do you notice	What do you notice most about people?	How they dress	How they sound and talk	How they stand and move	
What is a good time?	Do you have a good time when you are . . . ?	Looking at pictures?	Talking to friends?	Playing games?	
Playing new games	How do you like to learn to play a new game?	By watching other people play it first	By someone explaining the rules	By learning as you play	
Remember most	Do remember most when you . . .	See things?	Hear things?	Do things?	
Remember about people	What do you remember best about people?	Faces	Names	Things you have done with people	
Remember about people	Which of these would you like to do most?	Watch TV	Listen to music	Make something	

New Hi-Fi	If you got a new Hi-Fi, what would you do first?	Look at instructions and pictures	Ask someone how it works	Just start putting it together	

Calculate your score:

Add up the number of Vs, As and Ks here

Learning Style/ Modality	Visual	Auditory	Kinaesthetic	
Total				

Recommendation for you and your tutor

Visual Preference

- Show these learners what you mean/demonstrate
- Breaking down words and putting them back together will help them remember
- Use dictionaries where possible
- Will benefit from watching videos
- Learners may want to re-type/re-write notes
- Will write things down several times
- Will need silence whilst studying
- Will need a tidy environment to work in
- Remembers things they have seen

Auditory Preference

- This student will benefit from listening to your instructions
- Repeat the instructions or learning material being delivered
- The student will want to talk aloud
- Let them discuss things in groups
- This learner will read quickly and therefore may miss out/skip words or sections, encourage them to use fingers as a guide to slow themselves down
- May not understand illustration very well, especially in relation to maps
- They will be distracted easily by sounds

- Will remember things they have heard

Kinaesthetic Preference

- Allow this student to study in shorter periods
- Break up these study periods with lots of short breaks
- Allow them to move about a lot
- Let them experiment with ideas and objects
- Resources such as guidebooks using practical illustration will be really useful
- Will fidget whilst listening
- Will get distracted by movement
- Remembers things they have done

Lead with your strengths and develop your lesser preferences. Lead preferences suggest how you learn best. When you reflect on your learning, you should remember how you learned something so that you can use that method of learning again in the future. Remember to try to use the preference you are not so fond of, you will then start to learn using that preference too!

Chapter Six

Neuro-cognitive psychology and education: Mapping neuro-cognitive processes and structures to learning styles, should it be done?

Abstract

The application of neuroscience research to cognitive functions and behaviour has developed over a 30-year period. Michael Atherton and Read M. Diket (2005) for example, discuss the implications of mapping neurophysiological structures to cognitive and psychological processes, which they suggest started with the work of Howard Gardner (1983) and his use of developments in CAT scanning with which to underpin his theory of Multiple Intelligences. The recent developments in neuroscience have according to Atherton and Diket led to a wave of activity in this area in which theorists such as Geake and Cooper (2003) similarly suggest a collaboration between neuroscience and education to the point that training which incorporates both should be adopted if we are to equip teachers with the theoretical knowledge and skills they need to engage in teaching practice that facilitates effective learning. Indeed, 'brain teaching' is becoming the norm. In this paper, I intend to outline the mapping of cognitive neurophysiology to learning styles. The underlying fundamental question being: 'Does a one-to-one mapping of neurophysiological levels of brain activity to cognitive-behavioural levels really enhance educational pedagogy?' This question is posed partly in response to the way existing neurosciences are applied as educational pedagogy, which are 'predicated on an over-simplification of brain research' leading to unsatisfactory teaching practice (Geake, 2005, p. 11), and partly because I instruct students in the use of the VAK system and reflexive practice as learning styles for early year's practice as well as for use with the students in my own teaching practice.

Keywords *Reflexive Practice (RP), Visual, Auditory, and Kinaesthetic (VAK) Modalities and Learning Styles, Cognitive Neuropsychology and Educational Pedagogy*

> '. . . *there is clear evidence demonstrating that new neurons grow in adult monkeys, in cats, and in other mammals. This neuron growth takes place in at least two regions of the brain, namely the hippocampus and the olfactory cortex. The hippocampus is extremely important for memory functions, such as turning short-term memories into long-term memories.*'

Professor Kurt Fischer (August 1ˢᵗ, 2004) Harvard Graduate School of Education

Putting things in context

The information contained in the quotation above from Professor Fischer (2004) sounds as a comparative endeavour, promising to those involved in enhancing understanding of cognitive neurophysiological structures, learning and development; particularly for those who have interest in the relationship between neuroscience and education. But when drawing one-to-one comparisons between neuroscience and education what does it actually mean? Are we to assume that because neurons in the hippocampus and olfactory cortex continue to develop in nonhuman animals after birth then they will by comparison continue to develop in humans too? Those who work within the fields of neuroscience make comparisons of this kind to inform understanding of neurophysiological processes and structures. But what does this mean in terms of learning and development, for example, should we extrapolate from nonhuman research findings and then apply the insights drawn to human development? As Professor Fischer (2006) further suggests 'Journalists, educators, and even brain scientists too readily leap from brain research findings to an "implication" for education—which is typically nothing more than seat-of-the-pants speculation'.

If the scientific community decides not to develop arguments of relationality between neurophysiology, cognitive development and learning within the educational context then it will remain an unmapped area of knowledge. Yet the information available—'Bacons'; we should follow our senses, pick up the pieces of research/information that are being developed and try to place them in the jigsaw puzzle where they seem to fit in terms of relationality: whether it be similarity or some other coordinate with which they resonate. Indeed, when Professor Fischer (2004) states neuron growth takes place after birth I share his enthusiasm in placing such research findings in the jigsaw puzzle where similarity or resonance exists. It is for sure that similarity or resonance like correlates do not in any scientific way show cause but if you examine the scientific discoveries that have occurred over the centuries—many were built or are generative of intuitive reasoning about some or other resonance, similarity or correlate. A similar feat will be attempted in this paper, knowing that much of what is suggest is not supported as yet by scientific evidence but may be at some point in the future.

Indeed, Ian Sample, in 'The brain scan that can read people's intentions' (science correspondent, the Guardian, Friday 9th Feb. 2007, front page) documents findings from 'cutting edge' research in neuroscience that boasts brain scans can detect the intentions of volunteers as to whether or not they intend to add or subtract two numbers. Although the uses of this research are questionable for example, it was suggested that it could be used to assess intended future crimes (as in the film Minority Report, Steven Spielberg) the potential of it is remarkable and extremely innovative. Can such innovation in all honesty be disregarded as science fiction or should we endeavour to make that of it, which is of value, reality?

Fischer (2006) for example, suggests that growth curves for learning a task are influenced by individual learning styles characterised as 'novice chaotic learning', 'intermediate: scalloping' and 'expert stable'. Fischer suggests that students start out as novice learners but develop into experts with experience. Thus, for Fischer learners learn how to learn better. He further proposes that research shows growth occurs in cycles and that there are correlations between cycles of brain growth, cycles of cognitive growth, and cycles of learning (Fischer et al, 2005; Fischer et al, 2006). This is what one might anticipate but again, as Fischer himself points out, correlations are not cause and effect relationships and all such relationships do need to be held with scepticism despite their face validity. His research does nonetheless suggest that whilst learners are 'learning to learn' there is neuron growth in the hippocampus and olfactory cortex that shows correlates between the two: neuron growth and learning.

An understanding of cognitive neurophysiological structures and functions is useful and important when considering cognitive development and if scientists get it right, this has use-value or utility for informing practice in education. Researchers find themselves in a privileged position to be able to continue with the comparisons and the mapping of one discipline—neuroscience, to the other education, and it is possible that one can inform the other on a continual basis. Nonetheless, as Professor Fischer (2004, 2006) and Professor Geake (2003, 2005) contend, it is only now possible after years of gathering research data on the topic of neuroscience and its relations with education and it is still a precarious task.

A further point to consider, when applying neurosciences to education, is that the education system may not be the only place where learning happens, although evidence does suggest cultures that have education systems have populations with higher human capita indices. In addition, learning is itself a social construct and culturally specific. David & Powell (2005) for example, discuss the way constructs of childhood and learning through play are shaped by culture and economic status. In China, David & Powell asked participants from different socio-culture-economic backgrounds whether play for their children was 'banned, tolerated, encouraged or indulged' (David & Powell, 2005, p. 246). The researchers found that even in one culture answers were distributed across the four responses. Cognitive neuropsychological evidence suggests that during play activity synaptic growth is evident (Sutton-smith, 1997; in David & Powell, 2005). The conclusions drawn were that cultures that encourage play might provide a richer environment for childhood cognitive development. Yet again, does it not depend on the way play and learning is defined?

In western societies, a child may learn to fish or nurture a doll as play activity yet in eastern cultures a child will do these activities in the same way adults do. Therefore, whether the child is learning through play or by taking on adult tasks/ roles, both should in fact stimulate synaptic growth. So clearly, childhood, play and learning can have a number of definitions each one as valid as another and each definition/form of play or adult activity is capable of stimulating learning and development.

Vygotsky (1962) defined development as a biological maturational change in thinking and brain particularly when a concept is acquired on both the abstract and the concrete level of experience. Learning he suggested was the pathway to development. Everyday concepts are learned regardless of the social context but scientific learning takes place within the formal educational context as a cultural prerequisite for employment in industrial societies with capitalist economies. It seem reasonable therefore to presume that learning and development take place regardless of the context; either in or out of the education system and can in fact consist of information that is not necessarily that which is presented in the form of the national curriculum or that is of use-value to the present cultural ethos of a capitalist society. Therefore, whether cognitive neuroscientific understanding is applied to classroom practice or not, the learning and development that does take place may or may not be directly related to the intervention that stems from the unification of cognitive neuroscience and education anyway! It can only be speculated that it does although I would postulate that it contributes in a positive way.

Mapping cognitive neurophysiology to learning styles

Although there are many learning style systems or models if you prefer, I tend to work with two in particular: reflexive practice (RP) and the Visual Auditory Kinaesthetic (VAK) learning styles system and because of a deep interest in cognitive neurosciences; I cannot help but to map it to them. Like most people, I also have preferences based on my experience and knowledge of the education system, neuroscience and psychology, and indeed life. Thus, using this as a base, I intend to attempt the mapping of cognitive neurophysiology to educational behaviours, particularly, mapping learning styles with neurophysiological representations of them in the brain.

RP which involves thinking about one's practices whilst doing them, along with VAK learning styles (the latter styles being synonymous to the sensory equivalent) are used in Higher Education. The common thread here is that learning styles resonate with neurophysiological modulatory systems. It is argued here that RP is likewise a brain modulatory system, which can be described in terms of neurophysiological activity in brain-mind. It is also argued that RP and indeed other learning styles such as VAK have use-value to present educational practice.

The VAK system is useful when assessing learning styles. It has been mapped one-to-one with brain cognitive neurophysiology for approximately 30 years, and was applied to education in the 1980s by Gardner with his concept of multiple intelligences (Michael Atherton & Read M. Diket, 2005).

In 'Frames of Mind', Gardner outlined several different intelligences: Logical/ Mathematical, Visual and Spatial, Musical, Bodily and Kinaesthetic, Interpersonal, Intrapersonal, Naturalistic and Experiential. This system of abilities allows the individual to solve problems. Three of these intelligences are VAK modalities: visual, linguistic/auditory and kinaesthetic. His theory is widely used in schools today to enhance the teaching and learning process, and is often synthesised with Bloom's taxonomy (Scholastic, 2003). Bloom's taxonomy outlines the cognitive behaviour used to develop Gardner's multiple intelligences: together they are the intellectual modalities. In a similar manner, RP unites the VAK modalities and Bloom's taxonomy of skills in the cyclical movement of reflection and action (Lisle, 2006; Lisle, 2007). One could say that now we know the behaviours in Bloom's taxonomy we can get children (and adults) to engage them using stimulus tasks so that, as they describe, discuss, analyse, evaluate, synthesize, or engage in reflexive thinking it leads to furtherment in knowledge and in Gardener's multiple intelligencies.

When developing his theory, Gardner (1993) was mindful of the fact that: 'The sharp distinction between the "reflective" and the "active" is drawn in many cultures . . . a legacy of Western Cartesian thought as a universal imperative' (1993, p. 208). The fundamental error of this distinction reveals itself through the work of Vygotsky (1962) and the Marxian methodology. To Marx, and later Vygotsky, learning and development take place through the dialectic of theory and practice: the critique of material practice that involves both reflective and active learning styles. So to separate these styles is ridiculous. Indeed, any truly scientific methodology involves the integration of theory and practice, i.e. theory and experimentation. The bringing together of the abstract and the concrete: concept formation through reflective cycles of theory production and testing via experimentation is in itself learning and development. Both intelligences therefore are necessary. A final point from Gardner is:

> '[W]hile studies of perception and language have dominated published treatments in neuropsychology, the saga of the brain's role in physical activity proves to be as intriguing as reports about the aphasias or as accounts of the detection of edges, lines, colors, and objects' (1993, p. 210).

He thus applauds neuropsychologists who regard reflection as a means to directing action, a tool to refine actions and move towards adaptiveness and survival. To Gardner therefore, kinaesthetic intelligence—activity—is as valuable as the other forms of intelligence.

In the western cultural context, schools traditionally favour two of Gardner's intelligences: Linguistic (auditory) and Mathematic (spatial) (Gardner, 1993), the legacy of Piagetian education for example and the misuse of educational pedagogy. Gardner's multiple intelligences have a broader spectrum and are much more inclusive for a variety of learners. In this way, Gardner is one of a body of theorists to recognise the importance of what is now know as affective education. Affective education focuses on the modality of learning, for example individual learning styles and how the brain processes information in addition to how the environment affects the process of learning. Affective education is viewed as much more effective and conducive to inclusive education. Kinaesthetic learners learn by doing a task rather than through instruction of the auditory or visual kind, at heart, *they are* exploratory learners. Piagetian pedagogy is correct but gravely misunderstood, visual, auditory and kinaesthetic sensory input enhances understanding and learning and the three should be used in combination.

Cognitive neuroscience, learning styles and synaptogenesis

Neuroscience is about studying the brain as a biological structure, the neural mechanisms, sensory and motor functions it performs and the cognitive processes involved in recognition, memory, motivation and behaviour (Carpenter, 1996). Brain development starts at the foetal stage and genetically identical twins can have different brains at birth due to small foetal environmental changes (Pendrick, 1997). Approximately 100 billion neurons organised into bulb-like clusters form the network of nerve cells that makeup the biological structure of the brain. Neuron pathways are sparse at birth but flourish rapidly when the baby's brain as a biological structure interacts with its environment, and incoming stimuli such as visual, auditory and tacit flows in from the external environment, and from the internal environment in the guise of proprioceptual stimuli (the awareness of bodily occurrences).

The development of synaptic connections is so substantial in the first year of life that the brain triples in density and grows to almost adult size. Although the brain contains nearly all of the neurons needed for healthy functioning, neurons still develop in the hippocampus and the cerebellum after birth (Fischer, 2004; Blakemore & Frith, 2006). Those neurons that do develop after birth send and receive electrochemical messages between the brain and the body. Each neuron can develop up to 15,000 synaptic connections to other neurons. It is these connections that account for brain development, such as learning through interaction with the environment and via habituated and associative learning (Carpenter, 1996), what Athey (1990) termed the development of schemata.

The process of synaptic development is called synaptogenesis. By 6 months of age, a baby has more synapse than an adult has (Huttenlocher, 1990). However, after reaching maximum density, the neural connections are pruned, a process referred to as neural Darwinism. Via the process of natural selection, only those synapse that contribute to the baby's survival form permanent pathways whilst those that do not fade. Hebb (1949) and later Eliot (1999) suggests it to be a case of 'use it or lose it', meaning, use the information that led to the trace path developing or it will fade as will the trace path written in brain tissue. He also suggests that 'neurons that fire together wirer together'. The process continues up to 10 years of age and even into adulthood, synaptic connections can develop as the brain forms connections biologically between neurons that in consciousness are manifest as memorises and ideas, even words (Blakemore & Frith, 2006; Lisle, 2006). Blakemore (2007) points to recent developments in neuroscience whereby:

> 'Being able to read thoughts as they arise in a person's mind could lead to computers that allow people to operate email and Internet using thought alone and write with word processors that can predict which word or sentence you want to type. The technology is thought controlled. The computer appears to read words written in brain structures.' (Blakemore in Sample, science correspondent, the Guardian, Friday 9th Feb. 2007).

The interaction between the brain and the environments, both social (inter-psychological) and physical (inter-physio-natural) are the nature-nurture dialectics. A dialectic being the mechanism through which one thing interacts with another. For example, ability may be genetic (nature) but through instruction and effort (nurture), the latter transforms into the former thereby increasing ability and IQ (as discussed in chapter 4 Marxian Psychophysics). The interaction and formation of synaptic connections via the two processes of Long Term Potentiation (LTP) which it is suggested here, equates to prolonged synaptic activity and Short Term Potentiation (STP) to short synaptic activity, form part of the internal dialectic of brain-mind: The dialectic in which brain matter/structure produces ideas and new ideas in turn are written as brain structures (See diagram 4 this chapter). It is because of the dialectic processes that individual differences develop or are built on. In addition, individual differences can be associated with a sensitivity period (Bruer, 1999). If learning and the associated synaptic connections do not form within a given sensitivity period, then the baby or child may not develop sight properly or hearing or gross motor development can be impaired.

Blakemore & Frith (2006) for example, found that the development of vision is affected by environmental deprivation that is time relative. Similarly, the carousal kitten experiment (Held, 1965) showed that visual skills and motor skills develop in coordination and that deprivation of visual stimuli or gross motor movements affects motor skill development and eye-paw coordination. Indeed, any sensory deprivation—visual, auditory, kinaesthetic, taste or smell can lead to underdevelopment in terms of brain functioning and structure. Goswami (2004) more recently, discusses several pieces of research that look at the relationship between sensory deprivation and consequential brain area functioning. Depth perception for example, is influenced more by early deprivation rather than later (Fagiolini & Hensch, 2000).

What I am leading up to is an understanding of brain development that is sensitive to environmental affects some of which have a long lasting consequence. This discussion therefore also shows that neuron development within the brain is sensory dependent: visual, auditory and tacit. The visual cortex for example, 'develops selectivity to particular patterns of input from the external environment, the motor system (kinaesthetic) is developed through sequences of actions that obtain desired results in environmental interactions, and language (auditory memory) develops through being exposed to language (Carpenter, 1996). Thus, this suggests that a learning style system of development enhancement based on sensory modalities has more use-value than other types of learning style systems because of the affinity the VAK learning style system has with physiological processes, the visual, auditory and kinaesthetic perceptual modalities and equivalent brain and memory areas. Multimodal input can under certain conditions lead to multisensory synaptic firing and therefore wiring of synaptic connections in the brain that represent memory and learning. Multisensory memory and learning may be enhanced learning. Reading strategies that use the three modalities: auditory/hearing, visual/seeing and kinaesthetic/doing (writing for example) lead to greater language development in terms of spelling and writing for special needs as well as non-special needs pupils: i.e. see it, say it, cover it and write it, is a language development teaching strategy that has excellent results!

Schematic illustration of multisensory interactions

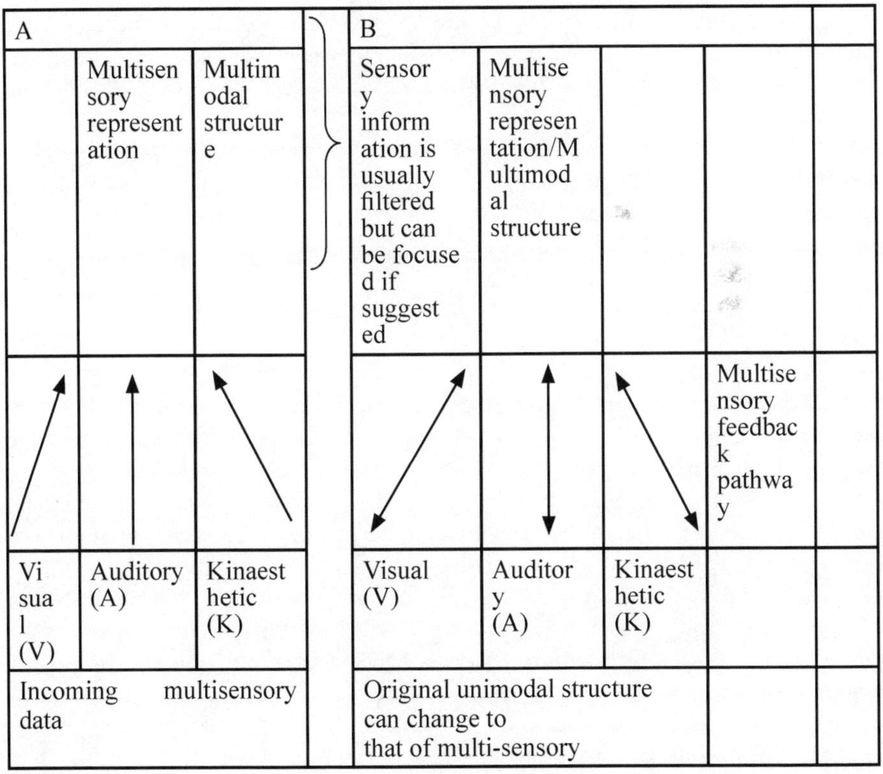

A				B				
	Multisensory representation	Multimodal structure		Sensory information is usually filtered but can be focused if suggested	Multisensory representation/Multimodal structure			
							Multisensory feedback pathway	
Visual (V)	Auditory (A)	Kinaesthetic (K)		Visual (V)	Auditory (A)	Kinaesthetic (K)		
Incoming multisensory data				Original unimodal structure can change to that of multi-sensory				

(Adapted from Roberts, figure 6, p. 354, 2002).

Figure 1

The visual, auditory and kinaesthetic sensory input pathways however do not automatically develop memory trace paths in unison: Roberts (2002) when discussing sensory integration, brings attention to the McGurk effect (1976) in which visual sensory input is dominant to auditory, tacit and proprioceptive. But does this therefore suggest a universal visual learning preference? It appears not because there are structures in the brain that have unimodal wiring. The superior colliculus for example, that is responsible for controlling attentive orienting responses shows increased firing rates when multisensory stimuli are presented at the same time, leading to the multisensory enhancement effect. In addition, it has been suggested that multisensory structures may affect unimodal brain structures (Roberts, 2002, p. 350-4). See figure 1. 'A' suggests a relationship between incoming sensory data via VAK and brain structures in which the brain structure—neurons such as those in the colliculus—store multisensory data rather than unisensory, making them multimodal. 'B' shows a relationship between multimodal structures that can also affect unimodal structures that may be explained in terms of the multisensory feedback pathways.

Therefore, it could be that using the VAK system as well as RP learning leads to more enhanced learning and development if used to focus multisensory perception. Multisensory teaching and learning using VAK would imply that learning is more likely to take place because it is more likely that memorises are stored in multimodal linked structures. This would imply that both VAK and RP are of value in terms of educational pedagogy, and as more discoveries in the neurosciences come to light, I think increasing evidence will afford biological foundations to support their existence rather than visual, auditory and kinaesthetic memories remaining semi-reified concepts.

Reflexive practice and educational pedagogy

Educational pedagogy concerns itself with the successful practice of teaching and learning. By successful it is implied that the outcome for the learners has some measure of enhancement in terms learning and development. One method of facilitating a successful outcome for learners is to get them to engage in RP. Reflective experience was first referred to as educational pedagogy by John Dewey (1916). Dewey believed that life was an experiential journey in which we come up against problems that we need to solve. To solve problems we think about them until we arrive at a solution. In this way for Dewey, we unite the brain and the body, theory and practice. Through the thinking process in which past experience is brought into the equation as a critical measure and catalogue of experience to choose from to guide ongoing actions, we can reach a state of reflection that involves a critical review of our actions. But beyond this state even, Dewey's reflective experience, involves experimentation and extensive analysis and evaluation of a problem in which all things are considered and hypotheses/theories are tested. One might call Dewey's reflective experience 'the retroductive method' of investigation—reflexivity (Lisle, 2000). In this way, Dewey's reflection was meant to be a means of change-action

(action leading to change) for social reform as well as educational reforms and personal development.

For Dewey then, reflective experience is distinct from the practice of thinking because like the scientist the reflective practitioner employs careful examination of the situation testing hypotheses stepping back and taking a holistic view before developing a plan of action with which to tackle a problem.

Schön (1987) later developed the theory of reflective-action particularly as educational pedagogy making a distinction between reflection-in-action, 'thinking on one's feet' and 'reflection-on-action', thinking about practice after the event. For Schön, reflection-in-action' comes about through intuition and can lead to 'knowing-in-practice' a state reached when actions have become routinised, automated and habituated and the practitioner spontaneous and professional. Sometimes, a practitioner's actions become so habituated that 'knowing-in-practice' is implicit (procedural) and hidden and the practitioner needs to reflect once more on practice to obtain the underlying meaning of the actions again, making it explicit. Indeed, as Berger and Luckmann (1966) point out, institutionalised actions that have become 'reciprocal typifications of habitualized actions' are social constructs, the patternings of social behaviours that we need to question in order to go beyond the confines of culture. In this way, both 'reflection-in-action' and 'reflection-on-action' are ways of maintaining a level of practice conducive to learning and development for the practitioner and the learner because they are cognitive strategies we can use to question the take-for-granted we sometimes see as reality, and initiate changes necessary for survival in an ever-changing environment and social niche.

RP is therefore imbued with survival potential, a prerequisite of cognition itself. It is in many ways instinctive but implicit and therefore needs to be made explicit through instruction. The explicit activity of RP has become so ubiquitous, that student learning is couched in RP as a meta-cognitive learning style, and used for planning and monitoring personal development. So, learning may start out as Pavlovian conditioning (habituated learning and associative learning) but through the practice of learning how to learn using RP as a meta-cognitive strategy, learning will progress from habituated though goal directed learning and finally to RP. Within the British education system self-reflexive learning is introduced from as young as five years old up to degree level, and indeed, is encouraged at post-graduate level. Post-graduate researchers for example, take part in reflexive practice exercises aimed at evaluating their own research and learning during the process of developing and executing the research proposals.

Reflexive practice as a brain modulator

As a learning style, RP is a fundamental: A modality for the acquisition of knowledge and learning that converts into development (Lisle, 2000; Lisle, 2006). As a modality functional to learning, it is not questioned in education. The VAK modality system can be shown to be a forerunner to RP, and integrative to it. Bloom's (1956) taxonomy of cognitive behavioural skills: knowledge/remembering, comprehension/understanding, application/ problem solving, analysis/seeking relations, evaluation/critically appraising and synthesising/creating hypothesis and holistic views (theories) are all cognitive-behavioural skills used in the acquisition of and manipulation of knowledge. RP would be seated at the top of the taxonomy fully incorporative of all other cognitive functions (Lisle, 2006). The VAK modalities are data input systems to the brain that convey essential information linking external environmental systems including inter-psychological data to intra-psychological meta-cognitive processes that take place in the cerebral cortex. It is because of this that it is suggested here RP is indeed, a high-order brain modulator that directs the VAK data input system. In other words, RP it is suggested is equivalent to or linked in some way to working memory (WM) as a hypothetical structure that theoretically directs VAK. Figure 2 is an adapted but familiar model of Brain, Mind and Behaviour (Morton & Frith (1995), which I will use to illustrate brain, mind and behaviour interrelations.

This model allows us to examine the relationships between brain, mind, socio-emotional factors and behaviour factors and environment: both the physical environment and socio-emotional environment. The environment can affect brain-mind on three levels: the physical (A), the social/emotional (B) and the behavioural (C).

ENVIRONMENT		BRAIN	
→		→	
	Examples of environmental factors i.e. stimuli	Examples of intra-individual factors (RP = WM +VAK)	FACTORS AFFECTED
A ENVIRON MENT FACTORS	Physical factors: i) Oxygen/ Nutrition/Toxin/ Light/ Temperature etc. i) Teaching resources	WM and VAK data input system multimodal synaptic connections	Brain
EMOTION AL FACTORS	Atmosphere and mood/welcoming behaviour of staff and pupils	Brain modulators serotonin/ dopamine adrenoline/ noradrenaline	self-esteem/ feeling of calm/ anger/ intelligence/fear
B SOCIAL FACTORS	Inter-psychology/ Teaching styles such as RP and VAK/ Authoritarian Democratic/ Lazes-faire	RP/WM to direct VAK (intra-cognition)	Mind
C BEHAVIO URAL FACTORS	Inter-psychology/ Learning styles such as RP and VAK	RP/VAK learning styles that lead to enhanced learning and development	Behaviour

Figure 2 An adapted version of Morton & Firth's model of brain/ mind/behaviour interrelations (1995)

If VAK multisensory learning and teaching are put into the model as well as the introduction of RP, we can simulate a situation that shows mind, brain and behaviour interrelations and development. The physical environment can affect brain via physical factors. The socio-emotional environment via inter-psychology and teaching and learning styles can affect mind and brain and indeed influence several brain-modulatory systems i.e. see figure 2. Lastly, behavioural factors such as inter-psychology and intra-psychology and learning styles affect brain modulation and mind too. The brain can affect the mind and the mind the brain, behaviour can affect mind then brain and vice versa. We can see the dialectic movement of brain-mind as brain matter produces ideas and incoming information and ideas result in the production of brain matter, that is, synaptic connections. What does the reflective cycle involve?

When we observe a situation, we also receive auditory information as well as visual and kinaesthetic. (A) We direct our attention and perceptual systems: visual, auditory, tacit, smell and taste, and then reflect on the data received (B). (C) From this we will formulate a plan of action. In this way, RP is, it is suggested, the behaviour equivalent to or linked with WM processes that theoretically direct the VAK perceptual system. Whilst WM is theoretically regarded as modality free in terms of sensory perception, it can hypothetically speaking modulate consciousness because of its relation to and manipulation of incoming perceptual data. The WM can when viewed as equivalent to RP in this way, not only modulate consciousness but prolong it, direct it and as a consequence enhance synaptic firing therefore increase wiring, that is, the development of synaptic connects between neurons—brain activity that leads to short term memories being passed into long term memory stores. There is as yet no research evidence to support these assumption but advances in research are leading in this direction.

Craik and Lockhart (1972) suggest that attention and perceptual processes are as important as the rehearsal of information for retention. Sensory osmosis is infinite so sensory information attended to by the perceptual systems whether exteroception, interoception or proprioception (kinaesthetic/vestibular) before rehearsal takes place is as important as rehearsal when receiving, remembering and learning information, indeed, the perception of information itself can lead to long term memories without rehearsal, for example, emotionally charged situations affect memory and retention.

In addition, the length of focused attention will affect retention in addition to learning modality. Martinez & Derrick (1996, p. 175) for example, have found that long-term potentiation (LTP)—prolonged and increased synaptic strength (neural activity in brain matter) leads to remembering rather than memory trace decay, forgetting (Hebb, 1949). What happens during LTP is that neurons fire in sequence according to Hebb's Postulate, when and if they are in the same area and close enough so one cell excites another. The activity when repeated causes metabolic changes that resemble growth; growth that I suggest is equated with LTM storage.

RP is behaviour that can focus VAK data input and assimilate the heightening of consciousness awareness resulting in global consciousness—the firing of neurons in sequence in a wider coverage of grey matter. It has been found that LTP is associated with the hippocampus, in particular, the storage of declarative memory. Damage to the hippocampus for example results in information not passing from the short-term memory to the long-term memory. Therefore, it seems reasonable to presume LTP is equivalent to long-term memory (LTM) and short-term potentiation (STP) equivalent to short-term memory (STM). In addition, information that is received during emotionally charged situations is either remembered or forgotten. Within the hippocampus emotions/brain modulators such dopamine and serotonin can act as motivators to inhibit potentiation thus leading to STP or excites it leading to LTP.

The registering and processing of information in the brain effects the way information is then retrieved, in that, information that is stored acoustically will more easily be recalled in the manner it was stored (Gardner, 1993; Smith, 1996). So, if you remember how to spell a word because you learned it by spelling it aloud, using the phonological-articulatory loop (Baddeley, 1995), you will verbally spell out the word on recall. If you learned how to memorise the visual-structural representation of the word, then you will more than likely visualise the word when you recall it (Tulving, 1972). If you learned a word using physical movements—spelling letters with your fingers for example, like sign language used by the hearing impaired, then you will use the same finger movements when recalling it, or write the letters when recalling it in line with the kinaesthetic mode (Aubusson, 1997). Again, this would suggest VAK enhances the teaching and learning process because it allows us to understand the process better. Nonetheless, research also suggests that information can be stored visually for example yet cued by auditory means, but it does take longer to recall because synapses rewire in the process. Finally, the Embedded Process Model (Cowan, 1999) of cognitive functions when applied to neurophysiological data (Chein, 2003) is useful for showing the relationships between cognition and neurophysiology. However, whilst Chein mapped the model with particular areas in the brain, referred to as LTM store, rehearsal and activated memory, I find it more useful to map it to the first and second messenger system of synaptic action. See figure 3.

This adapted embedded 1st and 2nd order messenger system model consists of two levels. The first level is when the action potential, a positive charge, known as an electrochemical message/neurotransmission, flows down the axon, a biological structure that connects one neuron to another in the brain, and builds up at the neck of the synapse. This is STP and it is suggested here, it equates to STM. At this point, several synapses may or may not be firing in sequence with other synapses at the same neuron. However, if attention is focused using RP/WM, then this will stimulate and enhance LTP, strengthening the action potential so that more neurons do fire in sequence leading to LTP therefore LTM, as the second level messenger system is activated when more neurotransmitter passes into the synaptic cleft forming a bridge and across into the neuron where it actions the nuclear protein and DNA. Furthermore, more Hebbian pathways/ traces of memory are developed, almost as if rooted deeper in the neuron rather than a shallow smattering of neurotransmitter that remains in the synaptic cleft and will dissipate as STMs do. The deeper penetrated neurotransmitter will connect to existing memory traces in the neuron.

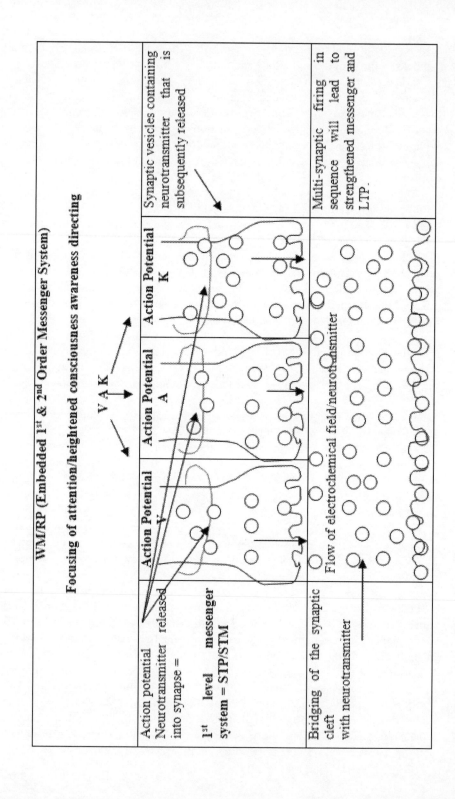

WM/RP (Embedded 1st & 2nd Order Messenger System)

Focusing of attention/heightened consciousness awareness directing

V A K

Action potential Neurotransmitter released into synapse = 1st level messenger system = STP/STM	Action Potential V	Action Potential A	Action Potential K	Synaptic vesicles containing neurotransmitter that is subsequently released
Bridging of the synaptic cleft with neurotransmitter	Flow of electrochemical field/neurotransmitter			Multi-synaptic firing in sequence will lead to strengthened messenger and LTP.

Bridging of the synaptic cleft with neurotransmitter	Flow of electrochemical field/neurotransmitter	Then LTM as electrochemical field/neurotransmitter acts on nuclear protein and possibly DNA
2nd Messenger system	Nucleus — Action on nuclear protein and DNA	

Figure 3 Focusing attention using RP/WM (Embedded 1st & 2nd order messenger system)

RP therefore as a learning style, directs the VAK sensory input (much like WM) and is thus useful as a meta-cognitive learning strategy. RP thinking is the process of practical-critical-activity (Newman & Holzman, 1993) through which ideas are products of material practice (Marx, in McLellan, 1977). From engaging in physical activity (kinaesthetic), and critical activity through dialogue, we conceive ideas, which the above shows are either stored in memory or are generative of it. The process Vygotsky referred to as intra—and inter-psychological activity in the zone of proximal development, when abstract and concrete experiences are brought together during concept formation, that is, when multisensory data is brought together when reflective processes direct VAK. The forming of the concept is therefore the bringing together of concrete/material experience with abstract/ ideas—thought, where one leads to the other and vice versa: the RP cycle (Lisle, 2000). This is the dialectical relationship, the psychophysics of brain-mind (see chapter 4 this publication).

Reification and scepticism

According to Geake (2003, 2005) 'the mapping of a neurological level of description on to a behavioural level is not simple or one-to-one' (Geake, 2005, p. 10) and he therefore is weary of the way this has been done with learning style systems such as VAK and then applied to education. He specifically brings attention to the way left-brain and right-brain functioning is theorised and applied to educational pedagogy such that females are regarded as left-brain dominant therefore communicators (auditory) and males right-brain dominant therefore are more kinaesthetic and spatial. It has also been suggested from such observations that Autism is an extreme form of the 'male brain'. If higher education (HE) practitioners are to impart educational pedagogy to budding educational practitioners, it would be beneficial to know just how much we can rely on the information we use to develop learners in HE who then go on to develop learners in primary and secondary education. Therefore, the mapping of cognitive neurophysiological levels of understanding onto cognitive-behavioural levels of understanding, as part of the supporting evidence of VAK's validity and usefulness, along with the usefulness of other brain modulatory systems such as RP (WM/VAK) could lead to profound consequences if the mapping or theorising is wrong.

Coffield, Moseley, Hall and Ecclestone et al (2004) after examining 15 or so learning style models suggest that as a measure of learning style, the models are usually subjective with little 'reliability, never mind validity' (2004, p. 45), and learning style assessments can be culturally biased as well (Coffield et al, 2004; Lisle, 2007). Recommendations are therefore that the theoretical robustness of each model as well as the quality of it should be analysed to assess usefulness as pedagogy; pedagogy that is within a broad sense made up of teaching performance, the theories and beliefs, policies, culture, ethos and structure and mechanisms of social control (Ball, 2004).

One reason being because the mapping of the cognitive neurophysiological level of understanding to cognitive-behavioural levels can lead to theory-practice pedagogy: concepts are social constructs and as such can impact on phenomena one-to-one construct for construct. For example, research has revealed that lack of auditory stimuli leads to fewer synaptic connections based on auditory stimuli in the brain therefore there are fewer auditory memorises (i.e. language unites or words). This is the same for the visual and somatosensory systems (kinaesthetic). One could conclude from this that if VAK learning programmes are not used properly and in the broader context outlined then it could lead to sensory deprivation rather than enhanced leaning. Teachers using the VAK system can for example, after diagnosis, perceive individuals as either visual, auditory or kinaesthetic learners thereby imbuing those labelled with those qualities (Hudak & Kihn, 2001; Coffield, 2004, p. 55). Individuals can be cloned as particular qualities and not as possessing a quality amongst others. This can lead to the self-fulfilling prophecy (Rosenthal & Jacobson, 1968; Hudak & Kihn, 2001) that entails not just the social environment affecting the child's self-esteem; it could actually affect the child's mind and brain. As is suggested by the Morton & Frith (1995) model, also Roberts (2002) and as I do here, behaviour—learning using just one sensory modality can affect mind and brain. If an individual is assessed, as have kinaesthetic preferences for example, will s/he be more likely to remain with just kinaesthetic preferences and not develop secondary learning style modalities, visual and/or auditory? There is a suggestion of a sensitivity period but as sensitivity periods go, there are degrees of effect and it is not always measurable or permanent.

Information about left and right brain functioning is interesting and informative, but it too can result in the social construction of reality and identity. An example of the social construction of identity comes from McDermott (1996, p. 269-300) who refers to 'The acquisition of a child by a learning disability' whereby the definition of the social context within which significant others manage the negotiation of identity formation of the child, operates as a framework for the self-fulfilling prophecy. Controlling both the defined context reality and identity therefore leads to social constructs that the child has difficulty negotiating its way through to a personally desired conclusion because of the manipulated social context (ill-informed practice) and power relations (Berger & Luckmann, 1966; McDermott, 1996; Hudak & Kihn, 2001).

Therefore, when using assessment tools such as VAK, one should be aware of the fact that perceptions and expectations can be distorted by the concepts in which one believes and uses. The point is not to ascribe statuses and identity through diagnostic concepts but to provide a learning environment that is functional for the development of healthy personalities. Thus, as part of the styles/modalities assessment, although individuals will be assessed and presented with information about their primary learning style, information about secondary learning styles should be given with an explanation of what the information means and how the individual can develop all learning modalities to their advantage. This is why RP and personal development planning (PDP) (also Individual Learning Plans) have been introduced alongside learning style diagnostics and multisensory teaching and learning strategies.

The kinaesthetic modality it should be added by no way incurs stigmatization. Spatial ability is one of the characteristics of those with kinaesthetic modality preferences. Spatiality is not just about visual aptitude as ethological studies using squirrels show and it is this intelligence that precedes mathematical ability, thought to be the purest of sciences involving the greatest amount of intellectual skill. Pattern recognition is spatial information for example as is movement in space and time. The unification of procedural (knowing how) and declarative (knowing that) information is essential for the acquisition of knowledge because it represents the synthesis of the abstract and concrete. It could be that individuals who are kinaesthetic—many children with ADHD and Autism for example, need more space and time orientated learning environments, in line with Piagetian child-centred learning. That is, 'the child-scientist' type of approach to learning, and guidance about how to develop other modulatory learning styles, for example auditory.

What is ironic is that in order to eliminate the problem of labelling and self-fulfilling prophecies one is faced with the task of deciding how to validate the concepts one does use and present them in a way that prevents misunderstanding and misuse. Geake (2005) suggests that cognitive neuroscience is useful when provided with a 'rigorous critique' because cognitive neurophysiological concepts can be just as construed as social ones (Berger & Luckmann, 1966; Parker, 1999; Hudak & Kihn, 2001). Although phenomena with biological foundations is believe materialistic therefore 'real' (Marxian materialism, in McLellan, 1977) and not socially construed (Hegelian idealism, Hegel, 1977) as the Morton and Firth's model shows, behaviour can affect biology, then brain, just like brain can affect mind, then biology.

Conclusions reached?

Doing VAK assessments adds to the learning process: Information not only of the individual's learning style preference but also of other learning styles feeds back into learning—self-reflective learning: Knowledge in light of practice you might say! This is one reason for using VAK assessments as part of the teaching and learning process, but alongside self-reflective learning to enhance development. Learners can be empowered because they can evaluate their strengths and weakness and build on both. In addition, by acquiring the skill of RP, students can not only apply reflective thinking to their own development but also to their teaching practice so that rather than just engaging in knowledge-in-use when they become practitioners, they will know how to engage in reflection-in-action and reflection-on-action to prevent the dissemination of misunderstood pedagogy.

Overuse of the one-to-one mapping of neurological brain areas and processes to behaviour such as left-brain, right-brain distinctions—scientific skills left, music right and so on, to such an extent that left handedness is associated with right brain functionings and right-handedness with left-brain functionings and behavioural identity characteristics, can lead to the self-fulfilling prophecy for those who are subject to left-brain right-brain theory-practice pedagogy, pedagogy that the Morton & Frith brain/mind/behaviour model, the Roberts model and the adapted one proposed here can be use to illustrate how the learning situation can be misconstrued and detrimental. The social, emotional and physical environment can influence learning as outlined indeed, emotions particularly have direct effect on brain modulatory systems such as the stimulated production of dopamine, serotonin, noradrenaline and adrenaline and likewise, the hippocampus as a relay system for the reticular activating system works as a brain modulator affecting memory thus learning.

The Marxian-Vygotskian methodology of learning and development: practical-critical activity as a 'tool' for understanding learning and development and a 'result' it can be an activity to spur development on and is people friendly (Newman & Holzman, 1993). Scaffolding learning for example, is Marxian-Vygotskian methodology. It involves building rapport and mutual respect. In addition, what I have referred to as the RP cycle of meta-cognition—the dialectic of mind-brain and behaviour in which the osmosis of sensory data through long-term potentiation converts into brain matter, the dialectic of mind-idea and brain-matter explain aspects of the RP process. Through the reflexive cycle: observe, reflect, plan and act, or plan, act, observe and reflect, then re-plan, ideas are generative of critiquing practical activity and also guide it, it is an ontogenic cycle of evolution of the individual's cognitive development. To map it to cognitive neurophysiology would be to describe it as the neurotransmissional activity in the brain as neurochemicals/transmitters flow through the nervous system into cell structures and the neurons—perhaps even DNA where information is stored as atomic particles; particles that have entered the biological system via the senses as well as produced within it. Indeed, Sample (2007) discusses the latest brain research in which microchips are embedded in the brains of wheelchair users for example, to the effect that the person with the implant need only think to move the wheel or activate a computer programme! Thus, microchips can read the language written in brain structure.

Smaller unit analysis thus is productive. The sensory molecular atomic data that is transposed into cellular structures and fuses with DNA via LTP is a possible truism and it seems reasonable to suggest that as a one-to-one mapping of cognitive neurophysiological material to language unites or memories is more tenable than trying to map a whole discipline onto a brain area such as music or science. But who knows, perhaps within the near future physics will enter the picture and as Penrose suggests we will be able to physically place consciousness at a given point in time and specific space in the brain. On the other hand, has this already been done—what exactly do fMRI show?

To continue the analogy of using physical atomic particles, one could suggest that quanta of brain matter will be developed from engaging the brain in higher order thinking skills i.e. reflexive practice for X amount of time it takes for the LTP to obtain embeddedness within the cellular structure of the brain: The embedded material could be representative of language units or sensory data—memories of pictures, sounds, smells, tastes and touch that can be unified via the hippocampus into coherent meaningful information elicited through cues in the internal and external environment: From double loop learning to the double helix.

On a more serious note, perhaps future research could examine whether or not using the VAK learning style system as well as RP as a meta-cognitive strategy does actually accentuate learning and development. Also, does the misuse of the VAK system lead to sensory deprivation? In that, if a child is said to be a kinaesthetic learner and only given kinaesthetic learning tasks, what effect does this have on the child? In terms of cognitive neurophysiological research, how can it be shown that RP is similar or equal to WM? And finally, if memories are stored multimodal are they retrieved the same way and are we creating an education system that actively contributes to the development of Autism in children, particularly males because of a belief in the postulate that Autism is an extreme form of the male brain?

Chapter Seven

The consequences of crossing disciplinary boundaries: Cognitivism, connectionism, constructionism and emergent intelligence

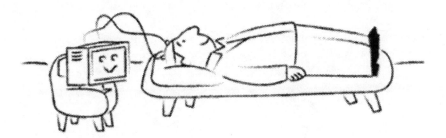

Cognition: When did it all start?

The study of cognition within psychology goes as far back as Wilhelm Wundt (1879) in Germany with the theory of introspection and William James (1875) in the USA, with the theory of 'the stream of consciousness'; even further back if we include theorists such as John Locke. Indeed the workings of the mind have been an area of intrigue, discovery, and conjecture for quite some time. It is no surprise therefore that its study has crossed disciplinary boundaries from physics and philosophy, through chemistry and biology to psychology, sociology and education. More recently within the last 80 years or so, the workings of the mind have been compared to machines and robots, computers in particular forming for some, the ideal analogy for the mind, its structure, processes and functions: An approach to cognitive psychology known as artificial intelligence and/or the information processing model. At present there are two main paradigms within the artificial cognitive systems approach, cognitivism that encompasses classical theories dealing with information processing:

consciousness, attention, memory and forgetting; and, the manipulation of symbols and systems. The second is made up of emergent theories of cognition that deal with connectionist concepts and enactive, self-organising systems.

Connectionism as a brain modelling approach refers to the brain structure as a system of neurons connected via neuronal wires, axons with dendrites, each neuron having developed since the onset of the foetuses' sensory consciousness, multiple connections between itself and other neurons. As an association is learned between two things then a corresponding biological neuronal connection, a dendrite, is formed. This type of neuron is known as a connector neuron, and they form approximately 97% of brain tissue. Emergent systems would be generative of Bloom's hierarchy of cognitive processes such as understanding, analysis, evaluation and self-reflexive learning: reflexivity, that is, brain modulatory processes the result of which is the emergence of top-down knowledge.

Early learning models of cognitive systems were modelled on the associationism of Aristotle, but the emergent systems approaches model the neurobiology of Hebb's postulate of trace path formation (1949). Piaget for example developed a constructionist approach with the theory of genetic epistemology that is an adaptive model of cognition allowing for the development of memory schema as brain structure interacts with its surroundings. Within this paper I have outlined my propositions about the nature of long and short term memory traces within brain neurophysiology building on the work of Hebb. In addition, I suggest brain neurophysiology responsible for the rehearsal loop that forms a connection between the short term memory (STM) and long term memory (LTM). Thirdly, I theorise ways in which genetic epistemology can develop from ontogeny through phylogeny to gene DNA. In preceding chapters I have outlined the way Bloom's cognitive processes result in the acquisition of knowledge or learning (for example the chapter on reflexive practices within the zone of proximal development) and the resulting neuropsychological changes.

Introduction

To begin, I would like to trace some of the roots of what is now a growing area within academia, an interdisciplinary study of the mind, focussing on the three areas of interest within the cognitive sciences: cognitivism, constructionism and connectionism. All three approaches to the study of mind have developed within psychology but through successive developments have incorporated into them research and understanding from adjacent disciplines: An interactionist endeavour the result of which is interactionist ontology and epistemology that can shed light on the interactions of mind, brain and robotics. The concern is the mapping of brain biology to concepts of mind such as information processing, and likewise using knowledge of cognitive psychology and brain biology to enhance understanding of computer technology such as robotics.

The latest development within the cognitive sciences has been the scrutiny of the brain's electrochemical activity allowing scientists to develop techniques for synthesizing the brain's biology with the metal mechanics of robotic limbs. When wired to a computer, the brain can for example, move a computer cursor—we now have no need for the mouse! Well actually, only if you prefer not to use robotic limbs to brain pads, robotic limbs that are in use for those people who for some reason or another have lost their biological limb or limbs.

Cognitivism and associationism in context

Associationism was developed over two and half millennia ago by Aristotle (384-322 BCE). His notions of how the mind worked incorporated elements of connectionism such as the way memories were structured and associated with one another via connections. The Aristotelian notion of association refers to a process of learning dependent on the association of one object/thing with another object/thing, so that a connection is formed and it may lead to a more complex idea/thing. The next addition to cognitivism as a paradigm can be traced to writings within cognitive science of John Locke (1690) 'Essay Concerning Human Understanding', where he outlines empiricism as an embryonic state of mind he refers to as 'tabula rasa'. Tabula rasa being the mind as a blank slate at the onset of consciousness (it was customary to say from birth until the discovery that a foetal brain can process information whilst still in the womb) and from that point on be responsive to external and internal stimuli i.e. data or information that is processed, stored and makes up our knowledge of the world. Locke was thus also a materialist, and was thus admired by Karl Marx!

There were five main elements to early associationism: 1) sensory information is presented as simple ideas, 2) ideas are associated with other ideas, 3) as ideas accumulate they become associated into complexes, 4) Sensations are made up of environmental conditions like space, time, objects, and similarities and differences between objects, 5) Complex ideas can be reduced to their simplest form. Such principles nonetheless were superseded although some of the principles are evident within the behaviourist approach. The behaviourist stimulus-response model of learning, following on from associationist principles, is one way of explaining how associationist ideas of connectionism operate. Based on the work of Ivan Pavlov (1849-1936), salivation produced by dogs when food is presented to them is an involuntary reflexive (automated) association between the food (a stimulus) and salivation (the response). But when the anticipation of being given food stimulates the salivation response, then the association is a learned one. Learning takes place on a number of different levels and the classical stimulus-response connection, was later developed into the theories operant and latent learning.

The importance of the stimulus response mechanism shows in the discovery of *stimulus generalisation*, that the conditioned response was not only associated with the stimulus but also other very similar stimuli: The more alike the stimuli the more likely the correct response and the larger the excitation response (i.e. referred to in a preceding chapter as short term potentiation or long term potentiation i.e. activation potential in the axon/dendrite synapse). These theories are just some of the learning operations that result in the emergence of connections within biological material such as neurons and dendrites. We can apply this to computation in that the computer will search for similarities in file content or programme content before retrieving information etc, or developing any new repairs, connections or actions.

The behaviourist Watson (1950) suggested that associated learning was basic to stimulus-response mechanistic type learning and he illustrated his point using a human baby 'Little Albert' in an experiment where he conditioned the child to form a connection between a loud noise and white rabbit. The child thus associating the noise with the white rabbit cried, and then, learning the connection between the two things started to cry even when he only saw the white rabbit and the noise was no longer presented. Such experiments are now regarded as unethical yet at the time led to some important discoveries within the field of behaviourism, and learning theory.

Jerome Bruner et al (1956) suggested however, that people were not 'passive' respondents. He regarded them as active participants whose actions are influenced by the *socio-psychological context* in which they find themselves, but at the same time people have agency and can influence the situation in return. His ideas led to the development of the *cultural model of education* and how it influences the learning process. And this is where the similarity between the brain and the computer ends—the computer cannot interact with its environment—well not as fully as humans do though it does develop a basic form of learning but thus cannot adapt or evolve at the same rate or level as humans.

Cognitivism and the systems approach: information processing

Fortunately cognitive sciences have been able to dip into biological as well mechanical sciences, even mathematics and physics, to underpin and/or explain connectionism complexities. Primarily biology was adept at explaining most of cognitive processes, but linked to the information processing model borrowed from artificial intelligence both biological and mechanical models have afforded a much richer and lucid field of information. It seems therefore according to Medler (1998, p 20) that biological underpinnings to information processing in the brain should form the roots of connectionism within psychology, and he cites the Symposium on Information Theory (1956) as the onset of cognitive science, graced by three eminent scientists: Miller with his theory of *'The Magical Number Seven'*, Chomsky with his theory 'The Three Models of Language', that signalled the onset of connectionist theory of synaptogenesis, and Newell and Simon's theory of the *'Logical Machine'*.

The information processing model deals with brain processes using the systems approach and is an extremely insightful addition. Starting with the senses that provide the raw data for perception, a sensory classification system was developed. For example, 1) exteroceptors deal with the sensory data from the external environment, 2) interoceptors deal with the data from the internal environment, particularly homeostasis and 3) proprioceptors deal with the bodily sensations of position within space and its movements in time. Incoming information via the sensory systems: vision, auditory, gestation (taste), olfactory (smell) cutaneous (skin/touch) and proprioception (kinaesthetic and vestibular senses), is conveyed to the brain for processing.

The corresponding processing units and areas of the brain the information is relayed to are: eye—occipital lobe-striate cortex, ear—cochlea-temporal lobe (via auditory nerve), tongue—taste-bud receptor via gustatory nerve to temporal lobe, nose—via transducers in olfactory mucosa to temporal lobe, skin corpuscles via nerves to parietal lobe/cerebellum and inner ear for proprioception via sensor-hairs in vestibular sensitive to gravity and relayed to the cerebellum see figure 1. Processing can be of several kinds, but starts with awareness, attention, perception, organisation of perceptual information such as short and long term remembering, as well as forgetting and of course retrieval of information using cues.

It became clear that information processing was organised and according to the Gestalt theory of organisation 'The whole was greater than the sum of its parts'. From recognising patterns within the environment the perceptual organisation of the data results in a whole picture being generated within the mind's eye, now known as Gregory's top-down processing. Top-down processing is thought to involve the synthesis of information from the long term memory to encode incoming information whether from exteroceptors, interoceptors or propreoceptors. Figure 2 shows areas of the brain top-down processing is likely to occur i.e. areas where secondary processing of sensory information takes place.

Figure 2 also shows areas mapped for sensory perception and it serves as a rough guide to illustrate top-down processing. Short and long term memory is present throughout the brain cortex and cerebellum that is, within all the areas illustrated. The exact positioning of STM and LTM is within the brain neurophysiology itself. I will return to this point later. Once information is encoded beyond the short term memory the processing of it involves top-down processing because it is synthesised with encoded information in the long term memory store. The processing of information from the bottom-up is thought to consists entirely of incoming data with no manipulation (Gregory, *'Eye and Brain'*, 1993), that is, it involves only information from exteroceptors, interoceptors and propreoceptors as in figure 1 above, information that has not entered the long term memory and been processed in any way. It will reach the hippocampus and areas within the limbic system and enter the STM but not beyond, see figure 3.

Figure 4 shows the limbic system as it appears with the brain cortex, thus one can see the inner structures responsible for bottom up processing and the out-structure responsible for top-down processing.

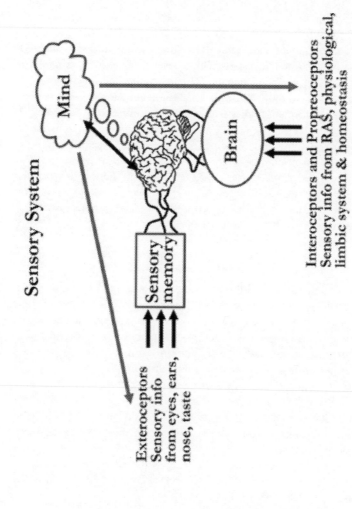

Figure 1

Areas of the brain top-down processing is likely to occur

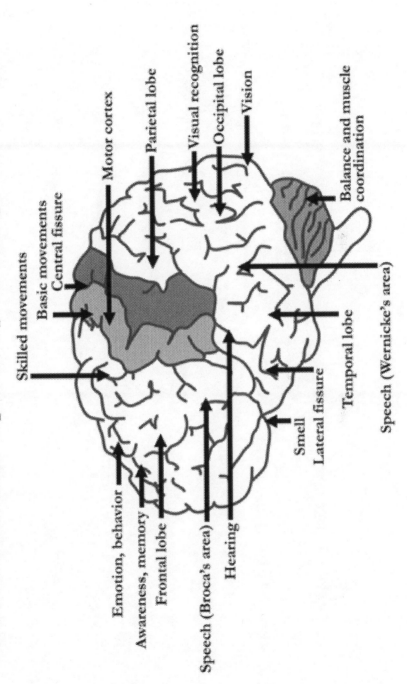

Figure 2

Limbic System

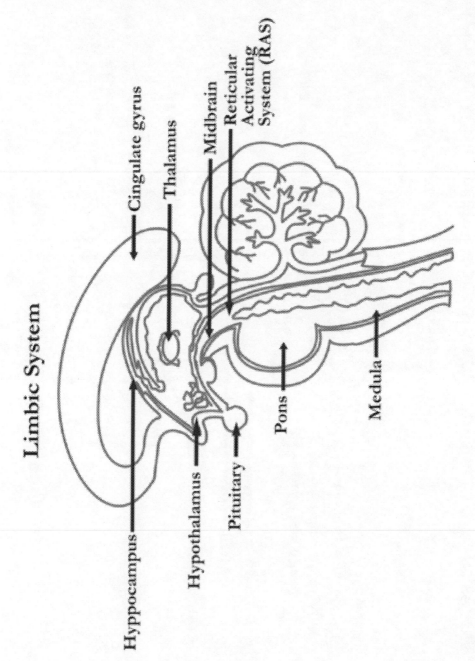

Cingulate gyrus

Thalamus

Midbrain

Reticular Activating System (RAS)

Hyppocampus

Hypothalamus

Pituitary

Pons

Medula

Figure 3

The Cortex with the limbic system within

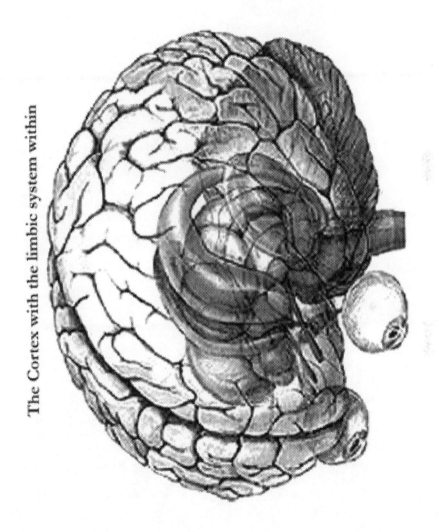

Figure 4

Figure 5

Gregory's theory of top-down bottom-up processing of information in the brain was developed further and is said to follow certain rules. Yes, there have been rules developed in accordance with the organising principle of Gestalt: proximity, closure, continuity, symmetry and similarity. In other words, things close together are perceived as part of the same object, if there are bits missing from a familiar shape the brain brings closure and we see a whole object and so on depending on the information about objects already stored in the long term memory. And so the theory of the optical illusion was formed and it was realised that perception was not always accurate. For example, what do you see in figure 5?

The picture is referred to as Leeper's 'Ambiguous Lady'. It is seen either as youthful women or old women. If you study the picture long enough you will experience both perceptions. It appears that information coming in to the brain is manipulated in this way because information the brain already holds, incoming information encodes with, referred to as top-down processing. In addition, the brain or mind is selective, a postulate that led Broadbent (1958) to develop the Filter Module of Attention.

Broadbent's filter model (figure 6) was an elaborate diagrammatic representation of the systems approach to studying brain processes for example: Input that refers to information coming in from the senses, the processing of the information i.e. whether it is selected for attention, whether it is processed—this may depend on the limited capacity of the brain. The limited capacity of the brain will determine whether or not information is passed into the LTM and the response to the processing of the information will be a reflection of that process either storage of information or loss. The main point being, that not all information is attended to or processed and even if it is processed it can be lost through trace decay, displacement and/or interference in STM and trace decay retrieval failure in LTM.

Miller's theory of 'chunking' was just as profound as Broadbent's contribution to this field. Miller however was concerned with the capacity of the brain to store information, how much information can we remember and for how long. Miller (1956) developed the idea that the brain can store seven pieces of information, plus or minus two. He called the phenomenon chunking. We remember birth dates for example, by chunking digits together either in threes '180'-'191' or twos '18'-'01'-'91', perhaps even in sixes '180191'. We do the same with telephone numbers and other information. If you can apply a rule to the chunking or a code, then you will remember even more. Dates are remembered as two digits for the day, two for the month, and two or four for the year. That is the rule for recording time using a digital calendar. For remembering multiples of numbers, we use the multiplication grid. If you know that multiples of nine always add up to nine, then you will remember the nine times table. Such patterns are the rules or codes that aid memory. Can you fill in the remainder of the multiplications' grid from memory see figure 7? Such mnemonic devices are used extensively in education as well other social context.

Through Miller's discovery then that chunking digits expands the short term memory, it was found 'the seven-bit bottle neck' could be bypassed. That is, chunking information using an encoding system aids the passing of information from the STM to LTM memory store. It was Atkinson and Shiffrin (1971) who found that rehearsal (repetition) extends the duration of memory. They developed the Multistore Model of Memory, with two divisions, STM and LTM. Again as Broadbent did, Atkinson and Shiffrin used the systems approach. Sensory data enters the sensory memory (SM) that is modality specific. If the data is selected for attention it enters the STM. Once in the STM information is either encoded with information already in the LTM or it is rehearsed and will pass into the LTM. If neither of these two processes occurs the information is more than likely lost. See figure 8.

The rehearsal loop is an important concept here because it led to the development of another model called the working memory model (WMM) of memory (Baddeley & Hitch, 1974). Baddeley & Hitch's (1974) model of memory which focuses on STM suggests it is a much more elaborate memory store than that suggested by Atkinson and Schifrin's multi-store model. Baddeley and Hitch see the STM as a working memory store.

The working memory (WM) is made up of the central executive—the control aspect, which is responsible for higher mental processes i.e. meta-cognition such as decision making, problem solving and planning; all the cognitive processes of Bloom's taxonomy including reflexive practice; and uses the other three aspects—visuo-spatial scratch pad, articulatory system, and phonological loop selectively as a guide. The executive can attend to information from one of the slave systems whilst at the same time inhibiting the other two. The central executive is flexible and modality free (i.e. can attend to and process any sensory information). The visuo-spatial scratch pad deals with visual information and spatial information such as depth perception, and movement. It is also involved in physical actions such as reflex-actions. It is responsible for mental-maps, i.e. photographic memory. The information can be rehearsed i.e. remembering the visual structure of a word for example, or the arrangement of parts in a diagram. In short, coding in the visuo-spatial memory is of visuo-spatial patterns.

The articulatory-phonological loop has received the most attention. Baddeley (1997) suggests that it is evidence for acoustic coding in STM. Actors use verbal rehearsal to remember their lines in a play and it is thought to act as an aid for beginner readers. Young children in the same way, use the articulation of language to learn it because the articulatory-phonological loop is a way of learning to say words they have heard and analysis the words they are saying to see if they are being pronounced correctly. The phonological store holds phonemic/sound information and is responsible for understanding words, and the articulatory process, speech production. See figure 9.

An Adaptation of Broadbent's Filter Model 1958

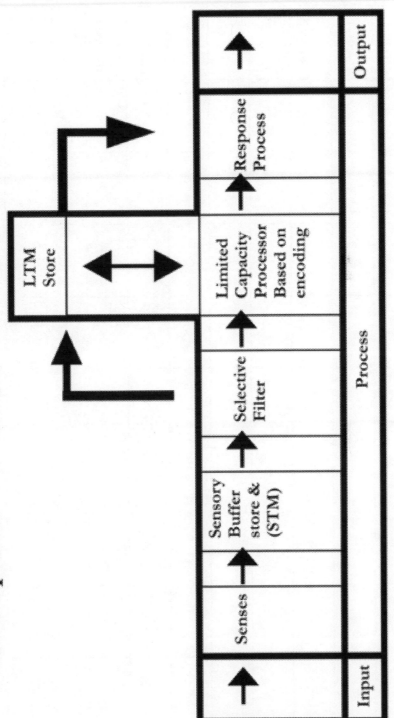

Figure 6

	1	2	3	4	5	6	7	8	9	10
1										
2		4								
3			9							
4				16						
5					25					
6						36				
7							49	56		
8										
9		18	27	36	45	54	63	72	81	90
10										100

Figure 7

Multi-store Model of Memory (Atkinson and Shiffrin 1968)

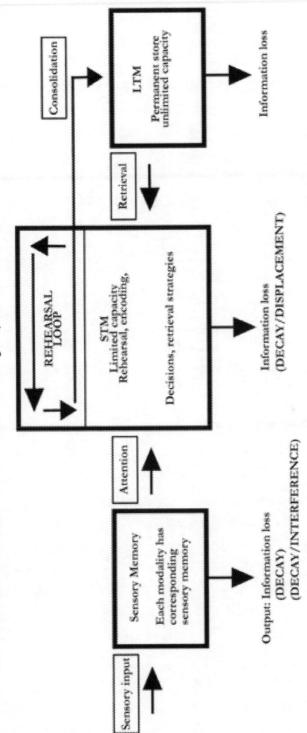

Figure 8

Working Memory Model: Baddeley & Hitch (1974, 2000)

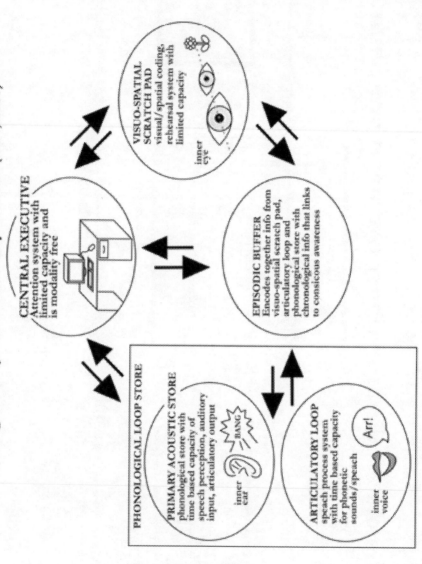

Figure 9

Locating the Rehearsal Loop in STM

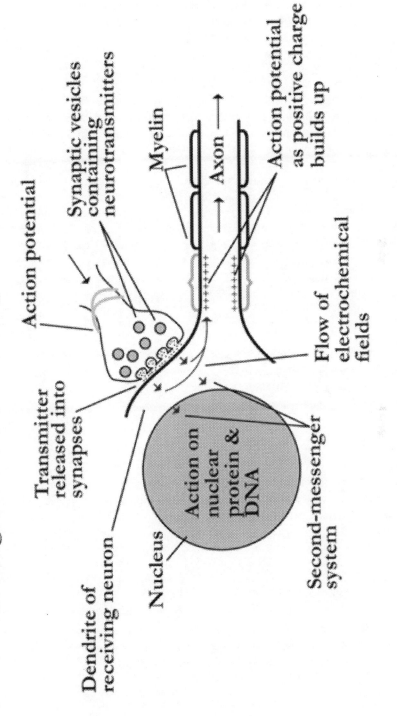

Figure 10

In 2000 Baddeley and Hitch further developed their model of memory. They added the episodic buffer. Using the addition of the episodic buffer the authors could explain the interactions between working memory or operations in the STM and the LTM as is indicated by the arrows in figure 10. Baddeley (1966) suggested coding in the LTM was mainly semantic. He designed an experiment to test this hypothesis. Subjects were tested under four conditions: acoustically similar word recall, semantically similar word recall, acoustic dissimilar word recall and semantically dissimilar word recall. Subjects recalled more words under the first condition therefore he concluded acoustic store occurs in STM. Baddeley's later experimental work suggested encoding in the LTM is semantic which can be visual, auditory or other sense data such as smell, taste or touch that has particular meaning for us (Braille for the blind). Tulving (1972) distinguished two types of coding in the LTM: episodic and semantic. Episodic memory is made up of episodes of experience, semantic memory consists of innate rule-forming mechanisms for perceiving reality (Kant, 1781) and constructing reality into meaningful categorises. Thus, whilst information in the STM is mainly auditory it can be visuo-spatial or any other sensory perception but if it is not organised in sequence with episodic information generative of epistemic brain structure responsible for meaningful categorisation (Kant and Piaget's genetic structures) that the LTM is composed of it will be lost. Therefore, RP/WM focuses attention on information from the STM that is most immediate to the needs of the organism for binding with episodic and semantic information in the LTM.

Nyberg, Habib, Tulving, Cabeza, Houle, Pearsson & McIntosh (2000) have investigated areas of the brain using positron emission tomography (PET). They were searching for a brain area where episodic memory might be located. However what they found was that although the pre-frontal cortex was involved in the encoding and retrieval of sentences and pictures, several areas in the cortex associated with sensory processing and also areas of the brain such as right prefrontal, medial temporal and parietal regions were also active. These researchers concluded that episodic memory takes place throughout most of the brain as large scale neuronal interaction is evident. See figure 2.

Graf & Schachter (1985) suggested a distinction between implicit and explicit memory. The memory used in laboratory experiments they suggest, is explicit and episodic memory or recalling previously unconsciously remembered things i.e. TV programmes, implicit memory. Explicit memory demands the use of WM that is meta-cognition or higher consciousness awareness (Vygotsky) and aids learning. These types of memory have been link to declarative and procedural knowledge systems (Cohen & Squire, 1911).

The attempt to theorise memory as an organising system goes back to Kant (1724-1804) if not before (Plato). It appears then that procedural knowledge (implicit or intuitive) is stored in areas of the old mammalian brain and declarative knowledge (explicit) in the cerebral cortex. It is the cerebral cortex that is said to house the WM. The latter theory I suggest has face validity given that the cortex area is the latest evolutionary change and at this point it can be assumed therefore that it will be responsible for further ontogenetic changes in the brain-mind dialectic as an ongoing workings of brain-mind. Collins & Quillan (1969) formulated a model that we can use to describe how memory is structured and organised. They call the model the hierarchical semantic network model. According to the model, concepts are organised in hierarchical order so that memory store is efficient and retrieval enhanced.

The fascinating thing about their model is that it synthesises nicely with Vygotsky's notion of concept formation and concept generality. For example, when discussing the teaching and learning context in a preceding chapter I outlined the way concept formation occurs. For example, during discussions with students using Socrates' teaching methods that combines episodic and semantic information; I observed students discussing topics until they found words within their existing language repertoire with similar meaning that helped them to understand concepts they had to learning. They were in fact examining their existing hierarchical semantic network synthesising new information with that encoded as episodic and semantic information in the LTM.

Thus developed the field of cognitive psychology and this research has been used to enhance the teaching and learning process. When I started teaching for example, having studied and taught cognitive psychology, I found myself applying cognitive psychology in my teaching practice. I was not just teaching it, I was doing it! Theories such as Miller's, and Atkinson & Shiffrins' were the filters through which I saw the teaching and learning process—as well as education theory too of course. But as I applied more and more cognitive psychology to my educational practices, I questioned how I could support the evidence I purported to believe. I found myself becoming more and more reductionist trying to explain things like short and long term memory until I developed the diagrams that now makes up part of the discussion in the publication. In other words, I found myself synthesizing neurosciences with cognitive sciences and education. I was doing what the connectionists had done all along—I was applying interdisciplinary knowledge to explain what I thought was occurring as learning took place. The process of learning became much more fluid and lucid by adopting an interdisciplinary approach. In chapter 6 of this book, the diagram of focused attention that depicts the first and secondary messenger systems in the neurons of the brain is there to illustrate the process by which I theorised sensory information is processes it short term and long term memory. One could also ask, 'where within memory is the rehearsal loop that aids the remembering of information?'

Having explained using a diagram, the process of information passing from the STM to LTM (see chapter 6) and having outlined several models of information processing in the brain, I should explain the biological structures where the rehearsal of information takes place in brain neurophysiology. In figure 10, where there is action potential at the synapses electrochemical transmitters are released into the synapses forming a bridge. When several synapses activate together in the same area or through connections of axons what develops is a long term potentiation (LTP) that is sustained enough to allow the flow of electrochemicals into the synapses and crossover and embed in the receptor sites of the adjacent dendrites. The electrochemicals can enter the neuron and at this point the electrochemical message is no longer a short term memory. It becomes encoded in the neuron as a long term memory. It appears therefore that rehearsal must take place at the action potential when a STP becomes a LTP. So what catalyses the change from STP to LTP? Focused attention can do this for example when deliberately engaging in reflexive thinking. Also, saying things over and over in the mind can sustain the action potential enhancing it and changing it from a STP to a LTP. Any kind of activity that maintains consciousness on a focused topic or object will enhance the action potential from a STP to LTP. Thus, rehearsal is extremely fluid encompassing action potentials and electrochemical activity in the axons and dendrites expanding the activity until it floods into the surrounding neurons where STP/STM becomes LTP/LTM.

However, further motivators and brain modulators also discussed in preceding chapters, for example, brain modulators (chapter 4) can change consciousness as our attention changes or our mood changes or even our motivation. The continuity of incoming information can change consciousness thus altering the action potential particularly if the incoming information is more important than that being processed in memory. Penrose (1992) suggested that consciousness is located in the axon or the myelin. I think it depends on the quality of consciousness one is talking about. For example, the sensory buffer would produce a type of consciousness and one could actually extend that placing it in the STM, which is within the neuronal circuitry. However, given that the working memory (particularly the central executive aspect of working memory) is mainly located in the frontal cortex it is quite possible consciousness is there. The olfactory bulb responsible for drives such as hunger, thirst and mating, including motivational and emotional needs and the fight-flight reaction essential for survival and adaptation resides quite close to the frontal lobe near working memory. Thus, if we re-examine figure 10, Baddeley and Hitch (1974, 2000) it is quite reasonable to presume that the central executive is in the frontal lobe and responsive to the olfactory bulb as well as other brain modulators. The central executive simultaneously controls all of the sensory information coming in from the sensory memory via way of the limbic system and hippocampus; including whether it will be processed in the specified areas as in figure 2 'Areas where top-down processing is likely to occur'. What is significant about the knowledge that is still evolving is its uses. Such knowledge can elucidate the workings of robotic limbs and so on and there is now a whole branch of educational psychology that utilises psychology research as a basis for what is called 'brain based teaching methods', some of which are very productive and some that I find non-productive.

Donna Walker Tileston (2004) has written quite an interesting little book called 'Learning, Memory, and the Brain'. She takes a creative look at the union of education and neuroscience using the visual auditory and kinaesthetic system, the learning styles that correspond to sensory modalities. Tileston also examines the concept of chunking and how we can use it to enhance storage in the LTM. On page 39 Tileston discusses the use of retrieving from the episodic memory as a way of cueing information from the semantic memory. The concept is quite interesting because what it involves is the use of Socrates' style teaching. It involves teaching via discussion whilst allowing the students to contribute to the full. Some suggest it involves teaching the students about how to access the knowledge they already store in LTM because the connecting of episodic and semantic retrieval gives that impression and the teachers therefore facilitates the student in the building of connections between episodic and semantic memory in different was to those already stored by adding to them incoming information. If you refer back to the chapter 3, this publication and read the discourse extracts you will see that actually that is what takes place. Discussion is used to cue episodic and semantic memories and via conjecture one could suggest at the same time new connections are being formed and trace paths developed in brain matter.

In addition, Tileston's discussion of procedural memory is interesting, also highly controversial and perhaps discriminate—she believes only children with learning difficulties benefit from this style of learning but anyway her book is useful. For example, Tileston talks about retrieving from procedural memory using role-play, debate and hands-on activities. This style of learning then is related to kinaesthetic learning the 'how to do something' knowledge we need whether we work in a space science laboratory and need to do experiments or work as a taxi driver who knows how to drive and memorise extensive areas in the form of cognitive maps, road maps. Declarative information—the knowing what something is usually made meaningful using diagrams—visual stimuli and/or auditory stimuli such as language and language related activities. Marilee Sprenger (2003) is another such author who uses the sensory modality learning style system in her teaching practice. Whilst she uses the system to differentiate and develop individual learning plans I personally would use knowledge of sensory modality learning systems to teach all students given as I do feel students should develop all modalities for learning.

Nonetheless, Sprenger examines some very complex concepts and teaching plans around the phenomenon of visual, auditory and kinaesthetic learning styles and she develops plans for the pupils that incorporate all three learning modalities. See chapter 5 appendices on assessing adults with learning difficulties in this publication for some examples of teaching strategies using visual, auditory and kinaesthetic delivery of information. The good thing about using all three of the sensory modalities for learning is that for example, procedural knowledge i.e. how to do something and declarative knowledge i.e. what something is can be brought together almost as if to enhance concept formation when the abstract 'what something is' it brought together with the concrete 'how we do something' knowledge. Yes, the process resembles Vygotsky's theory of concept formation. The bringing together of the abstract and concrete enables understanding to move from the implicit to the explicit. It appears that even Vygotsky's theory can be founded in reductionist explanations. Indeed is not brain based teaching another way of scaffolding learning by opening up the brain using information processing techniques and knowledge of brain-neurophysiology within the structural confines of education?

Connectionism, constructionism and interactionism

Connectionism then concerns the way the sensory information relayed to the brain is processed and further processed as reflection takes place what some call high-order thinking or meta-cognition (probably the activity of the central executive part of WM within the frontal lobe). Empirical knowledge, Locke's theory of knowledge, is suggestive that our understanding of the world comes from the senses as we interpret the information that enters perception via those senses. His theory stands contrast to Kantian *a priori* forms of knowledge or knowing that rationalist and nativist explanations adhere to—rationalism being the idea that we think before we act rather than merely respond to stimuli and nativism being the idea that knowledge and intelligence is inherent and passed to the next generation in DNA. The latter form of knowing is often regarded as intuitive understanding based as it is on the categories emergent of biological structures that are innate, for example, brain matter such as the limbic system and sensory brain areas that are directly emergent of the phylogenetic make-up of the species rather than ontogenetic make-up of the individual. *A priori* forms of knowing however may at times be a product of both phylogenetic materials as well as ontogenetic materials (the latter for example being composed of stored memories and synapses developed within a person's life time that reside within the neuronal matter), the form of rationalist knowledge one acquires from interacting with the world around us: reflexivity.

If you refer to chapter 6 once more, figure 3—'Focussing Attention Using Reflexive Practice/Working Memory, this publication, the diagram represents the idea that as sensory data is processed deeper within the neurons of brain cells, not only does the data convert into long term memory, the greater the understanding achieved the more likely it will become enshrined within DNA, that is, phylogenetic information. At the very least it will 'connect' when organised/encoded in the brain, with information that is already there. Hence the Kantian *a priori* form of knowing and intuition, that is often hard to explain. The biological structures themselves (such as the sense organs that perceive sensory information i.e. Sensory Memory: exteroception, interoception and proprioception) are written within the genotype; adaptive potentials developed within a generation will be stored in phenotype thus within the dominant-recessive gene and ideas developed within the individual's life time will be deeply embedded within neuronal cell structure, or our biological DNA. What this storage of information/ideas amount to is that a trace of understanding remains and can be unlocked via association or some other internal or external environmental cue/trigger. If the cue/trigger does not materialise then the idea within the gene, phenotype or ontogenetic store will dissipate. Thus explaining why behaviours can evolve into a species' repository and also out of it. A theory of course but it serves as an analogy that might explain both empirical and rationalist/ nativist epistemology and ontology. My theory in addition offers an explanation for how the information that is accumulated, further distributes to DNA that is present in all cells, and in particular, the DNA that contribute to the production of sperms in a male and eggs in a female, developed for reproduction.

To continue, the accumulated knowledge received via empirical means and that which is already *a priori*, works on the principle of Piaget's genetic epistemology: Genetic epistemology being the study of how we as biological organism develop knowledge through the interaction of the brain and body with its environment. This for Piaget was a process that took place in stages over an individual's lifetime but within the human species he theorised that there was universality to the development of knowledge owning to the inherited character of brain matter dictated by human phylogeny. At birth we may possess a collection of inherited behaviours such as crying, suckling and rooting. These 'schema' according to Piaget initially will be used to interact with our environment via the process of assimilation. If an object in the environment cannot be assimilated into an existing schema then we accommodate an existing schema (change it) so it can be used when interacting with a new object. As Piaget states:

'In its beginning, assimilation is essentially the utilisation of the external environment by the subject to nourish his hereditary or acquired schemata (schema). It goes without saying that schemata such as those of sucking, sight, prehension, etc., constantly need to be accommodated remains so undifferentiated from the simmilatory processes that it does not give rise to any special active behaviour pattern but merely consists in an adjustment of the pattern to the details of the things assimilated. Hence, it is natural that at this developmental level the external world does not seem formed by permanent objects that neither space nor time is yet organised in groups and objective series, and that causality is not spatialized or located in things. In other words, at first the universe consists in mobile and plastic perceptual images centred about personal activity.' (Piaget, 1954, p. 351).

The construction of knowledge as schema (bundles of information about an object or thing and how we act towards it/behavioural repertoire) then, is based on the process of assimilation and accommodation. From the interplay of perception to its environment, the adaptation of the organism to its environment helps to secure its survival. We have now all the elements of cognitive science: cognitivism, connectionism and constructionism as a unifying whole that explains the interactions of empiricism, rationalism and nativism. In other words, interactionism can be shown to be a truism. It is the 'truths' within science that lead to further scientific developments. Constructed schema emergent of connections and connections are emergent of cognitive structures in response to the social and physical environment: cognition connecting and constructing sensory information from exteroceptors, interoceptors and proprioceptors. That is, the development of ontological changes in brain-mind.

As mentioned earlier, Bruner (1966b) built on the theories of Piaget, agreeing that the child inherits biological structures through which it organises the world and helps it to survive and further adapt. Evolutionary theory for example, can testify that senses such as the eye have evolved over time to environmental conditions. As a species, we inherit sense organs, and the information needed to create them anew in every successive generation is passed from one generation to next via DNA. Bruner further suggests children are active rather than passive receivers of knowledge. Children are curious, they explore their surroundings and want to know what things are and what they do. Bruner was also a materialist. For example, he believed abstract thinking to be predicated on active experience and concrete experience, influences of Vygotsky's theory of concept development discussed in chapter 3 of this publication. Thus both Piaget and Vygotsky influenced the work of Bruner. Indeed, Bruner also extended notions of scaffolding, first developed by Vygotsky, who saw childhood development as an interaction of the child's psychology to its social as well as its physical environment, but Bruner applied it to educational context. One could say that Bruner, like Vygotsky was a social constructionist, whilst Piaget became known as a constructionist even though Piagetian genetic epistemology is concerned with the child's interaction with the physical environment—perhaps Bruner beat him to it!

Within evolutionary psychology Pinker (1997) came up with a theory of learning that incorporated the environment, culture and heredity, all interacting and influencing behaviour. It is suggested that humans have an instinct for learning; particularly that associated with curiosity, exploration, creativity, and reflection—particularly 'learning how to learn': Perhaps by remembering sequences and/or rules, then tracing back through them, until we hit on a sequence/rule that solves the immediate problem. Pinker further suggests that the rules or characteristics needed for learning, which might be I would suggest, Bloom's hierarchical skills for learning; analysis, evaluation, synthesis and so on, may over a period of time and successive generation within a stable environment, become innate—the Kantian postulate. His work incorporates elements of connectionist ideas used in mechanics. For example, he discusses the possibility of having multiple connections with corresponding innate learning skills, that can be switched on or off or undecided until needed and the environment, culture and our behaviour will be variables in the random selection of which learning mechanism is switched on or off. Nonetheless, because using computer simulations did not actually always obtain, in that innate learning did not always get selected for, Pinker thinks the passing of such an elaborate set of instinctual learning onto the next generation might be one million to one. Computer simulation is not always the best way to test a theory of human behaviour. Computer systems for example are closed systems and cannot fully reproduce the human condition as an open system, but in this case, a biological theory came up with the same conclusions.

Lynsenko building on the work of Darwin, formulated a similar theory of hereditary, also suggesting that characteristics might not always be in the second or third generation because not all of the social and/or environmental variables favour it (I have just discussed a similar process involving the retention and storage of memory in brain neurophysiology as LTM that may encode through ontogeny, phylogeny to gene DNA that are later retrieved by social and/or environmental cues/triggers and if not will disappear). Pinker concludes by suggesting learning leads to innateness of 'learning instincts' and innateness itself, but not complete innateness. Why you might ask? Pinker concludes by suggesting adaptiveness is 'adaptive' but not fully because adaptiveness is not always based on the power of learning and innateness. For example, looking at the case of the recessive gene for sickle cell disease, the cell is actually a 'fitness' in areas where malaria is endemic yet overall it is a weakness to the human biology. Thus one can see what Pinker is referring when he suggest adaptiveness is not always in a form we would regard as adaptive like we would consider 'learning instincts'. Who would have thought a cell defect would be fitness or a mechanism for adaptiveness?

If newly developed ontogenetic information is passed on, how does it circulate the biological organism such that it enters the phylogeny: DNA structure within the sperm and/or egg there to sexually reproduce future foetus? Well having pondered this problem I can see one analogy that might explain it. Like a viral infection that circulates the human biology via the blood stream, reaching most and sometimes all of the human body, so too can ontogenetic information. In a similar way that ontogenetic information enters brain cells, cells of the body experience a similar intake of sensory chemistry. New cells that also develop within the bone marrow, scrotum and/or ovaries are signalled to do so via the brain and they have to use the chemistry that is present within the human body, which now contains residue of the developing ontogenetic information as well as chemistry from the social and physical environment. The new cell growth thus will be patented with the new ontogenetic, now viable phylogenetic information: DNA. This will also apply to the sperm and egg cells that contribute to the DNA that is to be passed onto the next generation via those newly growing eggs and sperm containing the new DNA.

If this is the case, it would help to explain Pinker's postulate that adaptive learning mechanisms are not always passed onto successive generations. For example, viral infections circulating the body leave some trace: Either a scare or the aftermath of a viral infection, immunity to itself from the interactions between it and the human body. However, as with viral infections, after a period, given that cells renew themselves, the scaring or immunity will dissolve, unless the virus is circulating at a given constant and continuous pace. If it was a viral infection this might lead to death, very slow death or total immunity if the body is strong enough to develop immunity that is long lasting and perhaps even ontogenetic information that has converted into phylogeny, there by entering the genes: DNA. Conversely, if the viral infection is removed from the body short term via the bodies free floating anti-bodies, then it will not build up enough to enter the phylogeny or the gene pool, because such information has to be within the human body for the period it take ontogenetic information to enter new cells produced including those intended for sexual reproduction. As stated before even if the new ontogenetic information is converted into phylogeny it may enter the foetal DNA as a recessive gene and therefore not show through in the second generation, and not even pass into the third generation, if it is recessive in that particular environment—either social or physical environment. Here we have a truly interactionist explanation of cognitive development, a synthesis of biology and environmental conditions that influence the development of the individual: The interactive construction of the DNA within the bio-psycho-social environment. How can we not be interdisciplinary when the phenomenon we study is? This leads me into the next topic, that is, insights developed from mechanical cognitive connectionism similar to Pinker's led to development in the adjacent field of science too.

Insights and developments: Interdisciplinary cognitive sciences

Connectionism has become so interdisciplinary and current it is hard keeping up with the latest advancements in connectionist neural network research (Medler, 1998, p 19). The reason the two concepts of connectionism and associationism have been brought together is attributed to the work of neuroscientists trying to explain brain properties and corresponding processes.

There are branches of connectionism that bridge into engineering i.e. particularly the controlling of robotic limb movement. This form of stimulus response connectionism is also based on associationist and deterministic principles of behaviour, much like stimulus-response reflexive actions that are usually innate. Human behaviour is much more complex though because it is evolving and adapting to external as well as internal variable stimuli rather than prescribed fixed action patterns than make up the movement repertoire of robotic limbs. Indeed, human behaviour is problematic in this instance being as it is non-determinate and thus requires meta-cognition rather than just stimulus-response learned associations. This was also recognised by those working within the realms of artificial intelligence and Vernon et al (2006) have thus tabled the distinctions between what they call the classical cognitivist and emergent connectionist paradigms. To truly model the human brain, Vernon et al suggest artificial intelligence systems should have several characteristics that human brains have.

Classical computational theories of mind (CTM) were modelled on digital computers, those of von Neumann. These computers were serial processors that could only perform one operation as a time, and although they were fast, their speed was thus limited by the 'von Neumann bottleneck'. Within the mechanical branches of connectionism and cognitive science however, the Parallel Distribution Processing (PDP) model of information processing was developed by Newell and Simon (1976) and based as it was on the workings of the brain, with the central principle of connectionism, a brain made up of neuronal networks with multiple connections; it has become one of the most enlightening analogies for the brain-mind as well as for the development of computers:

> 'Under one central tenant . . . that the mind is an information processor; that is, it receives, stores, retrieves, transforms, and transmits information. This information and the corresponding information processes can be studied as patterns and manipulations of patterns. Furthermore, these processes posit representational or semantic states that are fully realised within the physical constraints of the brain' (Medler, 1998, p. 20).

The Newell and Simon information processing model PDP mirrored the system of symbols much like the way language operates as a form of communication for humans. Each symbol represents an object or some form of information that fits within a matrix of patterns of symbols that can be manipulated in some way. But unlike existing theories of connectionism that are based on hierarchical rules of information processing (particularly when we think of the rules for language), to deal with information, 'their system operates via the parallel processing of sub-systems, using statistical properties'. The eight functional properties of the PDP model illustrate nicely the 6 functional properties of the neuron, and how they function collectively to produce the information processing capacity of the brain. McClelland & Rumelhart (1985) have been noted as calling this model of information processing 'the neutrally inspired model of cognitive processing'.

The 6 processes of a neuron are: 1) input device—receiving signals from other neuron or environment, 2) the input is manipulated via integration device, 3) the neuron conducts information over distance, 4) the neuron acts as a output device conveying information to other neurons/cells and 6) it maps one type of information onto another like a computer. These processes have been incorporated into the PDP models. Medler (1998) summarises the three basic tenets:

> 'First, signals are processed by elementary units. Second, processing units are connected in parallel to other processing units. Third, connections between processing units are weighted. These three tenets are necessarily broad in their descriptions so as to accommodate all aspects of connectionism.' (Medler, 1998, p. 22).

Information processing accordingly includes reception, storage, manipulation and retrieval. Signals are transmitted via chemical, mechanical or electronic methods. The units respond to signals other than those generated internally. The processing unit can be symbolic of mathematical formula or a neuron with axon and dendrites and information can be encoded locally or distributed. Figure 11 is Medler's PDP model.

Medler (1998) Parallel Distribution Processing

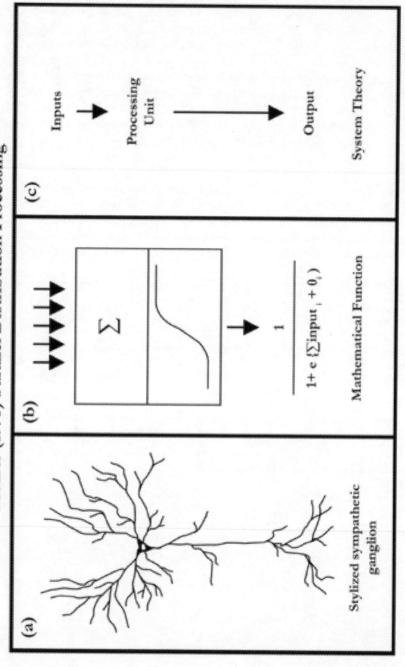

(a) Stylized sympathetic ganglion

(b)
$$\frac{1}{1+ e^{(\sum input_i + 0_i)}}$$
Mathematical Function

(c) Inputs → Processing Unit → Output
System Theory

Figure 11

Garnham (1991) Connectionist Representation of Processing Units

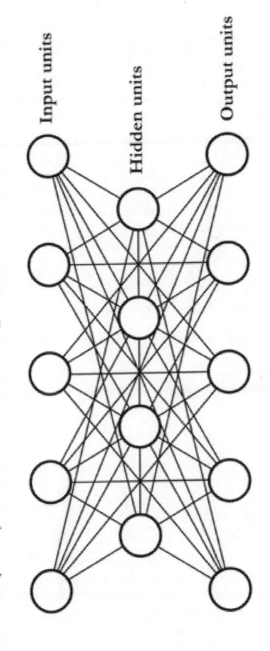

Input units

Hidden units

Ouput units

Figure 12

The model is impressive, and indeed based on the model by Garnham (1991), it can show communication between the input and output units, and the 'hidden units' that lead to distributed encoding or information storage—see figure 12.

This system mirrors the way the brain is wired. Rather than memory being in one cell, it can be recorded in any given number of cells/units that may or may not be distributed throughout the neuronal network. The system consists of elementary units that receive transmission from exteroceptors. The system also has hidden units that do not directly receive information from exteroceptors but instead deal with processing within the brain. These are the secondary sub-units that appear to process in parallel to others. Thus an excitation in one unit can trigger excitations in parallel units.

Although developments within PDP aid the understanding of how the brain works, because connectionist based machines are closed systems; in that, they cannot incorporate into themselves anything that is not programmed before hand by a human, they have to follow rules for example, Generalised Delta Rule (GDR) and thus cannot operate outside the system.

The human brain however, is an open system that interacts with the physical and social environment, synthesizing new information and making adaptive changes at random. So although the human brain has certain characteristics in common with mechanised connectionist systems it has emergent properties i.e. is capable of emitting emergent constructs, thus is not totally predicable as computers or robots are.

It is for this reason that despite the rather productive nature of computer type connectionism and its proliferation in terms the technology boom—world wide web, robotic limbs, brain chips and androids; with the hardware and software to support it, such technology it still searching for answers within neurophysiological principles on which to base future developments. According to Medler (1998, p. 64) a third generation connectionism should use 'neuro-morphic networks' as models to transcend the simplified components, layered architectures, and limited scale of the first and second generation networks.

By far one of the most important contributors to this multidisciplinary approach to cognition is Hebb (1949) 'the theory of trace decay' and the Hebbian postulate of learning, particularly within the biological branches of connectionism. Hebb suggested that interacting clusters or networks of neurons could be the basis of short and/or long term learning. Referring back to figure 12, Garnham (1991), the excitation of one unit can reverberate with another causing several units to activate in unison. Hebb however did not regard this as a site for the embedding of memory. Nonetheless, as discussed earlier, although the parallel activation of neurons does not necessarily develop into a LTM memory trace it will I suggest represent STM and may last up to 30 seconds without actually leaving a LTM trace. A process for which I suggest neurophysiological underpinning in chapter 4 and 6, where both short and long term memory can be placed within the first and second order messenger system of neuronal activity. Theories such as Hebb's have not only had an enormous impact on the social science branches of cognitive sciences, they still have had the most influential impact on artificial intelligence models. I hope my contributions are as useful, particularly those suggesting the rehearsal loop to be associated with 'cell assemblies/excitation cluster' and that of the first and second messenger system at the synapses being representative of STM and LTM.

Vernon et al (2006) outline some of the more recent developments within cognitive sciences, particularly the emergent paradigms of artificial intelligence that draw on neuroscience for inspiration, in order to develop a computer system with autonomous mental capabilities. It was found that cognitive systems had developed but could not reproduce ontogenetic development of the human brain. The emergent systems are the most dynamic, based on the connectionism of neurophysiology and the social constructionism of genetic epistemology as discussion here. What seems to be important is the development of a system that is not based on rules and laws that govern its behaviour, so that it has to adapt, with fewer *a priori* rule governed processes self-modification is more likely. We can now synthesis human biology with metal, or at least form connections between the brain's neurotransmission and receptor pads and/or microchips. For many the feat was rather scary in the beginning but like most resources we have learned to use the knowledge to advance robotic limb movements and computer cursors by thought. The union between the brain and the artificial intelligence of the computer has a long history and I hope any insights I have developed here will aid developments in the field and aid the continuity of it.

Chapter Eight

Agency-structure in social spaces: Reflexive practice & personal development planning

This paper developed from feedback from students on a BA (Hons) Early Childhood Studies Degree who were concerned the degree did not have practitioner status unlike the sister Foundation Degree. The romanticised liberal notion of higher education had become stale. As a new member of staff my knowledge of the sector was becoming more lucid. With a background in sociology, psychology and education the theoretical knowledge base was in place but needed linking to practices within educare. This is where the research began. Building on the portfolio of competences I acquired studying a PGCE-HE and Master of Arts in Education, Advanced Studies; and a sheet of competences left by previous staff, extensive mapping was undertaken to the BA (Hons) Degree in an effort to procure for it practitioner status. Key transferable skills were added to the mapping task as part of a government initiative outlined in the White Paper (DfES, 2003), consolidating competences aimed at graduate employability. As a Teaching Fellow in a Faculty of Education, I was responsible for developing a skills portfolio for the Early Childhood Studies Degree. Student discussion groups, questionnaires, consultations with staff, as well as information from the Early Childhood Studies Network and placement mentors all feed into the development of the portfolio of competences. Monitoring the process led to some interesting discoveries. In terms of sites of agency, Network members, staff, mentors and students have had an enormous impact and changes implemented. However, the process of developing a portfolio of skills has had its drawbacks. Some students have suggested whilst early years practitioner skills such as reflexive practice are desirable the breath of skills to develop when generic skills for employability are added including growth in the sector in terms of youth work and multi-agency working is an erroneous task. There are now five pathways through which students progress to their desired career tailored to the needs and strengths of individual student groups (CWDC, November, 2009).

Keywords Reflexive Practice, Personal and Professional Development Planning, Early Years Education, Self-reflexive Learning and Self-management, Agency-structure in Social Spaces

By way of an introduction

Monitoring the changes in curriculum and the processes of delivery within HE was quite unique as many of the changes were signalled from the bottom up i.e. came from practitioners and students. Thus rather than outcomes being tick-box type requiring closed responses; although the learning outcomes are academic, National Occupational Standards (including cross-sector units covering the Common Core Values) and Children's Workforce Development Council (CWDC, 2008) guided as an 'Integrated Qualifications Framework for Children and Young People', the evidence accumulated is based on student needs, context, interests and self-reflexive learning documented as part of the personal development planning process, back-up by written assignments therefore allowing students to bring together academic theoretical knowledge and practical experience from placement or work. The latter ensure that rather than practices remaining mixed and wide-ranging they can in addition be emergent, fluid and relative to practitioner context and needs. Indeed, the development of the five pathways through which the early years professional works, once again ensures that each student can study a pathway that suites his/ her requirements (CWN meeting, 5th November, 2009). Moreover, this amount of flexibility brings with it a certain amount of choice and agency that is important if students are not to be alienated from their daily practices.

Self-reflexive learning and education pedagogy

Educational pedagogy concerns itself with the successful practice of teaching and learning. By successful it is implied that the outcome for the learners is progressive with a degree of enhanced learning and development. One method of facilitating a successful outcome for learners is to engage in reflective practice. Reflective experience was first used as education pedagogy by John Dewey (1916). Dewey believed that life was an experiential journey in which we come up against problems that we need to solve. To solve problems we use thinking. In this way for Dewey, we unite the brain and the body, theory and practice. Through the thinking process in which past experience is brought into the equation as a critical measurement and catalogue of experience to choose from as a guide for ongoing actions, we can reach a state of reflection that involves a critical review of our actions. But beyond this state even, Dewey's reflective experience, involves experimentation and extensive analysis and evaluation of a problem in which all things are considered and hypotheses/theories are tested. One might call Dewey's reflective experience 'the retroductive method' of investigation—reflexivity (Lisle, 2000). Dewey's reflection was theorised as a means of change-action for social reform as well as educational reforms.

For Dewey then, reflective experience is distinct from the practice of thinking because like the scientist the reflective practitioner employs careful examination of the situation testing hypotheses stepping back and taking a holistic view before developing a plan of action for which to tackle a problem. Because of the rigour no doubt, Dewey's action framework for change greatly influenced the work of Argyris & Schön (1996). These two theorists developed a model for change-action that could be used to change any institution and/or organisation, and in addition, their model involved a distinction between theory and action and consists of two theories of action not just one. The first is 'theory-in-use' which is habitual actions that have become routine but of which we are not aware; and espoused theory (including values and beliefs) that we convey to others we believe our action to be. Their model also involves two types of learning: single and double loop learning. Both are ways of solving problems but with different outcomes. Their model for change-action revolves around the notion of solving problems for the benefit and development of institutions and organisations. The authors define single and double loop learning thus:

> "By single-loop learning we mean instrumental learning that changes strategies of action or assumptions underlying strategies in ways that leave the values of a theory of action unchanged . . . By double-loop learning, we mean learning that results in a change in the values of theory-in-use, as well as in its strategies and assumptions. The double loop refers to the two feedback loops that connect the observed effects of action with strategies and values served by strategies." (Argyris & Schön, 1996, p. 20-21).

Indeed, in single loop learning, a problem is identified and dealt with using existing theories of action (espoused theories) that leads to micro linear means-ends relational outcomes. The theory, values and policies that govern actions (governing variables) are not changed, knowledge-in-use and practice works as means-ends action. In double loop learning, problems are examined in a wider context. It involves taking a wider view assessing the macro objectives, policies and everyday taken-for-granted-routines that govern the single-loop model means-ends action. For example, when student attendance becomes an issue, monitoring attendance through the introduction of registers might lead to better attendance because students know that once this line of action is taken they have to attend to be entered for examinations (a confabulated scenario).

This is single loop learning based on existing routinised policy and practice. In double-loop learning, the situation would be viewed in a wider context: Questions such as 'Why do students not attend lectures?' would be asked and 'Is attendance in lectures fundamental to student learning and development?' What *ways* rather than *way* can we increase attendance, would be theorised and student motivation for example for attending and not attending would be examined. Teaching practice would also be questioned for example, what teaching methods are being used? And the context variables from outside the institution would be evaluated as influences of student attendance. In this way, single loop learning is about solving problems in the short term but double-loop learning is about changing practice for long-term use, which includes changes in institutionalised knowledge that has become the taken-for-granted social reality (Berger & Luckmann, 1966). The latter is more indicative as to what constitutes reflective practice. Indeed, distant learning and teaching methods are used extensively by some universities for example, the Open University, and some students may never attend tutorials, day schools or lectures but are very successful with their study because of the variety in teaching and learning strategies afforded by the breath of E-learning strategies the Open University offers. Education can be globally administered.

Schön (1987) later in life, focused in on the theory of reflective-action particularly as educational pedagogy making a distinction between reflection-in-action, 'thinking on one's feet' and 'reflection-on-action', thinking about practice after the event. For Schön, reflection-in-action' comes about through *intuition* and can lead to 'knowing-in-practice' a state reached when actions have become routinised and automatic and the practitioner spontaneous and professional. Sometimes, a practitioner's actions become so routinised that 'knowing-in-practice' is implicit and hidden and the practitioner needs to reflect once more on practice to obtain the underlying meaning of the actions again. In this way, both 'reflection-in-action' and 'reflection-on-action' are ways of maintain a level of practice conducive to learning and development for the practitioner and the learner. Tubbs (2000) suggests that 'knowing-in-practice' is enough based as it is on intuitive knowledge gained within the practitioner's field over a number of years. Although Tubbs might have a point reflexive practice is deemed the better option as it involves a re-evaluation of the situation in spirals of action on a continual basis therefore removing some of the doubt one might have about a particular situation. Tubbs (2000, p. 176) goes on to suggest that using reflexive practice as a teacher may lead to the state of self as a 'comprehensive teacher' but that it takes:

'[S]pirit or courage to risk losing herself in her service to her students. Secondly, that a truly comprehensive education may well be actual in the spirit of the classroom which respects dilemmas and works within the limits which contradiction and paradox determine for us . . . but the spirit of comprehensive teacher deserves to be pushed further than the "comfort zone" of reflection . . . to look at the dilemma of independence and dependence which is the self.'

Again, I have empathy for Tubbs on this point but I suggest that just as every investment in the early years to give children a good start in life has its benefits so too does the reflexive practice one takes to the teaching zone so that by the end of the first year at university your students are more independent learners which frees up time for staff rather than staff being inundated by constant requests for one-to-one tutorials because the students couldn't understand what went on the in the lecture theatre. One can then get on with the task of self-reflexive learning if one so wishes: I do. Philosophy is a beautiful thing—we all like to make predictions of the kind it takes scientific knowledge many moons to accumulate enough evidence to prove.

In addition, whilst intuitive knowledge might very well be the initial reflexive conversation with a situation somewhat like Locke's empiricism as a stream of consciousness (William James) living on Mead's knife-edge present, once it becomes routinised as Schön states when the situational context variables change (i.e. E-teaching and Learning) then so to must the routinised practices. Thus whether one wants to move beyond reflexive practice of comprehensive teacher or not at some point you will revisit the practice otherwise get left behind whilst others move in to an E-library, in an—E-university.

The double-loop model of learning when united with the theory of reflective-practice is useful for describing the sorts of practice practitioners are involved in, in education today. Through the use of action research and reflective practice, the theory, values and policies that govern action (governing variables) are questioned leading to change in government policy at institutional and practice based levels. Reflective practice has become so ubiquitous, that student learning is couched in reflective practice as a meta-cognitive learning style, and used for monitoring personal development and planning. In addition, student reflective practice as a trainee practitioner's pedagogical tool, involves double loop-learning. The development of professional skills involves using reflective practice to: observe, reflect on, plan for and act on plans in relation to issues and initiatives that can be analysed and evaluated in the national as well as the local (work experience) context; in relation to individual child development issues and issues around educational policy and practices (Lisle, 2000, 2005). Reflective practice has been fully integrated into the modular structure of degree programmes in the early year's workforce, including those on which I teach and also it is fully operational as part of work placement experience which is what this study is monitoring. Thus, for students, double loop learning is both applied to the work experience context as well being interwoven with their personal development planning, involving academic, personalised key transferable as well as work experience based skills, reflective practice being just one of those skills (Standards for Early Years Professional Status (EYPS) (CWDC, 2008). In this way, reflective practice is used as a meta-cognitive learning style for reflection for example, on how best to assess strengths and weaknesses and how to acquire the skills beneficial to personal and professional development (in line with standards that ensure Effective Practice and Professional Development, CWDC, 2008).

Reflective practice or emancipatory reflexive practice

Schön suggests that the effective professional needs to be self-monitoring and self-critical, that is, be a reflective practitioner. He refers to reflective practice as 'reflection in action', reflecting on the teaching and learning process for example whilst on the job. It involves internal dialogue, reflection, about the social context and appropriate action as it unfolds—learning in practice, and in the same instance learning through practice (Schön, 1983; Elliott, 1991; Eastcott, 1992). Through reflective practice, we acquire the skills of reflective practice and of the task at hand. This is why Ronald Barnett (1992) suggests that reflective practice has general validity and applicability to all students because reflective practice learning becomes part of the student's repertoire of transferable skills. The very skills demanded of them by prospective employers:

> 'Reflective practice is a vehicle of general utility, likely to command wide support in understanding what the development of the student's critical abilities might mean . . . it offers insight into the way in which skilled professionals are able to carry out informed interventions in the situations which they encounter in professional practice' (Barnett, 1992, p. 194).

Reflective practice is informed action; i.e. summarises drawn from the complexities of the situation. It indicates that professionals who use it are able to call upon a range of strategies in those situations, evaluate them then act. Reflective practice is in short, 'knowledge-in-use', (Schön, 1983). According to Schön (1983) and Barnett (1992), reflective practice involves interpersonal communication. Professionals listen to clients, evaluate what has been said along with existing knowledge claims, and then they reason with the clients in light of existing evidence. In doing this, they have to make sense of the problem, engage in effective communication, offer alternative solutions and act on the chosen one. Thus, by making students more aware of what reflective practice is and developing it, will equip them with reflective practice as a transferable skill and induce in them the ability to acquire deep learning and autonomous learning of the subject matter of their chosen discipline. Through reflection, students learn to 'evaluate knowledge claims and form their own, backed up by reasoned argument and empirical evidence' (Barnett, 1992).

Reflective practice is small-scale Marxist revolutionary activity—practical-critical activity aimed at producing change and is thus emancipatory. When the reflective practitioner critically analyses and evaluates a problem and/or government or local initiative it usually involves some kind of change to solve the problem. It may involve fine-tuning practice to meet expectations of initiatives or fine-tuning initiatives to meet expectations of context. As part of the individual practitioner's cycle of reflection, it involves 'reflection-in-action' (Schön, 1983), a process of reflective conversation to understand the situation and to change it in light of reflection (Elliott, 1991; Eastcott, 1992). Reflection-in-action not only brings about changes in material ways but also changes in intellect. According to Newman & Holzman, (1993) it is through practical-critical activity that humans experience the world and in the experiencing of it become change by it and in return can change it through the ideas that come to them whilst engaged in practical-critical activity:

Marx's dialectical historical materialism (Chapters 2 & 3 this publication). Reflective practice is one element in the cycle of action research.

Many educationalists use the term 'reflexive' rather than 'reflective'. Whilst reflective explains the mental activity involved in reflective practice, reflexive practice does this and emphasises the way in which our reflective practice works back in an effectual manner. In this study therefore, I will be using the term reflexive practice to prevent confusion.

To summarise, self-reflexive learning has a long history in education as well as professional occupations such as social work. More recently academics such as Gosling (2004, p. 9) see the value of self-reflection suggesting it allows the student to obtain greater meaning about their learning and the processes it involves. In this study students and staff within the subject area of Early Years Care and Education are afforded agency as self-reflexive learners involved in the process of developing not only themselves as learners but also as agents in the development of the subject area and the context of early years practices in an economic, cultural, global and international context. In this respect their self-reflexive learning involves personal and professional development planning to be over against the world in an ever-increasing global risk society.

Government guidelines for personal development planning

These research proposals although started as a response to student feedback about their learning and career context, became interlaced with government 'Guidelines for HE Progress Files', here translated in to personal development planning (PDP) in Higher Education, particularly in relation to the Key Skills Framework and the Key Notes Project (2004). It then developed into an evaluation of student's perceptions of Personal Development Planning and how they felt it should be integrated into Early Childhood and Young People Studies as a subject area. The intention for the main study was to propose a taxonomy of skills specific to the Early Childhood Studies Sector in terms of practitioner competences following mandatory statutory occupational standards, with generic overtones in terms of the expanding early years pathways and service sector as well as transferable key skills that could be developed then recorded as part of Personal Development Planning within a portfolio with the aim of improving employability.

Guidelines were prepared to assist universities and colleges of HE develop and introduce progress files to promote documented and enhanced learning. It was proposed Progress Files should consist of two things: 1) Monitoring of progress and 2) A recording mechanism/transcript (National Curriculum of Inquiry in HE, 1997). This translated to a transcription of student achievement (CV/Portfolio) and a means of monitoring, reflecting on and building on personal development (National Committee of Inquiry in HE, 1997). Universities set about introducing PDP across higher education institutions in 2003/4, and 2004/5 and then the Key Skills framework 2005/6 and 2006/7—I was one of several Teaching Fellows in a university that adopted the scheme, my task area set out above, although there were a number of areas covered: Employability, Assessment, E-learning, PDP and Key Skills, Teaching and Learning, Disciplinary Knowledge.

Personal development planning (PDP) was a title used by some but not all universities. As David Gosling (2004) points out PDP is one preferred by most institutions, as it tends to encapsulate variant definitions: Gosling defines PDP as:

'A set of activities which engages students in reflecting on their learning and personal goals, creating personal records, planning and monitoring progress towards the achievement of personal objectives and which is intended to improve the capacity of students to articulate their learning goals for themselves and to communicate the outcomes of their learning to others, for example to academic staff and employers.' (Gosling, 2004, p. 5).

Thus, Gosling's definition encompasses what was set out in the government White Paper, 2003, paragraph 4.7 (cited in Gosling, 2004, p. 6) concerning a system for recording learning that is durable, accurate and 'helpful' to students in their endeavours to gain future employment. An adaptable and most importantly, equitable and user-friendly system needed to be developed. Student learning autonomy yet sense of understanding their learning experience and the meaning behind it in addition to quality and measurable outcomes in terms of employability were the focus. What this amounted to was a system of recording personal improvement in terms of academic skills, subject knowledge skills and personal transferable key skills, later shorted to transferable skills (O'Connell, 2004, p. 15-27). What O'Connell also found from the evaluation of initial recording of achievement studies, a for-runner to PDP, was that student engagement with PDP had to be at a level of engage that employed meta-cognitive skills such as reflective-learning otherwise 'Recording of Achievement' had little impact. Self-motivated learners tended to engage with the process more, which was accounted for, as their desire to succeed.

Nonetheless, based on the principles of behaviourist linear learning the monitoring of achievable learning objectives is a motivator in itself and this is one of the theoretical models that underpins the modular system of education. In this respect, PDP of learning objectives using self-reflexive learning as a monitoring skill has beneficial qualities and thus as part of the quality assurance criteria the reflexive practice of PDP should potentially generate documentary evidence that can be used to enhance employability and personal development. For staff in Higher Education, PDP purportedly aids student tracking (Assiter, 2004, p. 31), and future development of learning programmes based on the student's level of understanding and needs. Likewise, involving work placement staff in the profiling process aids the synchrony of skills development with workplace transferable qualities.

One issue that needs attention, Assiter (2004, p. 33) highlights the issue concerning learning outcomes and workplace competences, suggesting that they are not fully interchangeable. Learning outcomes for example tend to be theoretically based if not knowledge based whereas competences tend to be practice skills based. Bearing this in mind, when developing a portfolio of skills/competences the issue was addressed by integrating theoretical knowledge and practice skills development using evidence from both theory and practice to substantiate competences. In this way, students were able to monitor their development of learning objectives on the modules that made up the course whilst at the same time the learning objectives could be taken into student work placements as a portfolio of skills to develop and be assessed by placement mentors as competences. It presents one of the biggest issues for staff, students and mentors. However, under the direction of Marxian-Vygotskian model of learning the unity of theory and practice is essential for learning: Theory is equivalent to abstract knowledge and practice is equivalent to concrete knowledge and both when brought together aid concept formation (see Lisle, A, 2000, 2006 and this book chapters 2 & 3).

Universities across the UK developed different systems for recording personal development. Some universities developed electronic journals situated on Intranet sites that both students and academics have access to, similar to what has now become the 'Blogging' sites we see such as 'MySpace', 'Facebook' and 'Mystuff'(OU). Whereas generic interfaces like MySpace and Facebook tend to record the journey through life in diary format (documenting individual's worldviews as it were), and as well acting as interfaces/portholes for socialising, the academic learning journals record skills development as a self-reflexive process that makes up the learning journey of the individual. Some universities still used paper-based portfolios as a means of collating evidence of skills development similar to the one I helped to develop as a Teaching Fellow. Liverpool University developed a web based electronic system called 'The Liverpool University Student Interactive Database (LUSID)' for monitoring student achievement, in terms of PDP as did Glamorgan University (2004). The E-journals consist as most do of a transcript recording student achievement and a means of monitoring built upon reflective practice (Strivens, 2004, p. 82).

Monitoring learning outcomes as well skills in a portfolio gives students 'clearly defined goals' (Assiter, 2004, p. 34). It appeared to me that as modules were driven by the assessment of learning objectives then the documenting of them in a portfolio seemed logical. The first mapping task undertaken therefore was of learning objectives that could be converted into transferable skills. The next step was to decide the evidence that would map onto learning objectives and transferable skills. What developed was a system of mapping subject knowledge based skills and key transferable skills onto existing programmes of study in a way that would utilise the structure of learning objectives that were in existence. Where learning objectives were not compatible they were phased out and new ones developed that could be integrated into the newly developing system for recording and monitoring purposes and the enhancement of student learning. The task was complicated by the fact that not only were there changes implemented on a generic basis across university in terms of transferable key skills, but also there were extensive changes ongoing in the early years sector in terms of developing programmes that equipped students with practitioner competences based on the mandatory national occupations standards. Between 2003 and 2007 the degree programme was mapped twice if not three times whilst delivery continued in terms of teaching and assessment. Since then, the entire curriculum has developed and expanded into five pathways of learning for students studying for employment with the early years and young people's employment sector in the UK.

Issues and problems arose that needed to be addressed as the subject knowledge skills and competences and transferable skills were mapped. For example, in monitoring and evaluating the curriculum to implement changes questions arose: If the degree is to be consumer led, what do consumers want: students, government, parents/guardians/carers, Early Years Service Sector Institutions? Also, what is successful PDP? Is it the synthesis of utilitarian (career orientated) and generic skills development? After numerous consultations with staff, students and members of the Early Childhood Studies Network over a 5 to 6 years period the development of taxonomy of skills for employability in the early year's sector, with generic overtones (safety net) seemed the main foci lending to the development of the five pathways of learning the multi-disciplinary curriculum.

Monitoring the development of reflexive practice skills and PDP of subject knowledge skills/competences and complementary transferable skills at University level was as follows for each student:

- *Level 4: Identifying and reflecting on existing skills and identifying skills needed*
- *Reflecting on progression through module structure*
- *Recording progress*
- *Level 5: Identifying career opportunities*
- *Reflecting on progression through modules*
- *Recording progress/development*
- *Level 6: reflecting on aptitude and abilities for employment*
- *Providing summary of PDP as basis for references and career planning.*

Student engagement in self-reflexive learning and PDP were essential to the monitoring process and to ease the workload of university staff.

Reflexive practice in the early years sector

Within early years practitioner literature there were a number of authors who offered guidance on what was regarded as reflexive practice. Jaeckle (2004) for example offers a rendition of what a reflexive practitioner is as well as the behaviours/meta-cognitive skills needed. Jaeckle suggests that reflexive practice entails 'Reflecting on the Key Elements of Effective Practice (KEEP). Similar to the guidance above, it involves assessing existing skills and identifying areas for further development. Jaeckle's formula is also interest motivated in that skills development is in terms of areas of interest. Both the personal and professional development of the individual is incorporated into the framework. Thus as with level 5 above, subject knowledge from academia can be integrated with that from work placements/ workplace practices. Jaeckle further discusses the process of reflexive practice as a way of improving practice through personal reflection and she regards it has a form of self-management. Some of the areas she suggests practitioners engage their reflexive skills are: relationships with parents, carers, children and colleagues and children's learning and development.

In the same book Spratt (2004, p. 295-307) and Moyles & Adams (2004, p. 308-317) outline the role of the manager in the context of early years provision. Using documentation such as the Every Child Matters (2003) policy and the National Occupational Standards that regulate the provision of day care (2003), of which there are14 standards, and the Curriculum Guidance for the Foundation Stage (2000) the authors enter into a discourse that summaries the way these documents guide practice within the early year's sector of employment. Miller, Cable & Devereux (2005) chapter 5 discuss *'Reflection in Practice'* outlining the role of reflection as a means of professional development and the way theoretical knowledge can be brought into practitioner spaces to develop evidence of competences in practice. It is the evidence for the competences outline in the National Occupational Standards and other government and early year's practitioner documentation that affords those working within the early year's profession the professional status they deserve. Through developing evidence of practice and practitioner skills, practitioners thus accord themselves professional status. However, does this documentary evidence procure an ascribed therefore given identity or is it negotiated therefore achieved involving agency which at the same, means that early year's workers are developing early year's institutions as a worthy and viable social institution of benefit to society?

Voices voices everywhere: Turmoil within early years

Not all those working within the early year's sector agree with the introduction of specified criteria just outlined in the latter section as the best way for improving early year's practitioner identity or their sector of employment. Jayne Osgood for example (2006a) argues against 'performativity', that is, a set of behaviours that are standardised and presented in documentation as professional practices against which all staff are judged, monitored and on which pay is performance related. Osgood refers distinctly to the kind of scientific management brought in by the Conservative government with the Education Reform Act 1988. She suggests it amounted to central government maintaining authority and power over the curriculum and institutional practices but any responsibility for the outcomes in terms of SAT results were devolved to local authorities and the schools themselves: Usually referred to in psychology literature as the diffusion of responsibility (Milgram, 1974). Professionalism as a measure of performativity Osgood suggests is a masculinised construct as is the whole discourse and culture of scientific management, beliefs she holds as an influence of the work of Foucault. Osgood also cites the work of Du Gay (1996) and what he terms 'controlled de-control'; meaning teacher's autonomy and control over their work becomes more and more regulated by government policy and routinised whereby teachers become 'proletarianised' as their work is de-valued in this way.

I would suggest however that there are a number of problems associated with scientific management that are not just government directed. For example, managers are not Saints. The personnel who do the work do not necessarily benefit. Managers have been known to 'cream' the most desirable tasks for themselves rather than allocate tasks according to credentials or ability. In addition, Managers have also been known to allocate the outcomes of work done in terms of the highest performance expropriated to their own performativity. What Foucault would refer to as a mechanism of control and dehumanisation. Thus, whilst I agree with the notion that with scientific management comes less autonomy and control, it does not necessarily function in the interests of central government. There are mechanisms along the way such as levels of management that expropriate finance and performativity that stands in contrast to government wishes. In this respect I agree with Osgood that early year's workers have no homogeneous agenda and personnel in the early year's sector are oppressed two-fold, because just as they have no control over the documentation of the developmental review process that underpins performativity and as such are driven not just by the documentation that measures performativity but also they are oppressed by managers who stand to gain more if personnel do perform above and beyond normal performance levels as they drive staff towards PDP/CPD whilst expropriating financial gains and performativity.

In addition, nor should the early year's sector celebrate collectivity in terms of the old discourse that women are naturally intuitive, nurturing and emotional. To remove the notion of professionalism from early year's practices under the assumption that it is a male discourse is defunct. I say this because although Osgood (2006b) rightly outlines this particular section of the occupational structure as having a long history of marginalization and exploitation, I think to resort back to a status of value, as a workforce based on 'emotional-labour' is an acceptance of that labour as less than any comparable male-labour. It is an acceptance of a gender distinction based not even on biology such as genetic phenotype, indeed, as it would suggest that altruism is something that only females are endowed with. If this is the case, then females are the rightful guardians of society and living in a patriarchy would bring imminent danger to the human species.

Similarly, to suggest that professionalism is a male discourse implying that females are not rational, logical, efficient, enterprising and/or industrious is suggesting that females and males are too dissimilar to be one race. I recognise that females are biologically fettered to carry offspring and lactate which males cannot but outside of this are we really any different? Males impregnate, and are thus regarded as aggressive rather than being penetrably passive but professionalism itself is not I think tied to biology in this way whether it is stated to be a male discourse or not. Societies are full of females who would regard themselves as professional and should we really deny the early year's workforce this privilege?

As Peter Moss (2006) points out that the early year's workforce is needed for economic reasons (also see Ball, 2004 'Sociology of Education') and this has become apparent particularly in the last decade or so as the economic recession has had devastating consequences. More and more women are finding they have to work to help support the family and pay the family mortgage, a legacy of cheaper, larger mortgages at a time when it was thought growth in the housing market would not stop. The extended early year's service sector according to Moss 'requires improved education and higher-level qualifications' for staff (Moss, 2006, p. 30). In the ever-increasing global world we live not only are we open to scrutiny by national government bodies, but international organisations aim to influence institutions such as the early year's provision particularly when in a global world economic crises are global too and any exemplar practice in one country can play a role in the transfer of knowledge and practice to other countries. Fortunately in Britain the early year's workforce is amongst the best. According to the Organisation for Economic Cooperation and Development (OECD) most early year's workforces are divided into the education sector and care sector. In Britain, the latter encompass health care as well as social care i.e. social work. The collaborative and collective communication between these compartments is fluid and the new early year's provision will continue in that capacity although Moss suggests changes might mirror those of other countries, and it would appear the most recent changes in curriculum are certainly broader and include youth work and social work.

Within the early year's sector of care and education then, there are several voices all examining, analysis and evaluating present practices and statues in an effort to develop a programme of study that mirrors the sector's needs in terms of standards, values and practices and the needs of staff, clients and stakeholders. This process is not unique to the UK. A similar process is going on globally in response to OECD monitoring and the people working within the sector as change agents. What is developing then is a framework that reflects the involvement of students, staff, sector employees and employers, the government and research done by academics and practitioners globally. One particular piece of research that investigated different discourse about the future identity of early year's practitioners was that by Lobman & Ryan (2007) in the USA. The main aim of the study was to assess standards of practice in existing documents and those regarded as essential and carried out in the field by practitioners. The key principles and values that were found are:

1) *Community orientated service delivery,*
2) *An inclusive system—multi-cultural and multi-social context and ability;*
3) *Qualified professional staff with management skills,*
4) *Good working knowledge of child development,*
5) *A child/client-orientated curriculum, especially fun for learning,*
6) *Developmentally appropriate practice, a facilitative role to enable 'knowing and able child/client',*
7) *Curriculum content that is co-constructed (active learning in sensitive, caring culturally aware context)*
8) *Teacher characteristics such as skilled educator, command of subject knowledge, creative, caring, healthy, passion for the job, open to learning;*
9) *Thus a self-reflexive learner who is action research supportive and continuing professional development orientated.*

After reading the literature on the subject it appears these qualities are almost universal. Hargreaves & Hopper (2006) in Britain examined early years teacher's perceptions of their status 'The Teacher Status Project (2003)' and it appears that 'dedication, expertise and competence score high as well as a strong liking for children' (Hargreaves & Hopper, 2006, p. 172). These qualities give teachers a sense of self-esteem. The formalising of the foundation Stage with documentation such as the Curriculum Guidance and Foundation Stage Profile Guidance (2008) enhance the status of early year's workers to, but these authors suggest that if care and education are brought together as is expected under the ten-year strategy of the now Labour government (2001) then the occupation will be down-graded. It will mirror the system elsewhere such as Denmark and New Zealand where the status is that of a social pedagogue, after the Greek meaning of a social pedagogue. However, managerial skills in nurseries were valued, as was subject knowledge and the regulation of the occupation by the General Teacher's Council. All of which put early year's teachers at 1.2 of the 2001 Census category with social workers, solicitors, doctors and barristers. So the occupation procures status as such but in terms of wage levels early year's practitioners earn far less than those listed. In addition, if the occupation is extended to include social workers who have a similar status and nurses then these authors think it would devalued the occupation.

O'Keefe & Tait (2004) conducted an examination of the British Early Years Foundation Degree in an effort to attain Senor Practitioner Status for the Degree and also to shed light on what is happening in this sector across the British Isles. Their main focus was the introduction of reflective enquiry-based study as a means of enhancing the status of higher-level teaching assistants to enable them professional credibility as senor practitioners. The Foundation Degree is now Sector-endorsed with a unique taxonomy of professional skills specific to Early Childhood Studies in Education (DfES, 2002). McCorwick Davis (2005) explored the development of reflective practice skills of pre-service student teachers using art as a median for illustrating the teaching and learning process—similar to the notions of reflexive practice used by O'Keefe & Tait (2004) where students engage in constant self-appraisal and development. McCorwick Davis found that art allowed students to develop creative skills and imagination adding to their reflexive possibilities. It enhanced motivation and countered the formality of classroom routines. Gaining insight into the child's perspective and family were enhanced as well as ways of interacting within the school world. Schön (1983) refers to this as reflection-in and reflection-on practice' (O'Keefe & Tait, 2004, p. 29)—reflexive practice as outlined in detail in the above sections. Unanswered questions remain though, for example, 'how well does the Foundation Degree pedagogy and practice equip the students with skills to deal with multi-agency/multi-skilled practice?' and 'What is the practitioner's role in relation to young children?' (O'Keefe & Tait, 2004, p. 33). It appeared then the Foundation Degree in Educare as a pilot degree equipped students with the skills for education-based practice but not for the inter-professional roles aligned to the early childhood studies sector.

All of the above contributions to early year's knowledge base in terms of research and practice have led to the development of the now developing five pathways of studying to become an Early Year's Professional. Within this study I will be referring to two pathways: the BA (Hons) Degree in Early Childhood and a work placement based Foundation Degree in Early Childhood leading to Senior Practitioner Status.

The study

This study aims to develop an understanding of early year's practices from the student's point of view, including their perceptions of Personal Development Planning and how they feel it should be integrated into their chosen pathway such as the BA Early Childhood Studies Degree. The information obtained can help staff in the early years, higher education and other agencies realise those practices in terms of HE delivery, guided also by government initiative and research within the national and international area. The study started out as one associated with a BA Early Childhood Studies Degree but was later expanded to include perceptions of students studying other pathways to Early Years Professional Status, such as those studying a Foundation Degree as a work based route.

Objectives

1. *To critically reflect on the barriers and issues involved in the implementation of ECS curriculum with practitioner options in HE*
2. *To monitor and evaluate personal development planning for successful student employment in the Early Years Employment Sector*
3. *The resulting curricula development will inform a taxonomy of skills that offers professional credentials for ECS at HE level with a genera for cross sector employment (and will follow CWDC & NOS criteria)*

Methodology

The methodological approach used in the study is a mixture of qualitative and quantitative measures brought together through the process of triangulation. The information from work experience assessment documentation filled in by mentors and students, discussions with target groups of students and discussions with mentors and tutors, will be triangulated and then cross referenced with the learning outcomes of the academic programme of study, for example, work and/or placement based assessments that detail students' reflexive practice and their engagement with personal development planning. The triangulation/cross referencing method involves obtain information of the research focus topic using different research techniques and then comparing or bring together the information gathered from the three or more sources and assessing it for similarity of features in itemised variables in the discussions recorded using free-style note taking and/or from the information obtained from thematic questionnaires; workplace portfolio assessments and work/placement assessments.

The method of triangulation/cross referencing used will be based on the work of Stephen Gorard (2004) and to some extend that of O'Keefe & Tait (2004). 'Various reasons have been advanced for the use of combined methods triangulation, including increasing the concurrent, convergent and construct validity of research' (Gorard, 2004, p. 43); triangulation/cross referencing in this study is used to enhance reliability and validity of the data collected. The table below outlines the mode of student assessment across the three stages of the degree programme. In actuality all of the modules have assessments that can be used as evidence for practitioner skills as well as academic skills development with the generic synthesis of transferable skills. Thus Figure 1 (See figures at the end of chapter) serves to illustrate theoretically, the breath of data that could be used in the analysis however I focused on just one or two modules per stage of the degree programme, because the amount of data produced is far too much to document in this paper.

Ethical approval is obtained via consent of participants in line with the criterion published by BERA (2007). There are no experimental trials. The consent forms administered to the participants: students, mentors and tutors, inform them of their rights to retract information submitted in questionnaires or discussions at any time during or after the research: All participants remain anonymous. Any information obtained does not affect the student's final degree classification nor is it to be used for any purpose other than for this research study. None of the participants are harmed in any way. Over three hundred questionnaires were sent out across three institutions and 27 were returned.

The age range of participants who opted in by returning the questionnaire and filling in the consent form is 19 to 57 years old. The majority of students on BA (Hons) degrees are within the 19 to 29 years age range and from this group 13 participants returned a completed questionnaire. Within the 30 to 57 years age range, there are 8 participants and one student withheld age. The participants from the latter age range were studying for Foundation Degrees as this type of pathway best suited their needs having as they do 5 years or more practitioner experience. Six of the questionnaires completed at the onset of the study were not used as the questionnaire content changed and they became incompatible.

Members of staff and 5 mentors contributed to the data collected either via discussion or by adding comments on the student's portfolio documentation. The data presented here is presented in a way that students remain anonymous thus certain data will not be displayed such as module grades as it states in the table above. It is too easy to lose anonymity where certain data sets are chosen for evidence and analysis. Aggregating student grades for individual learning outcomes although productive still breaches anonymity and confidentiality when examining data across pathways and backgrounds. Thus, although the data could have been examined using this technique, it will not be displayed here.

The educational background of participants was mixed. Nine students between 19 to 37 years old had mathematics, English Language and Sciences GCSE grade C or above. A further 9 participants had English and Mathematics; 2 had English and Science, 1 had Mathematics Science and English Literature and a further student had a General National Educational Qualification that was none UK. Thus, half of the students could have taken the Primary Bachelor Degree in Education had they wanted. The participants had a mixture of 'A' levels, Certificate in Management with 'A' levels, BTEC National Diplomas, Cache Diplomas and/or NVQ level 3 that were also relative to age of participant.

In relation to employment history and participant development in terms of career, 11 participants worked within primary care and/or education either as Nursery Workers or SEN classroom assistants. Participants also had employment experience in the service sector such as retail and administration such as reception work and one participant was a Reprographic Technician. Workplace preferences were varied: NHS working on the children's ward, nursery work and/or primary education, classroom assistant, SENCO, HE and FE tutor, Social Work and Adoption and Educare Management. Placements within education were easy to acquire but none of the participants who wanted to progress into Social Work obtained placements within the Social Services. Nonetheless, work with Barbados where such institutions are linked to SureStart centres offered placements with experience of working with families in a similar capacity to social work and they are regulated by Ofsted as are Child Development Centres that also offered placements that are structured; mentor supervised with an element of family work particularly with children with Special Needs. One participant was doing voluntary work as a mentor and 2 participants from the Foundation Degree were working as SENCOs who then went on to become tutor/mentors on the Foundation Degree.

For the majority of students, engagement with personal development planning before entering higher education appears to have been by way of action planning of skills development. However, 15 of the participants had considered things like the fit between placement type, existing experience of their chosen career field and the progression from the former to the latter in terms of knowledge and experience needed. The latter student group had encountered development planning in employment (i.e. CPD). Four participants were still undecided about their career path and two students had not considered it.

Reflexive practice and PDP using portfolio development

Stage one students who responded to the questionnaire had the three main GCSEs, Maths, English and Science and followed the 'A' level route into higher education and study on the BA in Early Childhood Studies. This could indicate any number of things. Their desire to work with young children however was given by both as a core motivator. Both students stated that they preferred working with young children from 3 to 8. Information presented in the questionnaires (see data table) showed progression in engagement with reflexive practice (RP) and personal development planning (PDP) of skill enhancement for employment within the Early Childhood Sector. Both students' employment history gave no indication of prior employment in the early year's sector. One student aspired to the teaching profession and the other social work. Both had work placements in schools. The fit between work placement choice and end result—career choice was apparent for the teacher orientated student but for the student who wanted to go into the social work profession it became apparent by comments indicating that experience with children was essential for social work together with a mature attitude to family life. Both students believed structured guidance with personal development planning was essential. Both chose PGCE as their postgraduate study. The pathway to this was seen as the completion of the degree. What is apparent about these two students is that one will follow a designated route to primary education with elements of ascribed status and thus identity (PGCE) whilst the other is striving to forge a pathway into social work using evidence based practiced as a student to acquire some credibility. The evidence developed from the student's site of agency within the early year's sector. In this way the student is also creating a space for agency as an early year's practitioner and at the same time extending the field for early year's practitioner employment.

However, planning transferable skills in terms of academic and work placement skills rather than being influenced by career choice and 'space of agency development'; was sequential and not a holistic approach to planning development. This was the tendency across those students who responded to the questionnaire as well those who did not which, for example, an examination of course work handed in for assessment by students generally showed development tended to be seen as engagement in action planning for transferable skills; academic and placement type skills and the input was formally structured at module level as learning outcomes. Both student respondents stated the Self-Management & ICT Skills development module that incorporated Personal Development Planning (PDP) within it as their source for personal development planning. Within this module action planning for skills development is highly structured. Of the 350 or so students taught this module over a period of four years only a few engaged in personal development planning beyond action planning pre-specified skills. Several students filled in the work placement skills compendia that matched theoretical learning objectives with equivalent practice based skills. At stage one the work placement compendia helps students to structure the portfolio for the placement skills developed. It consists of eight sheets for stage one, one for each of the eight modules and one sheet for overall reflexive-learning in the form of self-evaluation. Each sheet details the learning objectives/outcomes, with space for the inputting of grades obtained for the module, competence evidence generated can be described and placed behind the sheet with a further column for mentor comments.

Figure 2 contains learning objectives/outcomes for the practitioner module at stage one that I taught for four years. Attached to the back of this sheet were observations with reports detailing areas of development, observation technique used, developmental details such as cognitive, social and emotional or physical development including comments on student's role in the data collection process and areas which needed further work. For example the student to whom figure 2 refers wrote in her report "To enhance my practice I will write what I am observing in note form next time so that I can focus more on what the child is doing" . . . "From this observation I achieved my aims as child took part in a listening activity and responded to the instructions given" . . . "After observing an activity I planned I realised that part of my role was assessing children's development shown by the way they engaged with the activity" . . . "I had to change the role play area because some of the children couldn't reach the post office desk or write using the crayons" . . . . "I found that time and event sampling were the best ways for observing behavioural incidents", and so on. Figure 3 is an adapted version of the student's work changed to maintain anonymity of student, staff, institution and children involved.

The example in figure 3 is typical of any nursery and without doubt happens when children join a new social group and have to learn new rules. To deal with the child the student has used the reflexive cycle. She has *observed* a problem: A child expresses frustration and anger at having to stand in line, disrupts others in the line and starts to damage property. The student has then written a report analysing and evaluating the incident: *reflection*. From the reflexive analysis she decides what the problem is: 'Allan has difficulty dealing with frustration and anger'. To help Allan with the behaviour the student decides on a *plan of action*: 'the child should follow rules, and he will be guided on th*is*'. In the report the student suggests that guidance using the nursery rules will help him achieve the social skills of expressing frustration and anger in an appropriate manner without hurting others or damaging property. She has quoted theory to support her analysis and evaluation and has also drawn comparison between Allan's inappropriate behaviour and the behaviour of a child who has achieved these social skills. As a follow up I would expect the student to act on the plan to see if Allan responses in the desired way and then continue with another cycle of reflection dependent on the outcome.

As it states on the competence sheet the student conducted an activity aimed at communication skills, the task being to get the children to listen to instructions. The task thus was not only part of the curriculum for language and communication it very aptly served the purpose of dealing with Allan's social skills development in that it allowed the student to guide him with communication—listening to instruction—which he did not do during the incident the student documented. Thus, the student's plan of action was followed through with guidance using listening task and following instruction tasks and this time she achieved the desired response, the next step being to transpose the communication development to that of following rules that are also instructions. Figure 4 is a copy of the Instructions and listening task used.

The mentor who added comments to the sheets suggested that they were limited. She felt that with each observation, "the student developed skills and each observation reported really needed an area for comments". It is clear from the documentation that the student was greatly supported by her mentor. As a tutor however I considered the student's paperwork and competence compendia to have met the criterion, including the reports and the student and tutor input. Additional support by a mentor of the kind suggested is extremely beneficial for students and can form part of the weekly/daily diary or log, or can be added to comments on the evaluation section of the observation. In terms of this present research study, it shows that although the student was new to early year's practices in that she was an 'A' level student, she acquired placement skills and she enjoyed the experience. The skills she acquired fit the standards for Early Years Professional Status 'Effective practice' S10 'Uses close, informed observation and other strategies to monitor children's activity, development and progress systematically and carefully, and use this information to inform, plan and improve practice and provision'. In this respect, the competence compendia appeared functional i.e. fit for purpose. However, across the whole cohort group there were mixed responses to the work placement compendia. For example, students with placements outside education competence development had to engage in emergent competence development and at stage one this proved difficult without structured support from placement mentors and has this was a pilot study not all placement types were formally structured with mentors.

At stage two the work placement module was called 'Professional Skills Development (Personal Development Planning)'. This built on the skills acquired studying at stage one—see figure 5.

Students at this stage focused more on the development of reflexive practice skills that make up the reflexive cycle by applying it in a variety of different ways, the cycle itself of course being a research cycle of reflexive practice (see chapter 2). As a research tool the reflexive practice cycle can be used for small-scale reflexive practice that occurs daily and that daily all elements of the cycle can be entered into from observations, through reflections to planning actions for implementation. The cycle can also be used for medium term use that might span a term or two weeks; and it can also be used for longer term reflexive practices that might even span years. The main aim of using the reflexive practice cycle is to consciously engage with practice and document plans, reflections and observations so that with each cycle you can see clearly what you are basing your future actions on in terms of those plans, reflections and observations as you go through each cycle of action. When the reflexive practice spans weeks it can be written as a work placement diary/log. This module allows for both short daily reflexive cycles as well medium terms cycles that are documented in a diary/log and long-term cycles that can flow into the research project development module. For example, the student's work to be outlined here shows all three examples of reflexive practice.

The students' assessment I want to highlight at this stage is that of a student whose career choice was social work. This student had a placement with Banardos Children Centre attached to a SureStart Centre. Initially the work done was voluntary and it brought the student so much satisfaction as a career move the degree was to inform the placement practices and vice versa. For the practitioner module and the research module the student chose to reflect on the role of family support worker; commissioned as the student was with 'befriending' and supporting three families within an ethnic minority community. Because the student was checked by me using the CRB system, both Banardos Children Centre and SureStart were satisfied with the arrangement. The first part of the assessment for this practitioner module was the development of a poster that mapped out an issue the student had to deal with in the work placement. The student had then to write 750-words explaining the content of the poster with references/bibliography for learning outcome one. Some of the references listed by the student appear as a bibliography attached to the text written and are also referenced on the compendia sheet. For purposes of space here however only the poster is included see figure 6.

The families the student was asked to 'befriend' were asylum seekers. The student chose to assess the issues the families face on a daily basis. One family the student befriended was from Sudan. Figure 7 contains extracts from the student's work (it has been reduced for the purpose of limited space and brevity). The structure of the report followed the reflexive practice cycle and addressed learning outcome two (See Reflexive Practice in figure 7). As can be seen the work the student did with the family was invaluable. Her reflexive practice skills were very commendable.

Figure 7 only shows one cycle of reflexive practice but the student did write a work placement diary/log containing analysis and evaluation of the children's needs relating theory to practice. The student was moved so much by this type of placement experience that she decided to continue the work with the families and thus followed this piece of coursework through into her research project. She interviewed the family adults with the aim of giving this section of the community a chance to have their voices heard and to improve the developmental needs of the children by supporting the families. At this level (level 5) the student felt knowledgeable enough to develop emergent practices and also to synthesis those she felt were applicable for the assessment criteria with those skills the Banardos and SureStart team mentored her with. For example, as a Befriender she developed listening skills (Barnett and Schön). She was working in an area that was very little understood and an area that such innovation was highly sought. Her evaluations of the situation in terms of the family and children's needs were a direct reflection of the situation they faced and the emergent support structures and counselling from the student were tailored to the family's requirements.

The student produced a wonderful personal develop plan with medium term goals (written with the aim of gaining skills to do her research project with rationale aimed at career development) and short-term goals (skills needed). Her choice of career is social work specialising in early childhood that she states in the course work and the latter is her long-term goal. The skills outlined in figure 8 and on the compendia sheet details skills that satisfy NOS. But as the student was not monitored by a mentor who was appointed by the university it is difficult to say at what level the student achieve the NOS standards. The course work however does satisfy the course requirements to progress onto level six and these examples of student work act as a pilot for the further development of the early year's degree with practitioner's status. From this course work you can see why there is a need for flexibility of compendia practitioner skills and this student did well to develop those skills she felt would benefit her in terms of future career prospects.

Explanatory notes, books, and journal references to support the various types of development accompanied the personal development plan. Many of the skills the student developed were emergent of practice rather than being ascribed by the programme objectives developed by university staff. Thus, student learning from level 4 to 5 changed from ascribed skills develop at level 4 to achieved and emergent skills development at level 5. In this way the student played an active role in the development of her professional practice, developing skills emergent of practice as an agent in the social space of 'social worker/Befriender' within the early years sector. What Marx outlined as the development of ideas from critiquing practical activity—ideas that are emergent of practice and lead to changes in practice so that human behaviour is less alienated within the human condition one finds oneself: What Schön and Argyris refer to as double loop learning. Not all students achieve this level of engagement in reflexive practices because many of them follow pre-set competences within education for example but this student took the plunge as one of few who worked outside of education. There were others who achieved this level of reflexive engage with their placement practices particularly in Child Development Centres but they did not consent to take part in this study. In the final and third stage of the BA (Hons) Degree Programme, students undertook a module to develop 'Professional Practice and Management in Care and Education' (which is also the name of the module) with PDP/CPD incorporated into it and a further module 'Research Skills and Reflexive Skills Applied' will be discussed here. See figure 9. However, all of the modules that make up the degree programme have relevance to practice in terms of the learning outcomes. The third practitioner skills development module builds on the stage two modules. It is presented as a portfolio with essay assessments supporting practices as evidence of competence acquire.

In response to the first learning outcome documented on the compendia sheet figure 9, the student wrote the assignment response contained in figure 11. Only excerpts are included here however for brevity. Firstly the student outlines the skills the role demands then she outlines the initiatives she uses as guidance to practice, focusing in on one she uses to evidence its influence on the developmental needs of children.

Evidence for learning outcome 3 of this module was presented as personal development plan in response to changes in legislation and the role of the practitioner. The personal development plan took the shape of a selection of tasks to be completed successfully as part of the role of effective management in care and education. As can be seen from the last paragraph of the student's text summarised here, she set herself the tasks of organising meetings between nursery staff and parents/carers. The task also involved communication skills—she wrote a letter to parents/carers; developed a poster for the cloakroom wall, liaising with staff to co-ordinate the meetings and involvement of parents in the nursery day thus developing partnership working skills. The wall poster is figure 10.

For her main dissertation work, the student decided to investigate what it would involve to synthesise private day care assessment used such as the Foundation Stage Profile Assessment and the assessments used by state run nursery staff that are attached to schools. The main idea for the study was to evaluate measurements of readiness in terms of the assessment used. The title was on the lines of 'Early Intervention Programmes Improve Readiness for School: How does intervention vary across the private sector of day care and the statutory in terms of Foundation Stage Profile used as Assessment?' The findings suggest that private day nurseries use the foundation Stage Profile for Assessment purposes but statutory day care can use the profile or a similar tool developed by the staff in the schools. The latter situation according to the student's study is non-satisfactory because where two forms of assessment exist as measurement for readiness the one developed by the school takes precedence and the assessments done using the Foundation Stage Profile are regarded as incompatible and the children assessed as less than ready for school which is a problematic situation for those children and their position in the school hierarchy of learning competence.

The flexible approach to personal development planning and learning outcome requirements thus allows students to tailor their learning with the help of mentors and staff in a way that their developmental trajectory is career orientated and individualised. The NOS achieved in each module as it shows in the compendia sheet top left-hand corner can vary for each student but across each stage and breath of module learning outcomes all of the NOS are achieved and evidence from the other modules feeds into the practitioner modules.

Thus across the three stages a student can quite easily achieve all of the NOS provided the student has a placement with a fully qualified mentor-practitioner. The difficulty for the students was to select the tasks they needed to do so that the variety of task provided enough evidence for all of the NOS/practitioners skills to be developed. This information was actually within the learning outcomes of the programme but needed highlighting for student use. This could be one of the reasons why the students found the paperwork daunting. It was new to them and the mentor and staff. But as a pilot document it could be further developed and refined. At level 6 some of the students come from the Foundation Degree and thus have Senior Practitioner Status. The course work presented here is that of such a student. Her aim to synthesis the assessment criteria for readiness between private and statutory sector day care once again shows the student's engagement with her social situation/space is one of agency and also one that involves double-loop learning as it will lead to changes in practice should she achieve her aims. I happen to know that several schools have now started using the Foundation Stage Profile as a measure of readiness of children for formal education.

Although she has initiated the changes in practice so that within her catchment area both private and statutory nurseries use the Foundation Stage Profile Assessment as a measure for readiness for formal education it is very difficult to suggest that she has in this instance moved from ascribed to achieved or emergent practices as the criteria within the Foundation Stage Profile was set by government policy. In addition, as Osgood (2006a) points out, when government engage in influencing educational practices up to this level of direction then any room for reflexive and emergent practices are secondary and yet for practices to be least alienating for practitioners it is best if they are emergent and flexible. And this is the dilemma and why there is no single unified group of practitioners with the early year's sector. As can be seen, they have competing needs. Nonetheless, as a practitioner within private day care the changes initiated by the student do actually lead to enhanced practices for herself and staff and increased self-esteem for the children and their parents. This in itself is a move in the direction suggested by Moss towards the development of a more professional status and enhanced identity for staff in private day care.

Responses from questionnaire

In the main, the responses from the questionnaire suggested that a flexible approach to personal development planning was desired. Reflexive practice was deemed a necessity, but because students on the degree programme wanted to work in different areas, flexibility allowed for directional variation accompanied by variation in module choice to facilitate the proposed final destination in terms of post graduate study, whether PGCE, DipSW, MSc in Social Work, Counselling specialising in early years, or even a Child Development Centre or SureStart Nursery Manager. Therefore the information contained in the questionnaires and that of the compendia assessment the students engaged in suggests that flexibility of competences developed with mentor support and an element of structure is desirable.

From discussion with students across the cohort groups there were mixed feelings. Students who had a background in early year's curricula did not desire the practitioner option as they felt they had already achieved many of the competences. It was also commented on that even with practitioner options at this level those students with Cache diplomas for example, 'wouldn't gain much', as their aim was to go on to do PGCE and 'practitioner skills would be gained whilst doing it'. For 'A' level students without prior practical experience of working with children the work placement competence compendium was deemed useful. As the students said in response to the questionnaire 'the placements help to bring together theory with practice' 'they are an essential part of the degree'. The placement opportunities at this point were not compulsory. What was emergent was that students at stage one, level 4 were ready to engage in action planning and using the reflexive practice cycle but were either unsure of or not ready to fully engage with personal development planning (PDP). It was felt by staff that the degree would retain the name personal development planning as this gave the activity the individuality it entailed and did not over emphasize the nature of the course in terms of professionalism. Nonetheless, as it was proposed the next academic year the BA was to incorporate Early Years Professional Status then Personal and Practitioner Skills Development was to be adopted as a title for the development of skills within the compendium.

In addition, it appeared from the questionnaire that student knowledge of module choices at stages two and three was lacking. For example, the personal development plan in the medium term involved negotiating module choices through the degree reflective of the desired outcome of the qualification in terms of postgraduate study. Some modules were for example more suited to social work whilst others were more suited to health care and others education. It was found necessary to introduce information of optional modules the students could choose from and this was done using an additional lecture session in the evening towards the end of semester two to give students an idea of the modules they needed to choose depending on their postgraduate study choice. Only at this point did students get a realisation of the meaning of medium term development planning. Before this point learning the basics of the discipline involved in the stage one modules was enough and even though I tried to incorporate the options information into the Self-management and ICT module student knowledge of the discipline was still evolving. However, within the early years sector itself there were changes occurring and one of those changes was a move towards a curriculum that all students studied regardless of final destination so that all students would be knowledgeable of all areas of the curriculum in the event that should they change occupation their training would be regarded as sufficient and no re-training would be deemed essential. Following on from this then, all of the NOS were to be concentrated into fewer modules and all modules were to be made compulsory.

Supporting student portfolio of personal development

Support for student personal development planning as a university endeavour presented itself as notes available on line as part of the 'The Keynote Project' that could be used across the three years of the degree. These notes were to form part of the structured learning for PDP starting with level 4: to help students identify, reflect on and record existing skills and identifying skills needed for progression through modules, level 5: Identify career opportunities, reflecting on progression through modules, recording progress and development and level 6: reflecting on aptitude and abilities for employment and provide a summary of PDP as basis for references and career planning. In addition to the generic notes I piloted notes to support PDP on the BA programme. Student engagement with those I piloted would suggest that the level of progression expected by government documentation is sustainable and pitched at the correct level. Issues arose when Keynote Project Documentation for PDP was brought together with subject knowledge documentation for PDP. Not all students for example could plan their future careers or synthesis both types of PDP. At level 4 the action planning of personal goals was structured with learning outcomes modularised, listed and assessed with flexibility in terms of personal strengths and weaknesses. Thus when considering development needs in terms of level 5 and 6 modules students wanted to build on outcomes of strengths they were unsure of, because assessment was mainly summative. In addition, as student engagement with academia in the first year is often secondary to the development of personal social support structures in a new changing environment away from familiar people and surroundings, engagement with formative assessment was shrugged. Module choice lectures were set up with average student engagement. But even at level 4 students need to have a basic idea about their career choices in order to make module choices. As stated, most students at level 4 engage satisfactorily with action planning but many are not ready to engage with career choice planning preferring instead to keep their options open.

PDP, placement availability & post-graduate goals

Only two of the returned questionnaires were from level 4 students. Post-graduate career choice seemed straightforward in that, if you want to work in education you do a PGCE if you want to do Social Work you study CQSW, DipSW or MSc in Social Work and so on. But to progress through the degree choosing skills and modules proved tricky in that progression at times was based on work placement choice and availability that was itself dictated by maturity and disposition of student particularly for those who wanted to be social workers. Such students would study up to level 6 on the early year's course then move across onto the BA Social Work level 5 and 6 specialising in adoption in the early years or some other early year's specialism. These students could not start their academic career on the social work course because of their age. Thus they would do all three stages of the Early Years BA first. One of the respondents at level four had planned this route to career choice the other wanted to go into education and planned to do a PGCE. As can be seen from the course work and compendia skills developed for the stage two student in this study, developing skills specific to social work practice is attainable but monitoring the mentoring system would require further training of staff and mentors. Skills developed by the student were emergent and appropriate but not monitored as they should have been which is why students have to retake stages 5 and 6 if they progress onto a social work course.

At level 5, nine of the students had work placements in schools, five wanted to go onto to do post graduate teacher training and two wanted to do management courses so they could run their own primary day care nurseries. Two students were still undecided and two student planned to progress through the early years sector in education gaining skills and experience to take into social work. Those students who were undecided about their career choice preferred to vary their work placement experience.

Stage three participants mainly chose to go into education. Seven chose teaching; five at primary level and two at Further Education (FE) level. Stage three students were a mixed group some for example had completed the Foundation Degree in Education and it was the latter group who wanted to teach in FE and were mature students. One student wanted to progress in the direction of Social Work and another student had planned to work in education then progress onto a MSc in Educational Psychology. Across the three stages of the degree, although they did not return questionnaires, a number of students had placements on children's wards and wanted to develop a career path in health care. However, in the main from discussions in tutorial groups in comparison to participants in the study, education based professions were the majority choice.

The students who returned completed questionnaires may have had good reason to do so. For example, in the main, they had planned their future development and it was not necessarily within education. Few students across the three stages actually documented PDP as they felt it unnecessary and saw the progression from the BA degree onto a PGCE as straightforward. The degree content thus signifying their needs in terms of progression and only students who chose careers other than teaching tended to plan development in terms of module choice. In this respect, there appears to be a mixture of achieved identity and ascribed identity characteristics within the early year's sector and practices are both emergent and ascribed. It would appear that change is possible but in practicable measures. It could be possible that as Berger and Luckmann (1966) suggest we need an element of predictability in our daily lives to prevent stressful situations and thus ascribed reciprocal typifications of habitualised actions balance against the knife-edge present changes initiated by reflexive practices of students and staff in novel situations.

Perceived support required

Perceived support require for PDP tended to be structured guidance embedded in modules with tutorial discussions and an element of flexibility to cater for individuality—see figure 12. Overwhelmingly the choice was for compulsory placement and portfolio/compendium. However there was emphasis on flexibility, tutorial support and mentor support was seen as essential. As stated earlier, those students who returned questionnaires tended to complete portfolios and had chosen careers not necessarily in education. In other words, they were planners and individuals. The data suggest a balance between structure within the portfolio and flexibility to compensate for placement variation. Only one student felt mentoring non-essential: Most opted for a balance of taught structured support and tutorials. These result mirror those from the course work discussed in the latter sections.

Support available

Support available for PDP was extensive. At level 4 it was incorporated into two main modules: the 'Self-management and Skills Development' module and the 'Placement Skills' Module. The former module focuses on the development of generics transferable skills and the second on those skills essential to the placement experience. Nonetheless, in theory all of the modules on the course because they contain learning outcomes that can be mapped with practice based skills contain elements of PDP in terms of developing those practice-based skills. Student perceptions of the support available were mixed outlined in figure 13.

Student engage in PDP is seen as secondary to obtaining a degree and not always at unison with it. It appears that the structure of the degree is seen as enough to inform PDP and although the students who took part in this study engaged in PDP on the whole, given that there were essentially three to four hundred students sent the questionnaire, the majority of students I have taught within the early years find the present structured study pathways adequate in terms of the amount of personal development of skills essential for their employment in the sector; especially if there is a degree of flexibility. Whether staff can deal with the flexibility of skills development and number of modules and especially modules that are discretionary remains to be seen. Staff members spoken too suggested that a range of core modules with optional ones would be better as this would allow the team to consolidate the entire practitioner skills within the first two years of the degree leaving students time at level 6, stage three to enhance the skills they have developed.

Barriers and issues

From the student perspective, the main issue concerning engagement with PDP and reflexive practice is time. Ten of the students comment on time as an issue with comments such as 'limited time or opportunity to exercise new ideas', 'it takes time to reflect on a situation and then achieve goals set' and 'time is always an issue we have little time to reflect and plan'. In addition, students listed 'family commitments', 'family support', 'difficult to write down things and can get long-winded', as barriers to personal development planning and reflexive practice. 'Lack of knowledge and training' was given by two students as a barrier to PDP and reflexive practice, and 'a clear understanding of what it entails is essential'. A further student suggested that 'notes should be given in tutorials and lectures rather than have to be down loaded from the intranet'.

The learning outcomes portfolio with complementary practice based experiential learning was difficult to implement as one student found her mentor ignored them and used her own criterion as a yardstick. Whilst this is opportune for the emergence of practices the monitoring of it was unsuccessful without the correct amount of liaison between the mentors and the university. Nonetheless, this issue will be addressed in the future. Another student suggested that changes in government policy can influence the amount of reflect practice and PDP she engaged in because after planning one thing policy driven initiatives changed and her planning was disregarded. Another student gave 'intermittent relationship with mentor' as a barrier to PDP and reflective practice because 'there was no continuity; changing circumstance affects outcomes of PDP and reflective practice' and 'relevant support from professionals is a barrier', 'other people's judgements & views when dealing with serious situations might differ to your own', and 'sometimes pupils can be stubborn so even if you've tried to be reflective you can't always see plans through', and 'support from a supervisor or mentor can be an issue if it's not in place'.

Some students found reflective practice and PDP 'very boring when taught', 'too structured on specific learning comes', 'Doesn't take into account experience outside of setting', whilst other students thought that 'PDP should be structured', 'You need to be reflective—must set time aside to do it', 'there needs to be more content—reflective skills for stage one is adequate but more support needed for stage two for in-depth reflections on development and planning'. Thus a mixture of responses was noted. In the main, as this was a pilot for the incorporation of practitioner skills into early childhood studies pathways to graduate employment then the issues could be dealt with and changes could be made.

Further comments

Under the further comments section of the questionnaire were responses such as:

> 'Not enough placement opportunities in social services . . . there needs to be more content on social work on ECS course', more support is needed for students to reach their full potential, students should pick their own placements', 'placements should be compulsory because some student really don't engage at all', 'Reflexive Practice is important because it is important to plan, do and review what is made available for children and if you evaluate your work it leads to improved practice Self—evaluation forms are used at school we choose 3 things to improve and 2 things that have not gone so well—it is used with buddy groups, to reflect to get children to reflect on time in buddy groups it helps them with their emotional, social behavioural problems'.

This student was a qualified early year's senior practitioner and as you can see she understands what reflexive practice is. Perhaps those students new to the field are not as familiar with it. But in the main, all students regarded reflexive practice skills essential to practitioner development. One student responded:

> 'I do believe placements should be a little more structured in order for students to get more out of the experience. Similarly they should be compulsory, as it must be impossible to make a study of children if you have not experienced the numerous effects and demands a setting makes on them. Students should, however, continue to be able to choose their own placement', and ' . . . if they are not strong enough to make their needs known (i.e. some students complained of pencil sharpening a lot!) structured Supervisor/mentor is a good thing.'

Again, this response was that of a mature student who had worked in primary education for a number of year but who had studied the BA (Hons) pathway rather than the Foundation Degree. Her chosen career was educational psychologist. Thus on graduating from the BA she wanted to undertake a Master Degree in Educational Psychology. A further student responded:

> 'Having done the foundation degree professional portfolio which was very structured I felt it matched my work experience but was possibly too structured for students who have very different work experience I.e. childcare for children in hospitals . . . Portfolios are a good check on what you know and what you've learned and what you need more experience of, particularly for the younger students . . . Placements across all the Early Years Settings do not have the same needs . . . What

to include, time taken to achieve goals and how to identify weaknesses can be problematic . . ."

These comments are suggestive of the findings elsewhere in this study in that, portfolios/compendium need to be flexible with mentor support and an element of structure so that higher education staff can deal with the balance between flexibility and structure. Another Foundation Degree Graduate on stage three of the BA (Hons) programme said:

'RP is important for your professional development and improvement, I use it all the time to evaluate each lesson, helps me improve, also statutory reviews, getting other people's opinions is also a part of it, it helps you achieve goals and progress'.

Thus you can see the knowledge of senior practitioners and undergraduates is distinct but both groups see the benefits of portfolios/compendium, placements and mentor support.

Feedback from staff and mentors

From discussions with staff and mentors there appeared to be several issues and barriers involved in the implementation of the Early Childhood Studies Curriculum, for example, there was a diverse student intake that meant that for example, A level students wanted to do placements because they did not have the experience of working within the early years sector like the NVQ or Cache diploma students. In addition, because of the broad nature of the curriculum particularly in terms of optional modules to cater for the diversity of early years service sector institutions: education, welfare and health; a portfolio/compendium that reflected the learning outcomes at module level could be flexible and tailored to individual needs but the uniqueness of these portfolios made them hard to moderate and supervise for staff. Some of staff themselves where practitioners from the various institutions and felt that for some practitioner statues three years was not enough in terms of time to deliver all the curriculum content. For example, primary school teachers do a four year programme and we were expecting early years students to do as much study in a three year period, particularly since they were expected to develop portfolios for each stage of the degree, or at least for stage one and two to cover the number of practitioner hours deem essential for practitioner status.

The training of mentors and the co-ordination of placements was also a full time preoccupation in itself and was actually being delivered by one member of staff who was also a full time lecturer across the three stages and the CRB Counter-signature (me). In the end, as I was the one who was piloting the compendium of skills, I realised that my enthusiasm was greater than the energy needed to sustain the programme as it was.

Other staff members felt that it put too much strain on them as additional work when they already felt stretched. Several ideas were mulled over even the one of reducing the number of optional modules but in doing this student's career options were reduced. The final decision based on several discussions with staff and mentors was that portfolios should be flexible and learning outcome synthesised with reduced optional modules. This could be achieve by redeveloping the programme to include all of the learning comes essential for practices within the early year's sector but streamlined with core compulsory modules across the three stages of the programme. Sacrifices were made. Further amendments to the programme of study are in the offing. However, although it was deemed essential that placements should continue, it was felt that the BA programme if it was to deliver early year's professional status it could be achieved but if students wanted to be early year's teacher qualified then it needed to be a four early year's programme. The final year would then be the one that contained all the essential experience to obtain teaching skills equivalent to qualified teacher status similar to that of the primary B Ed.

This was but one study monitoring the changes made to higher education provision of training course for those students wanting careers within the early year's sector. Information circulated by Pamela Calder for the Early Childhood Studies Network suggested a move towards five pathways of Early Childhood Studies Degrees (ECSD) with Early Years Practitioner Status (EYPS):

1) *The BA (Hons) ECSD with the PGCE in Early Years (four years study in total).*
2) *The BA (Hons) ECSD with EYPS—2 years level 4 and 5 study 18 months to 24months developing practitioner skills in placements with fully qualified practitioner mentors for students new to early year's practices.*
3) *The three year Foundation Degree Work Based programme leading to Practitioner Status for student with practitioner status at level 3 or more.*
4) *A four year route for students new to the early years on a work based Foundation Degree.*

The fifth pathway is still to be developed (Email from Pamela Calder, 2009, CWDC, 2009).

Evaluations and conclusions

'Students wanted structured, compulsory placements, clearly defined learning outcomes and documentation, but flexibility, support on campus and in placement, variety in placement and career prospects and employment or access to further study . . .' reflexive practice skills, practitioner skills, academic skills, PDP skills, PTS skills, ICT skills, Portfolio/compendium development, Employability skills and researcher skill. It all seems a tall order. Nonetheless, government policy is signalling similar directional changes. For example, according to the Green Paper and the Every Child Matters' Agenda (2003) and included in chapter 6—Workforce Reforms

(2003, p. 83), there are several things on the agenda that need orchestrating within the early years workforce:

1. *Improved skills and effectiveness*
2. *Flexible and attractive Social Work options*
3. *Common occupational standards across the Early Years*
4. *High calibre leadership (MSc)*
5. *Multi-agency workers which is an evolving roles with common skills/ advanced skills*
6. *Information sharing and assessment*
7. *Generic workforce, common requirements.*

These suggested changes have thus been considered as part of the Children's Workforce Development Strategy as well as changes piloted and monitored within the UK by various university that feed information back to Pamela Calder who heads the Early Childhood Studies Network. Whilst this it is hoped will amount to a service that is second to none, it also needs to be sustainable. Indeed, the number of changes staff in higher education made in response to those suggested by government initiative and the children's workforce development council (CWDC) as well as those of students in this study and elsewhere in the UK were huge and many staff found the constant changes stressful. The result was further changes to curriculum offering a programme of study that encompasses all of the essential criteria suggested by the government and the children's workforce development council whilst tailoring the changes to meet the student needs at the local level of delivery. Thus, the BA (Hons) pathway is but one pathway with a three-year programme of study, but with a generic curriculum that feeds into social work, health care and education. Students who follow this pathway will go on to do post graduate studies in their choice of career. The other pathways outlined take a mixture of work based Foundation Degree Study and the length of time taken to complete choice of programme can vary but the average is four years full time study. The pathways are unique to each pathway-group needs whether EYPS/EYCD or EYCD/PGCE or one of the outcomes.

However, with the incorporation of social work and health care into a programme with educare, it appears that the role of the early year's professional is moving from one of educator to that of a Social Pedagogue. This has political implications for women who tend to be the main employees in the sector. For example, what can be said about the life-space they will occupy? And also, the generic base covers a breath of knowledge that cannot be covered to a level of that offered on a degree programme that specialises in one of the fields: either education care or health. Thus, students either satisfy themselves with EYPS or engage in post-graduate study to expand on the knowledge base of their chosen field. The changes therefore are at the EYPS level of practice only. How does this affect the early year's sector in terms of management and social work practices? Are students with EYPS up to level 6 deemed eligible to manage state run nurseries, as they are private day care centres? In addition, how have the changes affected pay levels? Has the development of practitioner skills to level 5 and 6 brought with them raises in pay and/or professional status as Moss suggests should be the case?

The social pedagogue is the model used in Demark and Germany. One only need look at the root meaning of pedagogue to see why the role is exploitative, i.e. a social pedagogue is a slave. The person who does all of the caring tasks within a household such as health care, education and social care. As far as the feminist perspective is concerned, within the household this role amounts to exploitation and second-class citizenship for women. Do we want this role for women in the public sector as well as the domestic sector? One can only suggest that if the role of the pedagogue is to be expanded to include all of the tasks the Greek Slave used to do then at least they want a professional title with the status and prestige of other professional occupations including a rate of pay that mirrors the amount and breath of work done. Ellen Galinsky (2006) 'The Economic Benefits of High-Quality Early Childhood Programs', has suggested that whilst early intervention is desirable, particularly using a well-educated, well trained workforce, if we try to incorporate too much into the programme then we may fail to deliver!

Thus, the inclusion of several professions within the rubric of early years leads me to question what is actually meant by the term professional. If a worker has to deal with an ever expanding knowledge base in terms of theory and practice then will this in the end down-grade the services provided and as the capacity of the individual to provide those services diminishes in a profession that is becoming a 'Jack of all trades'? Osgood suggests that a true sense of the word 'profession is one generated from practice' (Osgood, 2006a, p196). With this I am inclined to agree, particularly since such a statement is something I have argued based as it is on the Marxian notion that ideas for improving practice come from the practical-critical activity of engaging with practice, and as workers are stretched beyond capacity then we return to the old scenario first visited by Marx that is, a workforce that is alienated by their own labour. And has Osgood points out, we need an early year's workforce that is nurturing and caring rather than one governed by work overload. Thus, whilst as far as higher education programmes is concerned, we can offer a more encompassing curriculum that aids the interdisciplinary nature of care within the community in terms of generating discourses and practices that function for all workers whether social workers, youth workers or early year's workers; students should have the opportunity to specialise in particular work place practices. This would entail an act of negotiation that would give them control over their professional identity rather than it being ascribed by government or other similar outside forces. The choices would also allow for any emergent practices practitioners are confronted with that would signal changes in service needs—these emergent practices as it were would be generated by the practitioner as solutions to issues or problems reflected on. Such locally based initiatives may even signal piloting of the initiatives by local education authorities then government that can be monitored across various institutions to assess their usefulness. I think this way practitioners would be responsible for negotiating their professional identity and status rather than it being ascribed via an over-structured generic programme of study.

The demand for early year's provision has in fact outstripped its target. Gordon Brown set a target for the increased number of SureStart Centres/Child Development Centres at 2500 by 2008. The outcome in 2009 is 2900. Of the people who responded to the service provision enquiry, 78% said they used Children's Centres whilst only 13% used Health Care facilities (DCSF/Government, 2009). It would appear then that childcare and education is the major service demand. To bring all three occupational groups under one rubric may be far too broad a subject and perhaps to have several inter-related pathways would be a better option. Then youth studies and an integrated pathway that would enhance interdisciplinary working and communication would be a possibility, bring all types of care together but with specialist options at post-graduate level.

In some countries social welfare and education are brought together for example, in some Scandinavian countries such as Demark and places like New Zealand. Their early year's worker is given the title of pedagogue and the role is suggestive of a social pedagogue usually a female who looks after not only young children but also older children and the elderly (Moss, 2006). Do we in the UK want to re-visit this type of situation?

My point in the discussion is not to suggest Britain follows the same route. Esping-Anderson (1996) 'Welfare States in Transition', suggests the main problems for social policy makers is a growing disjunctive between existing social protection and needs. This is due to 1) changes in family structure—increase of single parent households, 2) changes in occupational structure, such as an increase in the service sector, 3) changing economic conditions—slow growth and deindustrialisation, and 4) changing demographic trends—ageing population. We have an ageing population with an increase in single parenthood and a social welfare system placed on the shoulders of a workforce that is predominantly female. Thus, it is feminist praxis not to allow the early year's workforce be a sector of exploitation by allowing any outside forces to negate the workforce into a catchall position for all the social welfare tasks a state welfare system services. So whilst the British welfare system is one of the most extensive it is one of the most comprehensive, compartmentalised but functionally exemplar models of state welfare.

To recap, whilst the notion of professionalism within the early year's workforce is desirable, it should not be a catchall profession. The latest curriculum changes that include youth work and elements of social work (2008) suggest a direction in curriculum that is government and/or workforce council directed placing a strain on a predominantly female workforce. Moss suggests that when males are employed in this sector they tend to work in the youth sector and social work sectors. It appears that if the work force is to expand then males within the workforce will lighten the load.

As I write this paper there are still changes going on in HE with the development of five pathways of progression. The BA pathway if studied by students with Cache diploma practitioner status or NVQ level 3 practitioner status will obtain practitioner status at degree level on graduation from the BA. For students with 5 years or more experience in the early year's field, on completion of the Work Based Foundation Degree students will gain practitioner status. Students new to the early year's sector of employment will study the BA degree and completion of their practitioner status requirements must be within 18 to 24 months period after two years of study at levels 4 and 5. These changes are not a direct result of this study alone but are part of a much wider study taking place across the UK as part of the Early Years Workforce Network and CWDC strategy for improving early year's work force status. Institutions not part of the Network or who do not subscribe to the CWDC changes will continue to provide the full time and part time BA (Hons) Degree in Early childhood Studies and the students will make their choice of post-graduate study in the third year based on what they learned during the degree programme and placement engagement.

Agency within the early years is a continuity that this study has made clearly visible. Whilst change is desirable and agency essential it can be stressful for higher education staff that have to respond to changes in curriculum and practitioner requirements. The children's work force is essential for economic development and although I have my reservations concerning the catch-all identity that is being negotiated within the early years, like Moss, I think if the early year's professional is to exist at all then the ascription of social pedagogue must still be developed until a desired result is attained that meets the needs of practitioners and others involved without the alienation that can amass when an identity is fully ascribed and not negotiated. What is very clear is that reflexive practice is essential to early year's practices and a media through which the negotiation process will continue. The UK has for some time known about the ageing population and the strain it places on the family. If as a nation we are to ride the recession through to a successful conclusion then respect and encouragement will ensure the support of a workforce that holds and rocks the countries cradles.

Figures for Chapter Eight

Figure 1

	STAGE 1 of degree Level 4	STAGE 2 of degree Level 5	STAGE 3 of degree Level 6
Assessment of module Learning Outcomes/ Course work Six Modules chosen two for each stage of the three year degree Grades across these modules could have been incorporated into the triangulation process but were not used for ethical reasons. The data below was consented to.	1 Self-Management and Skills Development Personal Development Planning (PDP) 2 Placement Skills development: Observing Children for Planned Provision of Learning (Research Methods for Observing Children and Reflexive Practice Skills)	3 Professional Skills Development (Personal Development Planning (PDP) 4 Research Skills and Reflexive Skills Development in Project Planning (integrated into PDP)	5 Professional Practice (Personal Development Planning (PDP)/ Continuing Professional Development (CPD) 6 Research Skills and Reflexive Skills Applied (Integration into PDP/CPD)
Assessment information and students' and mentors written comments in PDP Reflexive Practice Portfolios Sheets for the modules listed above	Evidence for skills development from placement/work	Evidence for skills development from placement/ work	Evidence for skills development from placement/ work

Questionnaires filled in by students	Student self-report in free response sections of questionnaire of perceived engagement with reflexive practice and PDP	Student self-report of perceived engagement with reflexive practice and PDP	Student self-report of perceived engagement with reflexive practice and PDP/CPD
Data from Discussions with Staff, Mentors and Students	Free-style note taking of discussions	Free-style note taking of discussions	Free-style note taking of discussions

Figure 2

COMPETENCES/ LEARNING OBJECTIVES Stage One Observing Children For The Planned Provision Of Learning	Evidence from academia (Grade obtained And/or work placement activity commentary) Grade:	Mentor's Comments
NOS Achieved Knowledge & Understanding Meeting a range of differing needs of children via Observation, planning & Assessment Skills Effective practice/ Relationship with children	I have helped with both lower and higher ability groups in year 1	Student worked and supported the SEN group and also the higher ability children with extension work
LO1) Explore a range of observational techniques within their workplace context.	I have read up on and looked at observation techniques used at school and discussed with mentor which observation technique I should develop	Student looked at relevant information and previous observations carried out on one particular child in the in her group Over the term several techniques were used
LO2) Construct a written report that identifies the focus of the observations, reviews and evaluates the selected techniques and accounts for the findings in an objective manner.	For each observation I did I wrote a report using the reflexive cycle Angela gave out a diagram on	Student has made good progress this term learning how to use various observation techniques and writing report to go with them

LO3) Reflect upon their own role in the data collection process and suggest possible modifications to enhance their own practice.	After each observation, as part of the report I added reflective evaluations of my role in the data collection process	The student has written report with good theoretical understanding of holistic development—very good work done here.
Additional work experience competences not commented on . . .	I carried out a worksheet where I gave instructions and the children listened and followed the instructions.	Student conducted a listening activities set with a small group of children helping them to complete work that relates to following instructions

Figure 3

Observation: Time and Event Sample

Setting: Nursery School
Date: 13/02/08
Aim: To observe Allan's behaviour when getting ready to go outside
Purpose: To note child's stage of social and emotional development
Time Started: 10.35   **Time Finished:** 10.40
Child Observed: Allan
Date of Birth: 10/9/04   **Age:** 3 years 5 months   **Gender:** Male
Immediate Setting: Nursery classroom and outside play area

Time	Incident	Previous happening	Who was there?	What happen next?	Comments
10.35	Allan was playing with the door handle, opening and closing the door having been told to stand in line ready for out-door play.	A nursery nurse help Allan put his coat on and asked him to join the line for outdoor play.	Five children were at the door standing line.	A staff member asked Allan to wait inside and join the line of other children. Allan does not respond so the he is taken to the end of the line.	Allan has to understand that he cannot always do things when he wants to. And then there are rules he must use at nursery for health and safety reasons.

| 10.39 | Allan although now standing in line has started to slap and bang the cupboard. | Initially he stood in line with the other children. | 21 children and 4 members of staff. At various places with the children. | A member of staff asked Allan not to slap and bang the cupboard as it was noisy and the other children would hear instructions if he continued. | Allan will receive instruction about how to follow rules such as standing in line quietly without damaging property or being disruptive. |
| 10.40 | Allan watched the staff member turn away and started banging the cupboard again. | Although he was told not to bang the cupboard he continued until staff spoke him a second time asking him not to. | 21 children and 4 members of staff. At various places with the children. | Allan was asked not to bang the cupboard a second time. | Allan will receive instruction about how to follow rules such as standing in line quietly without damaging property or being disruptive. |

Figure 4

Following Instructions Task: Simple Simon Said (SSS)

Whole Group Activity (Instructor to start the game)

Children have to listen and do the actions only if the instructor says 'SSS' before the instructions.

The Instructions says: 'SSS put your hands on your head' and then waits for the correct response.

Those children who have responded correctly are still in the game. Those who have not must sit down and watch.

The Instructor can give any number of instructions. Sometimes s/he will give instructions without putting 'SSS' in the sentence and when this occurs those children who were not listening properly and still follow the instruction must sit down and watch.

Figure 5

COMPETENCE /LEARNING OBJECTIVE Developing Professional Skills	Evidence from academia (i.e. Grade Obtained And/or work placement i.e. activity involved in) Grade:	Mentor's comments
NOS Achieved Team work & Collaboration Meeting a range of differing needs of children via observation and assessment skills Communicating and working in partnership with families and carers	A report was written which shows observation skills, reflexive evaluations skills and action-planning. Research method used was interview and free-style note taking.	The student has a keen eye for observation and is an active listener who shows empathy to people Befriended. The report produced by the student shows satisfactory evaluations of the situation with appropriate recommendations. In parts, excellent work done.
1) Students select a current development issue relevant to their workplace setting. Presented as a poster include the following elements: a) A brief summary with evaluation of the issue within the national context. b) A summary with evaluation of the issue within the workplace context. c) Evidence of reading and research.	The developmental issue chosen was concerning the welfare and development of two children whose parents were asylum seekers. I firstly Befriended the family as a volunteer working with Banardos attached to SureStart. I then researched the topic and found literature on the Every Child Matter's agenda (2003) that I put in the National context and International context in terms of Human Right's (2004) and Children's Right's (1998) (Essay Attached). See overleaf for the poster and the reflexive practice report putting the issue in the work place context. I have included some of the references used on the poster.	The student wrote a report detailing the work done with asylum seeker families that show engagement with the family enough to draw evaluations and suggest interventions.

a) STUDENTS PRODUCE a workplace log of practice experience noting tasks appropriate to the setting together with evidence of self-evaluation and critical evaluation of three issues related to early childhood development. The work must be supported with references. (1750 words).	See the Reflexive Practice log attached detailing visits to the families I Befriended over a period of four months. Some of the notes are interviews. I feel I developed coping skills dealing with stressful situations and time management skills. I also learned a lot from the team at SureStart and Banardos. I shadowed a Support Worker and learned about child development. For example one of the children I visited had global delay and with the supervision I planned activities for the child to overcome social skills problems and language problems; also self-esteem and behavioural problems. I feel the child would not have these problems if it were not for the family social position as asylum seekers.	Student has been a Befriender under my supervision for approximately three months. In that time I have found her to be very personable and pleasure to work with. The student is very motivated and shows great interest in the work. As a Befriender it is important to maintain up-to-date logs of every visit made, which the student completed accurately and in a timely fashion. Time keeping was always very good and the student has a very professional attitude; appointments are always kept. The student has good communication skills and tasks generally are undertaken with enthusiasm and without fear of asking questions about the situations encountered and always acts on information given.
b) Update your Personal and Professional Development Action Plan and describe in words how your professional practice experience has impacted on your professional development and planning.	I found it very difficult to find a placement but Angela suggested I try SureStart and Banardos. I thoroughly enjoyed this placement and it was relevant to my potential career choice, which was social work. As a volunteer I did some training and then started working with families. My Family Support Worker Supervisor said I was a very good worker and I feel I helped the families I Befriended. I have learned many skills that I can use as a social worker working with families.	Coping skills are good and the student can set boundaries. She always remains calm In all, I have found working with this student a pleasure and am confident in the skills acquired that the student is competent enough to be able to put into use at a later date.

| Additional work experience competences not commented on . . . | I have learned a lot about communication skills such as listening to people with an empathetic ear. I would like to continue working as a volunteer and want to do my dissertation on the topic of giving some of the asylum seeker families a voice so that their circumstances are improved which will improve the developmental requirement of their children . . . | The Banardos' Volunteer Induction Training, including the Ethos of Volunteering, confidentiality, Equality and Diversity, Health and Safety and Safeguarding Children. The student then met with the Family Support Workers at SureStart who mentored the student's work with the families allocated. |

Student Signature .... Mentor Signature ....

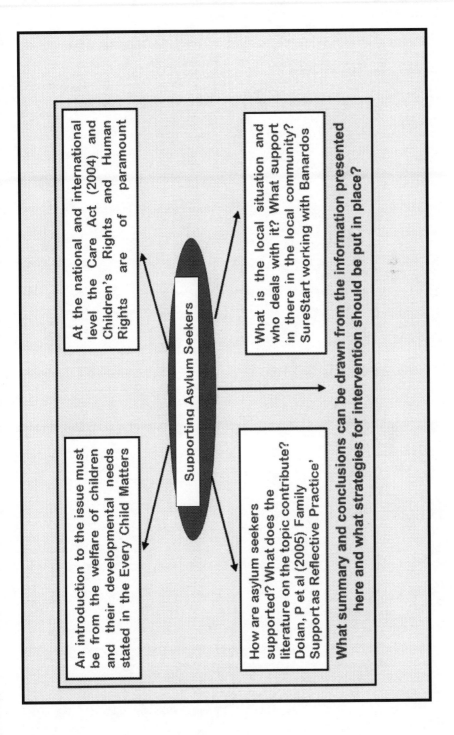

At the national and international level the Care Act (2004) and Children's Rights and Human Rights are of paramount

What is the local situation and who deals with it? What support in there in the local community? SureStart working with Banardos

Supporting Asylum Seekers

An introduction to the issue must be from the welfare of children and their developmental needs stated in the Every Child Matters

How are asylum seekers supported? What does the literature on the topic contribute? Dolan, P et al (2005) Family Support as Reflective Practice'

What summary and conclusions can be drawn from the information presented here and what strategies for intervention should be put in place?

Figure 6

Figure 7

INITIAL OBSERVATIONS

Having been in the UK for five years and been refused asylum three times the family were fraught. The family unit consisted of both parents: one female and one male with two children. As the student states 'one child is globally delayed and the younger sibling appears to have behavioural problems' (both Assessments were made by the staff at the SureStart Centre). The student's initial observations continue . . .

The family face several hardships:

1) Poverty—income is from the National Asylum Support Services (NASS) which is less then that needed to support the family and the parents go hungry.
2) Basic Accommodation—old furniture, old decorations, old clothes and the eldest child sleeping on a mattress on the floor with the mother so she does not fall out of bed. All items are donated by charities and the furniture project.
3) As a Muslim family the female wishes to keep the curtains and blinds closed so as not to be seen (fear is suspected). The mother also expressed concerns about her mental health, the description resembled anxiety and depression. These feelings affect her dealings with the children and she doesn't speak English particularly well so the children speak only Arabic affecting their schooling.
4) There are no toys or other activities for the children to occupy themselves except colouring books and crayons.

REFLEXIVE EVALUATIONS

The student made the assessment that the family was suffering from multiple problems. One of the children had global development delay.

1) The accommodation was basic and the eldest child needed a rail for the bed to prevent an accident.
2) The darkened house was affecting the eldest child's visibility and behaviour. She was globally delayed and aggressive to the younger child (Assessment made at the SureStart Centre). The children became very excited with each visit from the student. However the child's behaviour was difficult and distressful. Hair pulling and jumping on the back of the student was the norm. The student's evaluation was that the child needed stimulation.

3) The mother needs support to acquire English language and help her with mental health problems. The family suffer racial isolation and xenophobia.
4) The Children needed support—they have a right to play (Right's Act 2004). Although the problems were multiple and a few toys seemed a token gesture but these were the recommendations.

PLAN OF ACTION

The children's welfare was the mine concern. The global deal was dealt with mainly at SureStart but also in the home. For example:

1) The eldest child was provided with a bed rail so she could sleep in a bed and not on the floor.
2) The family were introduced to the toy library operated by the SureStart Team. The occupational therapist informed the student to assist the children in their choice of toys, particularly in terms of co-operative play aimed at promoting the development of social skills and family bonds. The latter was important because the eldest child craved the attention of the mother.
3) It was decided that the family were to be supported by the student, SureStart and Health Care professionals. The family were subsequently supported by the SureStart Team and the Health Car Team as well as the student.
4) The mother was introduced to staff at the SureStart Centre. It was arranged that she should attend mother and toddle group twice a week to prevent isolation and help the development of English as a second language for herself and her children.

Figure 8

Learning Objective	Presentation Skills	Skill Level Development	Development Opportunity	Evidence Objective Achieved	Time Scale
Placement Skills	Placement in school not relevant to career choice. Try to find relevant work experience. Good skills working with children.	To be able to successfully support families in need.	To work with relevant professionals gaining experience and confidence.	Currently supporting two families	Sept. to May
Stress Management	Gaining experience working to deadlines while continuing to raise a family and working in both paid and voluntary capacity.	To remain calm and keep things in perspective. Making sure enough time for family. Life and work balance is essential for good relations building with colleagues and families	Gain the relevant skills to remain calm when under pressure. Chosen career will be stressful so important to have the relevant skills to allow me to do it.	Gaining experience in situations that are new and stressful. Dealing with families in distress. Not taking stress home.	Jan. / ongoing
Research Skills	Completed Observing Children in 1st year.	To complete research project.	To improve research skills and produce good research project. To developing interviewing techniques.	Produced research project relating to my work placement— 'Giving asylum seekers a voice' with the aim of aiding child development and rights	Jan. to May

Time Management	Completed all essays in time first year and want to continue the same way	To start work experience with enough time to do research assignment—time plan needed	To gain experience working under pressure and dealing with deadlines.	Very hard to find placement but once found weeks of training followed leaving me a shorter time to research topic related to family support. Extension maybe required.	Sept. to May
Career Development	2nd year at university—gain relevant experience and contacts through work experience.	Continuing to support families.	Shadowing family support workers to gain knowledge of job. Interacting in a multi-disciplinary team.	Attend domestic violence group with support worker. Attend meetings with SureStart and Banardos	Jan./ Ongoing
Communication	Good skills at present but could be improved in terms of counselling skills.	To be able to communicate with families in an empathetic manner.	To learn essential skills from professionals around me.	Developing listening skills and reading books about support workers and counselling skills.	Jan./ Ongoing

Figure 9

COMPETENCE /LEARNING OBJECTIVE Professional Practice and Management in Care and Education	Evidence from academia (i.e. Grade Obtained and/or work placement I.e. activity involved in) Grade:	Mentor's comments
NOS Achieved **Professional Development** **Critical application of** **knowledge of procedure and** **policy to practice**	To complete this assignment I have chosen to examine the Every Child Matters (2003) policy, and the anti-bullying policy as they are applied in practice in primary education evaluating my role as a potential leader managing the changes the policies catalyse.	I am the area manager and first point of contact for this student. As such I act as supervisor/mentor.
1) Demonstrate an understanding of the impact of recent legislation on the developmental needs of children and the legal framework within which the educare manager works.	To complete the coursework for this learning outcome I outlined the role of the manager within an educare setting paying attention to the skills of a manager the role dictates within the legal framework of government initiatives and other government guidelines. I have written a bibliography for the essay I wrote. My reading for this learning outcome was guided by the initiatives I am working with in education.	The student has read documents concerning the legal framework an educare manager should know about.
2) Monitor and evaluate the implications of an aspect of recent legislation for parents and carers and/or educator and child care works and the skills required for effective management.	I chose to monitor the introduction of the new Early Years Foundation Guidance Document (2009) as a tool to assist transitioning for children into the education system as it acts as a mutual tool which parents/carers and nursery staff can monitor the development of the child and readiness for transitioning from the nursery into the reception class and key stage one.	The Foundation Stage Profile is used in the setting. The student uses it on a daily basis to plot the development of each child in her care.

3) Critically examine as aspect of change resulting from recent legislation reflecting upon you role in the process of change and suggest possible modifications to enhance practice and your PDP	As a potential manager in a childcare centre I felt I needed to outline effective management/leadership skills. These skills include critical examination of changes in legislation to implement modifications that enhance practice. I organised PTA meetings to develop relations between parents/carers and staff around the new Early Years Foundation Guidance documents. The documents service the purpose of partnership development between parents and staff as the document records the child's developmental needs and progress that can be discussed with parents/carers. The guidance notes in this respect aid the transition of the child from nursery into reception class. The introduction of enhanced staff and parents/carers relationships around the document enhance practice. For my personal development I have developed several skills in this exercise: organisational skills, communication skills, staff supervision skills, partnership development skills.	I was extremely pleased with the work this student produced for the setting and the arrangements made to develop working relationships between staff and parents. I hope the community spirit will continue.
Additional work experience competences not commented on . . .		
Student Signature .... Mentor Signature		

Figure 10

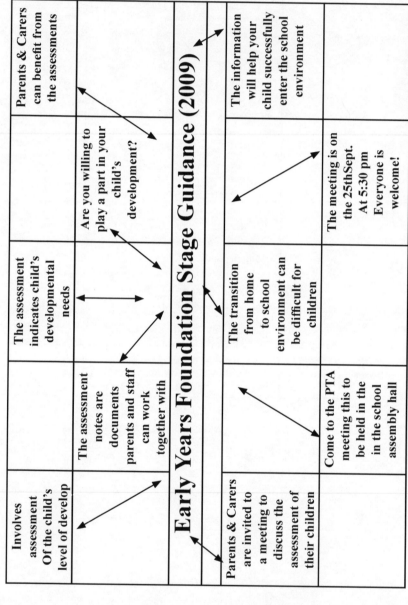

Involves assessment Of the child's level of develop	The assessment indicates child's developmental needs	Parents & Carers can benefit from the assessments
The assessment notes are documents parents and staff can work together with	Are you willing to play a part in your child's development?	

Early Years Foundation Stage Guidance (2009)

Parents & Carers are invited to a meeting to discuss the assessment of their children	The transition from home to school environment can be difficult for children	The information will help your child successfully enter the school environment
Come to the PTA meeting this to be held in the in the school assembly hall	The meeting is on the 25thSept. At 5:30 pm Everyone is welcome!	

Figure 11

Managing an educare setting is complicated, political and rewarding. Each manger will have a particular management style: democratic, authoritative, laizzes faire etc . . . The style of management can affect the running if the institution and characteristics that fit educare are those associated with leadership rather than authoritarian styles of management. Leading by example is very productive. Rodd (1998, p 6) suggests leadership and management are linked and both function together. The leader adopts a positive flexible approach whilst the manager is beaurocratic, often inflexible and authoritative but without the experience of the tasks they often give others to do. Leaders are more empowering (Handy, 2004, p28). Leaders empower the team allowing them to initiate changes collaboratively. Communication is important particularly when conflict arises and the 'micro politics' that go with it and a good leader who has the job of negotiating conflict can bring it to successful conclusions when they are abreast of the antecedent, behaviour and consequences (ABC). Counselling skills are useful as is the simple ABC cognitive approach to behaviour management.

A good leader will also be conversant with government policies and initiatives that have a direct influence on educare practices. Change can often be the harbinger of conflict, and a good leader will be up-to-date with investment in training and development initiative for staff that quite often resolve conflict (Muijs and Harris, 2003). Staff development is particularly functional to children's developmental needs. Walley (2007) for example suggests that the running of a day care setting can be determined by and influenced by the latest changes in government policies and initiatives. The Green paper for example that led to the development of the Every Child Matters Agenda (2003) has had an enormous positive impact on educare. It provides guidance for local authorities to procure five specified outcomes for all children: to be health, stay safe, enjoy and achieve, make a positive contribution and achieve economic well being. This policy was further developed in 2007 as the 'Every Child's Future Matters' (ECFM) report was published expressing the concern that the five outcomes are hard to attain. As O'Brian and Murray, (2006, p46) suggest however Forest Schools following on from Froebelian educational philosophy make an impact on the five outcomes. It appears that progression and improvement in provision are dependent on a combination of policy, leader and resources—not all schools for example have access to the type of environment Forest School commission. This type of provision is beneficial to children with kinaesthetic learning needs who are often at odds with the enclosed passive type of classroom-based environment.

Equally as productive is the Early Years Foundation Stage Curriculum Guidance (2009). The profile covers the six areas of holistic development with performance indicators that are now synthesised with the key stage assessment criteria. The synthesis is particularly important for the transitioning of children from nursery to reception and key stage one. Readiness is a product of emotional well being, cognitive and language develop, social development, knowledge of the world and physical development etc. This document is extremely important, as an indicator of the developmental requires for transitioning. Dockett and Perry (2004) conducted a survey to discover the perceptions and expectations of parents, carers and teachers of children's readiness for school. Whilst teachers' expectations were in terms of a child's disposition to adapt to the school environment, parents and carers expectations were in terms of disposition and cognitive needs of their child. The implications of this document for practice are enormous. The document aids communication and helps to develop the relationship between teachers and parents/carers, it indicates the development of the child, and how each member of the child's support structure can interact to support it with an enthusiasm on community support.

As a manger to further develop the relationship between parents/carers and teacher in the successful transitioning of children into the nursery school system I would organise PTA meetings where parents and teaching staff could get together to examine the Early Years Foundation Stage documentation. The document is a bridge between staff and parents/carers that can conveys valuable information about the children's development the two can mutually benefit from to the developmental benefit of the child. To further involve parents in their child's developmental journey as a manager I would invite them into the day to day care of their children on a rotary basis (to prevent overcrowding in the school) to see how their children are observed taking part in developmentally appropriate tasks and activities that are then assessed against the Early Years Foundation Stage Profile Guidance for development. The exercise for staff will benefit self-esteem as they will be able to demonstrate their role in the development of the children. The children will benefit from the partnership that will develop in terms of transitioning. For my personal development it will be a test indicator of organisational skills, communication skills, knowledge enhancement, staff management and partnership development skills. The exercise will also act as an exemplar for other childcare facilities that may like to develop a working relationship between teachers, parents and carers.

Figure 12 Perceived Support Required for PDP					
Type of Support	Structured Pre-planned Learning Outcomes in Modules with portfolio (I.e. like QTS portfolios)	Compulsory Work Placement	Non-compulsory Work Placement	Work Placement Mentor/ Supervisor	Mixture of Pre-planned Learning outcomes and flexible approach to portfolios	Tutorial Base Support
No of Students	6	20	1	18	8	9
Comments	Structured portfolios are best— something like those on the Primary B Ed. They should have clear boundaries They help with assignment work Degree impossible without one Better than assignments	The portfolios on the foundation Degree were very structured and useful They are useful for interviews	When you have to do a portfolio you get 'bogged' down in the additional work Can interfere with other work	Mentors are a good aid to progression Mentors in placements and specialist at university would be good	A flexible approach to the development of portfolios would allow students to collect work place evidence from a number of different placement types Students have individual needs/ are unique/ PDP needs to be tailored	Tutorial support is useful particularly if your placement is not in education One every 3 months would be good Tutorials help you catch up if you've missed something and this is needed for mature students who tend to do mainly evening classes because they work through the day

Figure 13

Actual Support Available	Students Engaged	Comments
Modular and Tutorial Based	21	All students referred to lecture and tutorial based available support but did not always specify which module.
Level 4	5	Five of the students referred to the Self-management of Skills Development module as available support for PDP. Reasons given were that the module outcomes incorporated PDP into them.
Level 4	None	No students commented on the module content of the Placement Skills module as one that was structured for PDP—perhaps it was seen as too obvious and thus most students stated module and tutorial based support.
Level 5	2	Two students commented on the content of the Professional Skills Development module as structured available support for PDP.
Level 5	None	None of the students commented on the Project Proposals Report module as containing structured PDP and yet the module outcomes specify the need for a rationale based on either placement choice or career choice. Again, perhaps it was seen as obvious.
Level 6	1	One student referred to the Professional Practice Module as one containing support of PDP.
Level 6	None	None of the students referred directly to the Independent Project modules as one containing structured support for PDP and yet students were instructed to choose a topic at level 5 for study that would reflect their career choice.
Induction Programme at level 4, 5 and 6	None	No students commented on the support available at inductions and yet students engaged in group brainstorming exercises linking project focus ideas to placement and career choice.
Module Choice Lecture Series	14 students went to the module choice lectures	Those who did not go to the 'choices of module' lecture commented: I was unaware of the lectures Didn't have time because of work commitments Made Choices on the basis of convenience because of the timing of the modules No comments made Two stated they did not plan modules
Mentor	7	Those who had mentors found their input invaluable—very support and necessary

Careers	1	Very useful when looking for prospective employers in areas you might not otherwise think of looking
Keynote Project Notes	1	These notes were useful but because the degree programme had notes also few students used the generic ones—two much information

Chapter Nine

The future of psychology and education

What is on the agenda for neuroscience, the cognitive sciences generally, and/ or psychological research and its insurgence into educational practices as we move into the 21ˢᵗ century? In terms of government policy, does the government stand as guardian to practices within education, or, is it but one influence inside the elaborate arena of negotiation? What place has psychological research within education? And what influences will practitioners themselves, and others attached to education in some shape and form have on its future?

One theme of this book has been the concept of reflexive practice and its uses in the enhancement of teaching and learning and/or personal and professional development, not to mention its uses as a research method. As a meta-cognitive style of learning it has face validity. This can be seen in the first chapter documented by sociologists, psychologists, philosophers and educationalists alike in response to the profound changes that took place within Western societies in terms of culture: the development of empiricism and rationalism and the onset of positivist methodology; witnessed a second time as the reflexive-turn when the critical theory of Marx became essential to the development of science in response to the developing knowledge that even sciences are affected by the same contingencies as culture *per sae*. Thus Parker signalled the need for a psychology that examines the discourses and narratives of people's lived experiences and Burman applied the reflexive gaze to developmental psychology. Stuart Parker discovered the anomaly of the way reflexive practice when operating within the framework of scientific management (bore of psychology and May experiments & Hawthorne Effect Research) can become a form of technical rationalism with values outside of its original prescriptive trajectory of progression. Although the notion of progression itself has been scrutinized as a concept that carries with it problems of inequality and hierarchical overtones, without it is society to spiral into oligarchical socialism and chaos? Haven't the Balkan states been through this once before (Littlejohn, 1984)? Then hierarchies have to be scrutinized along with other problems faced within the institutional world we have built around us.

The third theme therefore in this book was an examination of the dialectic of agency-structure as we develop as individuals within the institutional structures we have built: The personal and professional development of identities as an outcome of the agency-structure dialectic. As Foucault, Dahlberg and MacNaughton reveal, as individuals strive of personal development, power manifests itself in ways detrimental to sections of society. The reflexive turn thus started out as a critique to untruths and inequalities and was thought to break away from the progressive philosophies of the early enlightenment thinkers but it has in fact represented a reflexive-return to modernity as a harbinger of truth, equality, justice and freedom. The final dialectic therefore is one of the selfish-gene versus the selfish individual. The gene seeks unity within a kinship community of its manifestation and the individual seeks self-actualization as an exemplar of that community.

The 'phenomenology of spirit' unfolding (both that of Hegel and Marx, see chapter 4 on Marxian Psychophysics as the dialectic of brain-mind) within the social systems: cultural, political, economic, and social space (geographic location or otherwise) that surround us as individuals and groups is thus the dialectic of reflexive practice producing emergent ideas within the individual for change in institutions and the emergent changes within institutions thus working back on agents in a constant struggle for self-actualization as an individual or group. Indeed, the theories of Maslow and Rogers depict the needs of the individual of that of self-actualization within a community of people we seek recognition. The main social systems are in the end the most apt characteristics of identity formation because of the very reason we live in social groups from which we want recognition as actualizers. As we develop our own ontogeny we develop community and social institutions: 'the phenomenology of spirit'. Religion is not lost—it has become reflexive and modern as the communicative liquid that oils the systems and is a reflection of them and the people within them: the historical religions have lost charm only to be succeeded by the core values and principles they upheld now enshrined within the legal system and other social institutions emergent and functional to justice, unity, freedom, equality and truth: The enlightenment project.

In the present economic climate as western societies embrace their margins; the bounded nations and othernesses; twinned sites of local, and local with global changes, of emergencies, bubble up in a glowing spectra; the UK is but one physicality of many as 'all that is solid melts into air . . .' (Marx, *Economic*, 1890). The final encounter may well be one of total eclipse or a unified glorification as the global capitalist economy struggles for its feet, hovering beneath its own carriage on a blanket of air without the support of the industrial base. Money—paper alone—will not support the march of capitalist accumulation. As inflation rises and gross national product falls, mindful of the fact that debit accounts are debt in the guise of growth without anything but words and hot air to support them; where will the funding for education, or indeed, a welfare system come from? What does the future hold for education? Is it to be a personal endeavour as the individual identity connects to the web of information the Internet offers whilst at the same time waxing and waning with the move into global pockets of socialism? Where within Adam Smith's *'Wealth of Nations'* did it suggested that the state should dictate social-co-operative support to monopolistic and/or dictatorial ex-appropriation of taxes in the guise of government expenditure? The 'invisible hand' has now lost its glove: have monopolies and oligarchies become the new socialism or is it just another way of working for Ford? These questions are paramount in an ever-changing world in which reflexive practice is the only way through.

King (1992) outlines the hybridisation process of a global world culture in which the individual as an identity becomes one of a diasporic identity that consumes on both a global and local level. The motivating force is capitalism with all its expectancies of employees as human capita—employability skills are one form of identity expression.

Newman & Holzman in *'The End of Knowing'* discover that in the postmodern matrix we call the human condition; society fosters its own identity problems in many forms. Psychological problems for example, are conveyed through culture as a re-enactment of everyday life, as everyday life becomes more and more routinised. What Berger & Luckmann outline as the process of re-enactment of social relations that get passed down through the generations as reciprocal typifications of habitualised actions. The end result being as we saw in a preceding chapter, the development of learning styles that can become one-sided identities: i.e. either solely auditory learners, visual learners or kinaesthetic learners if educators are not fully conversant with the theory behind the practice. But in addition, Newman & Holzman address the needs of people, many of who are now children and young people, with psychological problems such as psychotic and neurotic disorders that are fostered in much the same way. Their solution to the problem is 'activity theoretic'.

Basically, activity theoretic is a starting point from which there is no practice underpinned by theory. Any theory there is, according to these two authors, should be emergent of the practices engaged in. In other words, their approach is about the production of new theory from practice, using action research and reflexive practice. Whilst their work is to be commended, the complete decomposition for all existing theory is hard to deliberate. Once again, a return to reflexive practice as a means of developing theory and practice appears to be just as insightful if not more so. In addition, although within a discipline such as psychology there are numerous approaches that do not always interact because of the differences in methodology: ontology and epistemology there has been a demand for inter-perspective research. Crossing boundaries has a tendency to generate insights that we need. For example, the unification of neuroscience and education with all the interpretations of its combination along a continuum from strict neuroscience through neurophysic, neurochemistry, neurobiology, neurocognition, cognition, cognitive psychology and not least psychology of education continues to flourish because of the insights generated. There is still much needed research in these areas. Technology is developing rapidly and the cross fertilisation between it and cognitive psychology is essential. Work done in this area opens windows for neuroscience and other fields to connect such as the way intellectual impairment has been brought together with artificial intelligence, neuroscience with mainstream education and education with cognitive psychology and last but by no means least, meta-cognitive psychology with the social psychology of identity formation. The list is endless.

We have the old theories from Froebel, Reggio Emilia, Piaget, Bruner, Vygotsky, Holzman & Newman, Usha Goswami, Foucault, Dahlberg and many more—an international collection of eminent people—most I have discussed within this book and once again the range of theoretical base is profound and broad but society does change as part of the struggle between self-actualising individuals and the institutions they manifest and as a consequence new synthesis and research that situates the synthesized theory within a global economy necessitates itself. For example, the education system in Britain is predominantly Piagetian in culture but is synthesised with the theories of Vygotsky and those of neuroscience: brain based teaching and learning strategies. The information processing approach to cognition is one of the chalk-face areas for research.

International perspective: International peer reviewed research & practices

According to the Organisation for Economic Cooperation and Development (OECD) most early year's workforces are divided into the education sector and care sector. In Britain, the latter encompass health care as well as social care i.e. social work. The collaborative and collective communication between these compartments is fluid and the new early year's provision will continue in that capacity although Moss suggests changes might mirror those of other countries, and it would appear the most recent changes in curriculum are certainly broader and include youth work and social work. Universal child development is both psychological as well as social and health related and we find that on continents globally the care and development of children is approached in slightly different ways. Understanding of the Nordic, UK, Reggio Emilian, Te Whariki and Froebelian preschool philosophies/frameworks on which the care and education of children rest has thus become the preoccupation of social psychologists, developmental psychologists and educationalist. Examination of the similarities and differences of the preschool philosophical frameworks in view of the global international nature of preschool provision taking into account cultural relativism and universality seems to be their preoccupation.

The cultural characteristics of Nordic preschool as outlined by Johanna Einarsdottir (chapter 7, 2005) shows there are a number of themes that characterise Nordic preschools. Strand for example (same publication, chapter 5, 2005) discusses how the cultural context influenced the development of education provision along with Nordic history and cultural values. Because Nordic societies value their cultural heritage some adopt Froebelian and Reggio Emilian frameworks i.e. are less structured and but more adaptive in terms of community context. There is a struggle between Nordic preschool provisions local versus nationally prescribed provision. Einarsdottir (2005) suggests in Norway early year's philosophy and practices are inward looking i.e. too local and community based that they become isolated and insular. 'Social games' by elitist groups who hold authority seem to be at the root of some of the tension. There can be friction between the language/cultural needs of the local community level and political/economic needs at the national level. The main characteristics of the Nordic preschool philosophy are (Johanna Einarsdottir et al, 2005):

- *Preschool influenced by postmodern ideas—constructionist,*
- *Framework is thus changing and adaptive to contemporary society and relationships between preschool and compulsory education,*
- *Children's rights are important (Brostrom, chapter 9, 2005),*
- *Play is central for development and learning (Hakkarainan, chapter 8, 2005),*
- *The right to play,*
- *Relationship building is important,*
- *Ethical methods of assessment and observation are central to professional training,*
- *Curriculum is free-flow play based but changing to structured pre-planned activity in some Nordic Nations (Pramling-Samuelsson, chapter 5, 2005).*

Postmodern feminist influences such as female nurturing role is challenged and children are seen as investigators of their own world (Taguchi, chapter 10, 2005). Like most international perspectives the Nordic tries to cherish Nordic values and culture whilst maintaining pace with early year's provision at the global level. Thus the process of hybridisation is observable.

The history of UK preschool provision in comparison has taken the opposite course. In 1870 with the implementation of the Education Act elementary school became compulsory for children age 5 and over, in 1880 for all children aged 5 to 13. Children under 5 were admitted for their own protection—the onset of the industrial revolution was not a place for children. In 1905 children under 5 were excluded from elementary school because it was seen as unfit. 1911 Margaret MacMillan opened a nursery for poor children to keep them safe and off the streets; feed them and improve personal hygiene. Play facilities were available and free health care. UK cultural influences are that traditionally the curriculum in England and Wales has been "child-centred" i.e. influenced by the work of Piaget. The value of play to assist development was widely adopted but in the 1960s family size declined as did the number of nurseries. Playgroup facilities increased from then on. Government influences on the curriculum were developed within the Rumbold Report (DES, 1990) 'Starting with Quality' & Royal Society of Arts Report (1994) 'Start Right' which continued with HMI Publication i.e. the curriculum from 5 to 16 years. The implementation of a curriculum with 8 main areas of learning (1) aesthetic and creative (2) human and social (3) language and literacy (4) mathematics (5) physical (6) science (7) spiritual and moral, and (8) technology was a starting point for the curriculum we have today.

In 1994 high-quality provision was to be available to all 3 to 4 year olds with emphasis on cognitive and social benefits to children. The partnership between parents and schools was seen as important. The then Conservation government introduced the Nursery Voucher scheme in 1996 i.e. vouchers of value £1,100 for 3 terms to 4 year olds for preschool provision to demonstrate ability to move children towards desired developmental outcomes (1996, SCAA). The Early Learning Goals (QCA, 2000) were brought in as part of the UK cultural context for Preschool Development with the main philosophical pedagogy of: 1) Individualism—influenced by Western culture—Dewey, 1959. 2) Montessori, 1972—spontaneity and independent learning. It was meant to be child-centred learning (Issacs, 1933; Piaget). The approach to early year's education was criticised by Galton (1987) as unrealistic and romantic. The philosophy of free-play came from Rousseau, Froebel, Owen, MacMillan and Issacs. In Oxford Syva et al (1980) in 'The Oxford Study' put forward changes for early year's education to be more structured and developmentally challenging distinguishing between the old philosophy as ordinary play with little adult input and challenging play with adults scaffolding child's play within the zone of proximal development. It was still the developmental philosophy of Piaget but with the introduction of Bruner's work on the role of adults which was to be emphasized.

The next changes were seen in the Foundation Stage Curriculum documents (2000). The 2000 Curriculum Guidance for the Foundation Stage (Qualifications and Curriculum Authority Publication) introduced 'Stepping Stones'; that is, examples of what children do and what the practitioner needs to do to help children achieve them. The government demands for raising standards means preschool educators are required to conform to Ofsted inspection criteria. Smidt (2002) suggest this leads to learning as a passive process that resembles the old style rote learning and it appears to be on the increase and his comments have had some influence because for a period in 2008-9 even child minders were brought under Ofsted inspection. But already in 2010 they no longer need to process child development documentation as rigorously as SATs or as other assessment are documented higher up the school curricula. It is too much pressure place on children and their minders alike. The New Foundation Stage Guidance (2008) nonetheless is to stand as one of the main guidance documents. It combines previous Foundation Stage Curriculum and the Birth to Three Matters framework as well as influence from the Every Child Matters (2003) strategy and changes to the Rights of Children (2004) that are now a global preoccupation. Beverley Hughes the minister for education regards it as essential for all aspects of childrens preschool development.

Views of the conservatives and Liberal Democrats are that the Early Years foundation Stage Guidance is still too prescriptive. It does however incorporate into it elements of the Reggio Emilia and Froebel's Kinder Garten approaches. New Foundation Stage Guidance (2008) additional features:

- *It is incorporative of the Reggio Emilia and Froebel's Kinder Garten approaches,*
- *It fosters Citizenship, it is community orientated i.e. Reggio/Froebel,*
- *Play is valued i.e. Froebelian influence naturalism,*
- *Language/mother language Froebelian influence,*
- *Creativity and free play valued,*
- *Co-constructed project work from Reggio,*
- *To cater for multi-ethnic communities.*

The UK approach then is also a story of hybridisation with a curriculum culture and philosophy extrapolated from several mainly European but extremely international approaches to child development.

The UK is not the only one to do this. For example, the Te Whariki Framework in New Zealand (1993) was brought in as an early childhood pilot curriculum. Te Whariki translated into English "The Woven Mat" originating from New Zealand's native language Maori. Te Whariki later became an approved framework and was introduced as a national curriculum in 1996. The Whariki curriculum was written as a bicultural framework for early childhood education, written partly in Maori. Te Whariki main values and philosophy are: 1) Te Whariki incorporates a flexible national curriculum providing the set essentials of education, 2) Puts great emphasis on children's well-being, ensuring that children learn how to communicate confidently, enabling them to feel that they belong and empowering them to offer positive contributions to their society. New Zealand is a melting pot of many diverse cultures and ethnic groups, so at the heart of the Te Whariki ethos teachers endeavour to educate children to appreciate and respect other cultures, sharing their beliefs and ideas as they interact in society. Up until the 2008 changes to the UK early year's curriculum, the Te Whariki was a unique philosophical curriculum sourcing much of its belief system from Maori language and cultural surroundings that was multi-cultural. The characteristics of Te Whariki at the chalk-face are:

- *The children attending school are not monitored in the same way as many western early childhood models,*
- *Te Whariki does not measure children by a step progression but patterns which are all equal points of success,*
- *Te Whariki is as the name suggests a woven mat consisting of principles strands and goals all of which are woven together make patterns—no pattern is of lesser value than another,*
- *At individual centres teachers follow the curriculum but the direction in which they decide to implement provision is left to the discretion of practitioners,*
- *The cultural diversity of the community that children are from has a big impact on the style of the teaching methods for example, centre based in a Samoan community would be run differently to that of a Centre run in a predominantly European community,*

- *The common feature is that Children are encouraged to have "learner centred" curricula running alongside mandatory curriculum elements.*

It can be seen therefore that this community has also experienced global hybridisation and in fact the original pilot was the work of two British early year's practitioners. But in addition, one can see influences from the Reggio Emilia Approach.

Understanding of the Nordic, UK, Reggio Emilian, Te Whariki and Froebelian preschool philosophies on which the care and education of children rest has allowed the hybridised early year's education philosophies to develop leading to a richness of practitioner knowledge. The Reggio Emilia approach developed just after the second world war in the late 1940s and early 1950s with its emphasis on the 100-languages of children, developed for the needs of multiple cultures and it now influences most preschool provision. In postmodern communities children are given a voice and empowered through the process of co-constructed curriculum. The UK Piaget structured learning is likewise a big influence and Scandinavian countries use both approaches to early year's develop. Froebelian naturalism i.e. Forest schools have re-entered early year's educational culture and following the Children's Rights Agenda the focus is on children being allowed to play not only at school but also at home. The Kinder Garten value of naturism is spreading. The framework of Ofsted inspections and the use of a report published (2007) outlining the notion that Every Child's Future Matters in which outdoor activities were thought to be lacking in present school arrangements because of the fears of health and safety that deterred practitioners from operating within the naturalist philosophy are being dealt with. The adoption of Forest Schools is on the increase as advocates of this philosophy suggest they can make a positive contribution to 4 of the Every Child's Future Matters Agenda's outcomes: Children can make a positive contribution, be healthier than without naturalistic school arrangement, are safe because of the practice of a more rigorous health and safety framework, and children certainly enjoy the activities associated with naturalistic type schooling (O'Brien & Murray, 2006; William-Siegfredsen, 2005).

The developments within early year's education have thus been rapid, international and mutli-perspective in approach. The dialogue is richer and discerning. Problems that have arisen have tended to be linguistic in that multicultural communities need multiple levels of communication and Reggio provides several answers to this problem: art, drama/role play, project work, mother tongue teaching are some of the ways practitioners overcome language barriers experienced in Nordic cultures as well as European and other continents' cultures. There can be friction between local and global needs for all hybrid approaches and these are often economic in nature.

An area where psychologists and educationalists need to investigate is the development of education systems in countries in East Asia, Africa, and parts of South America. What the countries in the Occident have learned through the exchange of philosophical ideas concerning child development can be transposed to developing economies as a starting point for further development towards their own hybridised educational philosophy.

Reflexive practice, the dialectic and the spirit of change

In 1993 Mestrovic argued that it was becoming increasingly clear that the predominantly economic cold war between capitalist and communist nations was being replaced by a predominantly religious war between the Christian West and the Islamic Diaspora as an ethno-nationalist movement. Mestrovic proposed the Balkan war produced the 'Balkanization of the West' with the leading Western powers seemingly paralysed by the spectacle of interethnic warfare. He therefore claims that the Balkan war has derailed the movement for unification in Europe, and within Europe there would be considerable debate and concern over the rise of 'new racisms' which rely on notions of cultural difference rather than scientific notions of race marking ethnic boundaries. Is this a case of folk devils and moral panic (Cohen, 1972) or are Western societies doomed to fall apart at the seams?

In the era of late modernity, the dynamics of interethnic relations between nations and between majority and minority groups within nations, is complicated by globalism. Diasporas such as Islam and African are becoming more politically motivated with an increase in identity politics. In the last two decades revolutionary developments in communications such as Internet facilities: E-mail, Information Newsgroups and World Wide Web, including satellite transmission 24 hours, 7 days a week, and world news congresses to scientific research, have been matched by the tendency for a variety of institutions, groups and individuals (corporations, universities, writers or terrorists) to 'position themselves globally' in relation to markets, media or global cultural politics. It is in these conditions that much of contemporary culture is produced and they are the 'contemporary conditions' for the representation of identity (Anthony King, 1991). These are the conditions in which cultural groups stand in power relations to one another—being pulled together by national identity and stretched apart by diasporic identity: yet another dialectic.

In looking at globalisation in relation to English culture and the British experience, Professor C. Husband (1991) shows how 'Englishness' was formed in the context of Imperialism and along with it the colonized other was constituted as part of English identity. But in the present period of globalisation, Stuart Hall (1991) sees the relationship between the state and identity eroding. The old political and social terrain of Englishness is being broken up by the enormous, continuing migration of labour in the post-war world. With this erosion is a backlash, a narrower and more dangerous definition of identity both national and diasporic, driven by xenophobia and racism (S. Hall, 1991, p. 23-26).

Hall argues that when nation states begin to weaken and are less powerful, they go local and global in the same movement. Alongside the narrower local definition of Englishness is global mass culture production (the American style nonetheless), satellite TV and so on, which is centred in the West, speaks English, and is a part of the homogenisation process (what Walerstien calls the movement toward an homogenous global culture). Its aim is to absorb those differences in other cultures within the larger, overarching framework of what is essentially an American conception of the world, in order to maintain its global position (S. Hall, 1991, p. 27-29). I would suggest a hybrid culture and not necessarily just an American/English concept of the world. The English culture was already a hybrid before America transported it a new to the margins. As Jan Pieterse points out: `The most celebrated European philosophies, political principles, forms of Knowledge, technologies, arts and styles turn out on closer examination to be multi-cultural in character, origin and composition . . . the Occident was historically multi-cultural long before it became demographically multi-cultural' (Pieterse, p. 146, 1994). Indeed, the process of homogenisation is really that of hybridisation in disguise.

Hall regards the new forms of globalisation as different from preceding manifestations. While remaining in terms of technology, capital and advanced labour centred in the West, he suggests that the most profound cultural revolution has come about because of the margins coming into representation in the arts, in painting, films, music, literature, politics and social life generally. In this way 'marginality has become a powerful space' (1991, p. 34). He argues that the discourses of the dominant Western powers have been threatened by the de-centred cultural empowerment of the marginal (Third World countries culture) and the local (ethnic minorities cultural identity in Britain for example).

At the opposing end, when the movement of the margins are so profoundly threatened by the global forces of late modernity, they can themselves retreat into their own exclusivist and defensive enclaves. This is when the local ethnicities become as dangerous as national ones. A situation develops in which global homogenisation is resisted by traditionalism and old identities are rediscovered both ethnic minority identities and mainstream cultural identity. These re-found traditional identities constitute a form of fundamentalism i.e. religious and nationalist (S. Hall, 1991). Alongside this regression into the enclaves of traditionalism, we get cultural hybridisation—the mixing of, selection of, different cultures from different parts of the globe, in terms of music, dress, eating habits, arts and so on. The culture flow is mostly from the centre to the margins, such as the nation state and its institutions, but there is a movement from the margins to centre also, such as music, dress style and eating habits (Ulf Hannerz 1991, sees the interchange of culture as asymmetrical).

This interplay of culture is contingent on culture politics. Hall argues that when the margins begin to contest the centre, the local comes into representation because of the identification of diaspora in the West with their mother culture at the margins. Ethnic minorities in Britain cannot fully identify with aspects British National identity; they have experienced a similar marginal and subordinate position as other ethnic minorities and peoples on the periphery of the globalisation process (i.e. the margins). However, I heard only the other day (January, 2010) that Firth a representative of the British National Party in the UK regards Nationals as those who are born in the UK thus this encompasses anyone regardless of racial heritage. The counter-politics of the local nonetheless, through the diversity of identifications become a struggle that is conducted positionally, as a war of positions (like the Gramscian notion of the war of positions). S. Hall calls this positional political resistance (1991, p. 32). It represents the way ethnic minorities in society use their diasporic identity to contest the majority culture in that society.

Interestingly, we have come to the end of the book and once again I must return to the notion of dialectics. I have just outlined the dialectic display of cultural changes taking place within early year's developmental psychology as educational practices and philosophies take on a hybridised and global form. Hall sees the hybridisation process as part of identity politics as individuals that make up diasporas compete in the social arenas for cultural space. The dynamics of identity politics on the local and global levels are often problematic and although we can educate people and develop a citizenship culture there are areas that remained undocumented where people are falling through the net of welfare. In the chapter on 'Agency-structure in social space' one of the students working for SureStart and Banardos discovered a family of migrants who were living in conditions less that function for the developmental needs of the children. The mother spoke no English and her knowledge of British culture was poor that she did not know how to get help for herself or children. These are identities living in the UK who need help for their children now. There is a shortage of social workers in the UK—this area needs attention before it gets worst. Since the government implemented the Every Child Matters Agenda (2003 revised 2004 & 2007) the improvements have been slow: another area for research. What is the history of social welfare practices in the UK in meeting the needs of ethnic minorities and native poor communities? How can we use this history to elucidate the problematics of today's social welfare institutions and what part does psychological research play within this agenda? These questions are pertinent in the present climate of cultural change and where the education system remains the foci for service provision.

Bibliography

Ager, R (2000) *The Art of Information and Communication Technology for Teachers*. London: David Fulton Publishers.

Akrill, T. B., Bennet, G. A. G. and Millar, C. J. (1979) *Physics*. London: Edward Arnold Ltd.

Allan J. (1997) 'Learning outcome-led modular design: an analysis of the design features which influence students' perceptions of learning', in Rust, C. and Gibbs G. (1997) *Improving Student Learning through Course Design*. Oxford: Open University Press.

Ameriks, K. (2000) The legacy of idealism in the philosophy of Feuerbach, Marx, and Kierkegaard, in K. Ameriks (Ed) *The Cambridge Companion to German Idealism*. Cambridge: Cambridge University Press.

Argyris, C. and Schön, D. (1996) *Organizational Learning 11: Theory, Method and Practice*. USA: Addison-Wesley Publishing Company Inc.

Aristotle in M'Mohon, Rev. J. H. (MA) (1879) *Aristotle's Metaphysics*. Bradford: Central Library.

Assiter, A (2004) Principles for Profiling in Gosling, D. (2004) *Personal Development Planning*. Selly Wick House, Birmingham: Staff and Educational Development Association Ltd (SEDA).

Atherton, M (2005) *Applying the Neurosciences to Educational Research: Can Cognitive Neuroscience Bridge the Gap?* Part 1. Paper presented at the annual meeting of the American Educational Research Association. Canada: Montreal.

Atkinson, R. C. and Shiffrin, R. M. (1968) Human Memory: A proposed system and it control processes. In K. W. Spence & J. T. Spence (Eds.), *The psychology of learning and motivation*. Vol. 2. London: Academic Press.

Aubusson, P., Foswill, S., Bart, R. and Perkovic, L. (1997) *What happens when students do simulation-role-play in sciences*. Research in Science Education 27, 565-579.

Baddeley, A. (1966) The influence of Acoustic and Semantic similarity on long-term memory for word sequences, *Quarterly Journal of Experimental Psychology*, 18, 302-9.

Baddeley, A. (1997) Memory, in C. French and A. Colman ((Eds)) *Cognitive Psychology*. UK: Longman.

Baddeley, A. (2000) The episodic buffer: a new component of working memory? *Trends in Cognitive Science*, 4, 417-423.

Baddeley, A. and Hitch, G. (1974) Working Memory, in G. H. Bower (ed.) The *Psychology of Learning and Motivation*, Vol 8, Academic Press.

Ball, S (2004) (Ed.) *The RoutledgeFalmer Reader in sociology of Education*. London: RoutledgeFalmer.

Barbe, W. B. (1985) *Growing up Learning*. Washington D. C.: Acropolis Books.

Barnett, R. (1992) *Improving Higher Education: Total Quality Care*. Buckingham: Open University Press.

BERA (2007) *Revised Ethical Guidelines for Educational Research*. Nottingham: British Educational Research Association.

Berger P. and Luckmann T. (1971) *The Social Construction of Reality: A Treatise in the Sociology of Knowledge*. England: Penguin.

Berger, P. and Luckmann, T. (1966) *The Social Construction of Reality: A Treatise in the Sociology of Knowledge*. London: Penguin Books.

Bhaskar, R. (1983) *Dialectical Materialism and Human Emancipation*. London: New Left Books.

Biggs, J. (1990) *Teaching: Design for Learning. Annual Conference of the Higher Education Research and Development Society of Australia*. Brisbane: Griffith University.

Blaikie, N. (1993) *Approaches to Social Enquiry*. Cambridge: Blackwell.

Blakemore, S-J, and Frith, U. (2006) *The Learning Brain: Lessons for Education*. Oxford: Blackwell Publications.

Bloom, B. S. (1956) *Taxonomy of Educational Objectives 1*. USA: D. McKay Incorporated.

Bouldin, A. S. and Myers, S. M. (2002) *Learning Style Preferences Revised at the University of Mississippi School of Pharmacy*. Mississippi: Mississippi University.

Briggs, A. R. J. (2000) Promoting learning style analysis among vocational students. *Education and Training,* Vol. 42, No 1, 2000, pp. 16-24. Milton Keynes: MCB University Press.

Broadbent, D. E. (1958) *Perception and Communication.* London: Pergamon.

Bruer, J. T. (1999) *The Myth of the First Three Years: A New Understanding of Early Brain Development and Lifelong Learning.* New York: Free Press.

Bruner, (1993) The *Culture of Education.* US: Harvard University Press.

Bruner, J., Goodnow, J. & Austin, A. (1956) *A study of Thinking.* New York: Wiley.

Bucuvalas, A. (2004) *Learning and the Brain: An Interview with Professor Kurt Fischer.* USA: Harvard Graduate School of Education.

Burman, E. (1992) Developmental Psychology and the Postmodern Child. In: Doherty, J. Graham, E. and Malek, M. (Eds) *Postmodernism and the Social Sciences.* London: Macmillan Press.

Calder, P. (2009) *Early Childhood Studies Degree Forum & Net Work Coordinator.* Imperial College London.

Carpenter, R. H. S. (1996) (3rd Edition) *Neurophysiology.* London: Arnold-Hodder Headline Group.

Carver, T. (1991) (Ed.) *The Cambridge Companion to Marx.* Cambridge: Cambridge University Press.

Cassidy, S. (2004) Learning Styles: an overview of theories, models and measures. *Educational Psychology,* Vol. 24, No. 4, August 2004, pp. 419-444. London: Routledge.

Chaiklin S. and Lave, J. (1996) *Understanding practice: Perspectives on activity and context.* Cambridge: Cambridge University Press.

Chappell, V. (1994) *The Cambridge Companion to Locke.* Cambridge: Cambridge University Press.

Chein, J. M., Ravizza, S. M. and Fiez, J. A. (2003) Using neuroimaging to evaluate models of working memory and their implications for language processing. *Journal of Neurolinguistics,* 16, 315-339.

Child Education (April, 2003) *Every Child's Potential.* UK: Scholastics ltd.

Chohen and Squire (1980) Preserved Learning and retention of pattern-analysing skills in amnesia: Dissociation of knowing how from knowing that. *Science*, 210, 207-10

Chomsky, N. (1968) *Language and Mind*. New York: Harcourt Brace Jovanovich.

Coffield, F J, Moseley, D V, Hall, E and Ecclestone, K (2004) *Learning styles and pedagogy in post-16 learning: a systematic and critical review*. London: Learning and Skills Research Centre/University of Newcastle upon Tyne.

Coffield, F., Moseley, D., Hall, E. & Ecclestone, K. et al (2004) *Learning styles for Post-16 Learners. What do we know? A summary of the report to the Learning and Skills Research Centre*. University of Newcastle. http://www.Isda.org.uk/files/pdf/Unplearnstylespost16.pdf.

Coffield, F. (2005) *Kinaesthetic Nonsense*. Times Educational Supplement. 14th January 2005, p28.

Cohen, L and Manion, L. (1994) (4th Edition) *Research Methods in Education,* London: Routledge.

Cohen, R. (1994) *Frontiers of Identity: The British and the Others*. Essex: Longman Sociology Series.

Cole, Michael, et al (1978) *L. S. Vygotsky: Mind in Society: The Development of Higher Psychological Processes*. London: Harvard University Press.

Collin, A. M. and Quillan, M. (1969) Retrieval time for semantic memory. *Journal of Verbal Learning Behaviour,* 8, 240-7.

Collins, W. (1989) *Collins Concise Dictionary Plus*. Glasgow: the Bath Press.

Coon, D. (1983) (3rd Ed) *Introduction to Psychology-Exploration and Application*. England: West Publishing Company.

Cornforth, M. (1949) *Dialectical Materialism and Science*. London: Lawrence and Wishart Ltd.

Cowan, N. (1999) An embedded-processes model of working memory. In A. Miyake, & P. Shah (Eds) *Models of working memory: mechanisms of active maintenance and executive control* (pp.62-101). New York: Cambridge University Press.

Craik, F. and Lockhart, R. (1972) Levels of Processing. *Journal of Verbal Learning and Verbal Behaviour,* 11, 671-84.

Curtis, A. (1994) Play in different cultures and different Childhood. In Moyles, J. (1994) *The Excellence of Play.* Berkshire: McGraw-Hill Education in Association with Open University Press.

Dahlberg, G., Moss, P. and Pence, A. (Eds.) (2007) *Beyond Quality in Early Childhood Education and Care: Languages of Evaluation.* London: Routledge (Taylor and Francis Group).

Darwin (1859) *The origin of species by means of natural selection.* London: John Murray.

David, T. and Powell, S. (2005) Play in the Early Years: the influence of cultural difference. In, J. Moyles (Ed) (2nd Edition) *The Excellence of Play.* Berkshire: Open University Press.

DCSF (May, 2008) *Practice Guidance for the Early Years Foundation stage: Setting the Standards for Learning, Development and Care for children from birth to five.* Nottingham: DCFS Publications. Copies obtainable from: www.teachernet. gov.uk/publications

Department for Education and Skills (2000, 2008) *Curriculum Guidance for the Foundation Stage.* Nottingham: DfES Publications.

Department for Education and Skills (2002) *Statement of Requirement for Sector Endorsed Foundation Degree.* Nottingham: DfES Publications.

Department for Education and Skills (2003) *Every Child Matters: A Framework to Support Children in their Early Years.* London: DfES Publications.

Department for Education and Skills (2003) *White Paper.* London: DfES Publications.

Department of Health (2001) *Valuing People, White Paper.* London: HMSO.

Descartes, R (1961) *Rules for the Direction of the Mind.* New York: Bobbs-Merrill Company INC.

Dewey, J. (1916) *How We Think: A Restatement of the Relation of Reflective Thinking to the Education Process.* Chicago: Henry Regnery.

DfES (2004) *Pedagogy and Practice: Teaching and Learning in Secondary Schools: Unit 19: Learning Styles*. UK: Crown Copyright, Department for Education and Skills. REF: DfES 0442-2004 G

Diket, R. M. (2005) *Applying the Neurosciences to Educational Research: Can Cognitive Neuroscience Bridge the Gap?* Part 2. Paper presented at the annual meeting of the American Educational Research Association. Canada: Montreal.

Donaldson, M. (1978) *Children's Minds*. St. Ives, G B: Clays Ltd.

Dreyfus, H. L. (1991) *Being-in-the-World: A Commentary on Heideggers Being and Time, division 1*. London: the MIT Press.

Eastcott, D. (1992) *Evaluating Your Teaching*. SCED.

Einarsdottir, J. & Wagner, J.T. (2005) *Nordic Childhoods and Early Education: Philosophy, Research and Practice in Denmark, Finland, Iceland, Norway and Sweden*. Charlotte, NC, USA: Information Age Publishing.

Ekman, P. and Friesen, W. V. (1975) *Unmasking the Face*. Englewood Cliffs, NJ: Prentice-Hall.

Eliot, L. (1999) *What's going on in there?* London: Allen Lane.

Elliott, John (1991) *Action Research for Educational Change*. Buckingham: Open University Press.

Engels, F. (1934) *Dialectics of Nature*. Moscow: Progress Publishers.

Engestrom, Y. (1996) 'Developmental studies of work as a test bench of activity theory: The case of primary care medical practice', in S. Chaiklin, and J. Lave (1996) *Understanding practice: Perspectives on activity and context*. Cambridge: Cambridge University Press.

Esping-Anderson (1996) *Welfare States in Transition*. London: Sage.

Fagiolini, M. & Hensch, R. K. (2000) Inhibitory threshold for critical-period activation in primary visual cortex, *Nature*, 404, 183-186.

Fischer, K. W. (2006) Dynamic Cycles of Cognitive and Brain Development: Measuring Growth in Mind, Brain and Education. In, Battro, A. M., & Fischer, K. W. (2006) *The Educated Brain*. Cambridge, UK: Cambridge University Press.

Forman, D., Nyatanga L, and Rich, T. (2002) E-Learning and educational diversity. *Nurse Education Today.* 2002 Jan; 22 (1): 76-82; discussion 83-4. UK: Academic Press.

Foucault, M. (1994) *Power.* Series Editors, Faubion, J. D. & Rabinow, P., USA: The New Press.

Foucault (1980) *Power/Knowledge, Selected interviews and other writings 1972-1977.* Brighton: Harvester Press.

Fraser, G. (2000) *Antimatter: The Ultimate Mirror.* Cambridge: Cambridge University Press.

Fukuyama, F. (1992) *The End of History and The Last Man.* New York: Free Press.

Gadamer, H-G. (1989) (2nd Ed) *Truth and Method.* New York: Crossroad.

Galinsky, E. (2006) *The Economic Benefits of High-Quality Early Childhood Programs.*

Gamow, G. (1966) *Thirty Years that Shook Physics: The Story of the Quantum Theory.* New York: Dover Publications Inc.

Gardner, H. (1993) *Frames of Mind: The Theory of Multiple Intelligences.* London: Fontana Press.

Garnham, A. (1991) *The Mind in Action.* London: Routledge.

Geake, J (2005) Educational neuroscience and neuroscientific education: in search of a mutual middle-way. *Researchintelligence: News from the British Educational Research Association.* August 2005, Issue 92. UK: British Educational Research Association.

Geake, J. and Cooper, P. (2003) Cognitive Neuroscience: implications for education? *Westminster Studies in Education,* vol. 26, no. 1, June 2003. UK: Carfax Publishing, Taylor and Francis Ltd.

Giddens, A. (1987) *Social Theory and Modern Sociology.* Cambridge: Polity Press.

Giddens, A. (1991) Structuration Theory: Past, Present and Future, in C.G.A. Byrant and D. Jary (Eds), *Giddens' Theory of Structuration: A Critical Appraisal.* London: Routledge.

Giddens, A. (1992) *The Height of Modernity.* London: Routledge

Goddard, J., McNamee, S, James, A.L. & James, A. (Eds.) (2004) *The Politics of Childhood: International Perspectives, Contemporary Development*. Basingstoke: Palgrave McMillan.

Gollwitzer, P. M. (1999) Implementation Intentions: Strong Effects of Simple Plans. *American Psychologist*, Vol. 54, No. 7, 493-503. USA: American Psychological Association, Inc.

Gorard, S. and Taylor, C. (2004) *Combining Methods in Educational and Social Research*. Glasgow: McGraw-Hill Education, OUP.

Gosling, D. (2004) *Personal Development Planning*. Selly Wick House, Birmingham: Staff and Educational Development Association Ltd (SEDA).

Goswami, U (2004) Neuroscience and education and special education. *British Journal of Special Education*. Volume 31, number 4, 2004, pp. 175-183. Cambridge: NASEN.

Graf and Schechter (1985) Implicit and explicit memory for new associations in normal and amnesic subjects. *Journal of Experimental Psychology: Learning, Memory, and Cognition,* 11, 501-518.

Gregor, A. J. and McPherson, D. (1965) A study of susceptibility to geometric illusions among cultural groups of Australian aborigines, *Psychologica Africana,* 11, 1-13.

Gregory, R. L. (1993) *Eye and Brain*. London: Weidenfeld & Nicholson.

Gregory, R. L. (1966) *Eye and Brain*. London: Weidenfield and Nicolson.

Gross, R. (2000) *Psychology: the Science of mind and Behaviour*. Great Britain: Hodder & Stoughton Education.

Gumbrell, C. (1983) *Karl Marx*. Evergreen Lives: Tonsa, San Sebastian

Guthrie, W. K. C. (1967) *The Greek Philosophers from Thales to Aristotle*. London: Methuen & Co Ltd.

Habermas, J. (1970) Knowledge and Interest, in D. Emmet and A MacIntyre (eds.), *Sociological Theory and Philosophical Analysis,* p. p. 36-54. London: Macmillan.

Habermas, J. (1972) *Knowledge and Human Interests*. London: Heinemann.

Hall, S and Gieben, B. (1992) *Formations of Modernity*. UK: Polity Press.

Hargreaves, L. and Hopper, B. (2006) *Early years,* low status? Early years teachers' perceptions of their occupational status, in Early Years, Vol. 26, No. 2, July 2006, pp. 171-186

Harre, R. (1970) *The Principles of Scientific Thinking.* London: Macmillan.

Harre, R. (1972) *The Philosophy of Science: An Introductory Survey.* London: Oxford.

Head, J. (1996) Gender Identity and Cognitive Styles, in Murphy, P. F. and Gipps, C. V., *Equity in the Classroom: Towards Effective Pedagogy for Girls and Boys.* London: Falmer Press UNESCO Publishing.

Heather, N. (1976) *Radical Perspectives in Psychology.* London: Methuen.

Hebb, D. O. (1949) *The Organisation of Behaviour.* New York: Wiley.

Hegel, G. (1977) *Phenomenology of Spirit.* Oxford: Oxford University Press.

Heidegger, M. (1962) *Being and Time.* Oxford: Blackwell.

Held, R. (1965) Plasticity in sensory-motor systems. *Scientific American,* 213 (5) 84-94.

Hobson, A. (1999) *Consciousness.* New York: Scientific American Library.

Honey and Mumford (1986) (2nd Edition) *A Manual of Learning Styles.* Maidenhead: Peter Honey Publications.

Hudak, G M and Kihn, P (2001) *Labelling: Pedagogy and Politics.* London: RoutledgeFalmer.

Huttenlocher, P. R. (1990) Morphometric Study of Human Cerebral Cortex Development. *Neuropsychologia,* Vol. 28, pp. 517-527.

Iles, I. K. (2003) Becoming a learning organisation: A precondition for person centred services to people with learning difficulties. In, *The Journal of Learning Disabilities* (2003) Vol. 7 (1) 65-77 031985 ISSN 1469-0047 (200303) 7:1. London: Sage Publications.

Ingelby, (1982) *Critical Psychiatry.* Middlesex: Penguin Books.

Jaeckle, S. (2004) Managing Yourself and Your Learning, in Bruce, T. (Ed) (2004) *Early Childhood: A Guide for Students.* London: Sage Publications Ltd.

James, W. (1890) *Principles of Psychology*. New York: Holt.

Joshi, R.M., Dahlgren, M., & Boulware-Gooden, R. (2002). Teaching reading in an inner city school through a multisensory teaching approach. *Annuals of Dyslexia,* 52, 229-242. Brooklyn, New York: The Orton Dyslexia Society.

Kant, I. (1933) *Critique of Pure Reason*. London: Macmillan.

Karpel, M. (2004) Student Profiling embedded in a First Year Undergraduate Unit: A Case Study in Gosling, D. (2004) *Personal Development Planning*. Selly Wick House, Birmingham: Staff and Educational Development Association Ltd (SEDA).

Kehily, M, (2003) *Children's Cultural Worlds*. Milton Keynes: John Wiley & Sons Ltd. and the Open University (Book 3).

Kelly, G. A. (1955) *A Theory of Personality-the Psychology of Personal Constructs*. New York, Norton.

Kemmis, S. and McTaggart, R. (Ed.) (1988) *The Action Research Planner*. Australia: Deakin University Press.

King, A. D. (Ed) (1991) Culture, *Globalisation and the World-System*. London: Macmillan Press.

Kolb D. A., Rubin, I. M. and McIntyre (1973) *Organisational Psychology: An experimental approach*. Englewood Cliffs, NJ: Prentice Hall.

Kolb, D. A. (1984) Learning Cycle and Learning Style Inventory, in D. A. Kolb *Experiential Learning*. London: Prentice Hall.

Kuhn, T. S. (1970b) Logic of Discovery or Psychology of Research, in I Lakatos and A. Musgrave (Des) *Criticism and the Growth of Knowledge,* pp. 1-23. Cambridge: Cambridge University Press.

Lacey, P. (2000) (Editorial) Don't forget education! In *The Journal of Learning Disabilities* Vol. 4(2) 99-103 013654, ISSN 1469-0047 (200006) 4:2. London: Sage Publications.

Laing, R. D. (1967) *The Politics of Experience and the bird of Paradise*. Harmondsworth: Penguin.

Leach, J. (1991) *Running Applied Psychology Experiments*. UK: Open University Press.

Lee, D. and Newby, H. (1994) *The Problem of Sociology*. London: Routledge.

Lewin, K. (1946) Action Research and Minority Problem. *Journal of Social Issues,* 2 (4), 34-46.

Lichtheim, G. (1961) *Marxism: An Historical and Critical Study*. London: Routledge and Kegan Paul.

Lisle, A. (1997) *Inter-ethnic Relations and Social Change in the Late Modern Era: Integration or Segregation*. University of Bradford Library: Unpublished M. Sc. Dissertation.

Lisle, A. M. (2000) 'All hail reflexivity', in I. Parker (Ed.) *Annual Review of Critical Psychology: Action Research,* Vol. 2, pp. 109-129. Bolton: Discourse Unit, Manchester Metropolitan University.

Lisle, A. M. (2005) Marxian Psychophysics: the dialectic of brain-mind. EDUCATION-LINE Database of conferences and working papers. Available online at: http://www.leeds.ac.uk

Lisle, A. M. (2006) Maintaining Interaction in the ZPD through Reflexive Practice and Acton Research. *Teacher Development: an international journal of teachers' professional development.* Vol. 10, No 1, 2006, pp. 117-143. Oxford: Triangle Journals Ltd.

Lisle, A. M. (2007) Assessing Learning Styles of Adult with Intellectual Difficulties. *Journal of Intellectual Disabilities* Vol. 11 (1) 1-23

Littlejohn, G. (1984) *A Sociology of the Soviet Union*. London: Macmillan Press.

Lobman, C and Ryan, S. (2007) Differing Discourses on Early Childhood Teacher Development, *Journal of Early Childhood Teacher Education,* 28:367-380, 2007

Locke, J (1690) in Chappell, V. (1994) The Cambridge Companion to Locke. Cambridge: Cambridge University Press.

Locke, J. (1690) *Essay Concerning Human Understanding.*

Locke, J. (1690) *Two Treatises on Government.*

M'Mohon, Rev. J. H. (MA)(1879) *Aristotle's Metaphysics*. Bradford: Central Library.

Mac Naughton, G. (2005) *Doing Foucault in Early Childhood Studies: Applying post-structural ideas*. London: Routledge (Taylor and Francis Group).

Martinez, J. L. and Derrick, B. E. (1996) Long-Term Potentiation and Learning. *Annual Review of Psychology*. 47:173-203.

Marx Weber (1920) *The Protestant Ethic and the Spirit of Capitalism*.

Marx, K. and Engels, F (1848) The Communist Manifesto in McLellan, D. (1977) *Karl Marx: Selected Writings*. Oxford: Oxford University Press.

Marx, K. in Meikle, (1991) History of Philosophy: the metaphysics of substance in Marx, in T. Carver *The Cambridge Companion to Marx*. Cambridge: Cambridge University Press.

Maybin, J. & Woodhead, M. (Eds) (2003) *Childhoods in Context*. Milton Keynes: John Wiley & Sons Ltd. and the Open University (Book 2).

McCorwick Davis, S (2005) Developing Reflective Practice in Pre-service Student Teachers: what does art have to do with it? *Teacher Development,* Volume 9, Number 1, 2005

McDermott (1996) The acquisition of a child by a learning disability. In S. Chaiklin, and J. Lave (1996) *Understanding practice: Perspectives on activity and context*. Cambridge: Cambridge University Press.

McEvoy, J. P. and Zarate, O. (1996) *Introducing Quantum Theory*. UK: Icon Books.

McGarrigle, J. and Donaldson, M. (1974) Conservation accidents. *Cognition*, 1974, 3, 341-50.

McLellan, D. (1977) *Karl Marx: Selected Writings*. Oxford: Oxford University Press.

Medler, D. A. (1998) A Brief History of connectionism. *Neural Computing Sureys,* 1(2), 18-72. US, Berkley Education: Lawrence Erlbaum Associates Inc. Http://www.icsi.berkley.edu/jagota/NCS

Meikle, (1991) History of Philosophy: the metaphysics of substance in Marx, in T. Carver *The Cambridge Companion to Marx*. Cambridge: Cambridge University Press.

Middleton, E. m. (1989) *Ideology, race and Mental Health. MSc dissertation, Social and Economics Studies Department*. Bradford: Bradford University.

Miller, G. (1956) The magical number seven, plus or minus two: some limits on our capacity for processing information, *Psychology Review,* 63, 81-97.

Miller, L. Cable, C. and Devereux, J. (2005) *Developing Early Years Practice*. London: David Fulton Publishers Ltd.

Montgomery, H. Burr, R. & Woodhead, M. (Eds) (2003) *Changing Childhoods—Local and Global*. Milton Keynes: John Wiley & Sons Ltd. and the Open University (Book 4).

Morton, J. and Firth, U. (1995) Causal Modelling: A Structural Approach to Developmental Psychopathology. In, Cicchetti, D. & Cohen, D. J. (Editors), *Manual of Developmental Psychopathology*. New York: Wiley. Vol. 1. pp. 357-390.

Moss, P. (2006) Structures, understandings and Discourses: possibilities for re-envisioning the early childhood worker. *Contemporary Issues in Early Childhood,* Volume7, number 1, 2006

Moyles and Adams, (2004) Developing and Managing the Professional Role in Bruce, T. (Ed) (2004) *Early Childhood: A Guide for Students*. London: Sage Publications Ltd.

Myers, I. B. (1962) *The Myers-Briggs type indicator manual*. Princeton, NJ: The Educational Testing Service.

Newell and Simon (1976) *Human Problem Solving*. Englewood Cliffs, NJ: Prentice-Hall.

Newman, F and Holzman, L (1993) *Critical Psychology: Lev Vygotsky: Revolutionary Scientist*. London: Routledge.

Newman, F. and Holzman, L (1997) *The End of Knowing: A new developmental way of learning*. London: Routledge.

Novikov, I (1990) *Black Holes and the Universe*. Cambridge: Cambridge University Press.

Nyberg, L. Habib, R. Tulving, E. Cabeza, R. Houle, S. Persson, J. and McIntosh, A (2000) Large Scale Neurocognitive Networks Underlying Episodic Memory, in *Journal of Cognitive Psychology*. 2000:Vol. 12, pp163-173.

O'Brien, L. & Murray, R. (2006) *Such enthusiasm—a joy to see: an evaluation of Forest Schools in England*. Report to the Forestry Commission by the New Economics Foundation and Forest Research.

O'Connell, C. (2004) The Development of Recording Achievement in Higher Education: Models, Methods and Issues in Evaluation in Gosling, D. (2004) *Personal Development Planning*. Selly Wick House, Birmingham: Staff and Educational Development Association Ltd (SEDA).

O'Keefe, J and Tait, K (2004) An Examination of the UK Early Years Foundation Degree and the Evolution of Senor Practitioners—enhancing work-based practice by engaging in reflective and critical thinking, in *The International Journal of Early Years Education*. Vol. 12, No 1, March 2004

Osgood, J. (2006a) Professionalism and performativity: the feminist challenge facing early years practitioners, in *Early Years,* Vol. 26, No. 2, July 2006, pp. 187-199

Osgood, J. (2006b) Deconstructing Professionalism in Early childhood Education: resisting the regulatory gaze, in *Contemporary Issues in Early Childhood,* volume 7, Number 1, 2006

Parker, I. (1992) 'Discourse Discourse: Social Psychology and Post-modernity'. In: Doherty, J. Graham, E. and Malek, M. (Eds) *Postmodernism and the Social Sciences*. London: Macmillan Press.

Parker, I. (1999) (Ed) *Deconstructing Psychotherapy*. London: Sage Publications Ltd.

Parker, S. (1997) *Reflective Teaching in the Postmodern World. A Manifesto for Education in Post-modernity*. Buckingham: Open University Press.

Pavlov, I. P. (1927) *Conditioned Reflexes*. Oxford: Oxford University Press.

Pendrick, D. (1997) The New Phrenologists', *New Scientist,* 155:2091, pp. 34-47.

Penrose, R. (1997) *The Large, the Small and the Human Mind*. Cambridge: Cambridge University Press.

Perry, C. and Ball, I (2004) Teaching Subject Specialisms and their Relationships to Learning Styles, Psychological Types and Multiple Intelligences: implications for course development. *Teacher Development: an international journal of teachers' Professional Development*. Vol. 8, No: 1, 2004, pp. 9-28. Oxford: Triangle Journals Ltd.

Piaget, J. (1954) *The Construction of Reality in the Child*. New York: Basic Books Inc.

Pinker, S. (1997) *How the mind works*. New York: Norton.

Popper (1934) *The Logic of Scientific Discovery*. London: Sage Publications Ltd.

Qakes, P. J., Haslam, S. A. and Turner, J. C. (1994) *Stereotyping and Social Reality*. Oxford: Blackwell.

Ratey, J. (2001) *A User's Guide to the Brain*. London: Little, Brown and Co.

Riding, R. and Douglas, G. (1993) The effect of cognitive style and mode of presentation on learning performance. *British Journal of Educational Psychology* 63, 297-307. Ingenta, UK: British Psychological Society.

Rinaldi, C. (2001) Documentation and Assessment: what is the relationships? In Guidici, C. Rinaldi, C. and Kerechevsky ((Eds)) *Making Learning Visible: Children as Group and Individual Learners, Reggio Children,* pp. 78-89

Roberts, D. (2002) (Ed) *Signals and Perception: The Fundamentals of Human Sensation*. London: The Open University Press.

Rose, C. (1985) *Accelerated Learning*. USA: Dell Publishing.

Rose, C. and Goll, L. (1992) Accelerate Your Learning Action Handbook, Accelerated Learning Systems, in, Sears, J., Chapman, J., Hamer, P. and Cozens, P. (2001) *Non-Judgmental Differentiation*. Herts: The Association for Science Education.

Rose, C. and Nicholl, M. J. (1997) *Accelerated Learning for the 21st Century: The Six-Step Plan to Unlock Your Master-Mind*. USA: Dell Publishing.

Rosenthal, R. and Jacobson, L. (1968) *Pygmalion in the Classroom*. New York: Holt, Rinehart and Winston.

Rutter, J. (2003) *Supporting Refugee Children in 21st Century Britain*. Stoke on Trent: Trentham Books.

Sample, I (2007) The Brain scan that can read people's intentions: call for ethical debate over possible use of new technology in interrogation, science correspondent, *The Guardian* front cover. Friday, 9th Feb., 2007, Published in London and Manchester.

Sayer, D. (1991) *Capitalism & Modernity: An excursion on Marx and Weber*. London: Routledge.

Schön, D. A. (1983) *The Reflective Practitioner: How Professionals Think in Action*. London: Basic Books Ltd.

Schön, (2000) *The Reflective Practitioner: How Professionals Think in Action.* London: Basic Books Ltd.

Schön, D. (1987) *Educating the Reflective Practitioner.* Presentation to the 1987 meeting of the American Educational Research Association: Washing DC.

Sears, J., Chapman, J., Hamer, P. and Cozens, P. (2001) *Non-Judgmental Differentiation.* Herts: The Association for Science Education.

Shand, J. (1993) *Philosophy and Philosophers: An Introduction to Western Philosophy.* London: Penguin.

Shaywitz, B.A., Shaywitz, S.E., Blachman, B.A., Pugh, K.R., Fulbright, R.K., & Skudlarski, P., et al. (2004). Development of left occipitotemporal systems for skilled reading in children after a phonologically based intervention. *Biological Psychiatry,* 55, 926-933. Elsevier Sciences Inc, USA: Society of Biological Psychiatry.

Shelley Aldridge (2005) *Support Guidance for Implementing Policy for Work Place Learning.* University of Derby. University of Derby Intranet, URL: www.UDO. Derby.ac.uk

Shelton, L, Kaufman, L., Price, L. and Clary, J. (2002) *LD Resource Guide: Making Sense of Learning Difficulties, Disabilities, and Differences.* California: California Library Literacy Services.

Smith, A. (1996) *Accelerated Learning in the Classroom.* UK: School Effective Series, Network Educational Press.

Smith, Adam (1776) *Wealth of Nations.*

Smith, N. (1992) 'Geography, Difference and the Politics of Scale. In: Doherty, J. Graham, E. and Malek, M. (Eds) *Postmodernism and the Social Sciences.* London: Macmillan Press.

Soja, E. W. (1989) *Postmodern geographies: the reassertion of space in critical social theory.* London: Verso.

Spratt, (2004) Practical Projects: birth to 5 years in Bruce, T. (Ed) (2004) *Early Childhood: A Guide for Students.* London: Sage Publications Ltd.

Sprenger, M. (2003) *Differentiation through Learning Styles and Memory.* California: Corwin Press, a Sage Publications Company.

Steinberg, S. and Kinchloe, j. (Eds) (1997) *Kinder Culture: The Corporate Construction of Childhood.* Westview Press.

Strivens, J. (2004) The Liverpool University Student Interactive Database (LUSID): A web-based System for Recording Achievements in Higher Education in Gosling, D. (2004) *Personal Development Planning.* Selly Wick House, Birmingham: Staff and Educational Development Association Ltd (SEDA).

Swingewood (1975) *Marx and Modern Social Theory.* Great Britain: The Anchor Press Ltd.

Szasz, T. (1974) *Ideology and Insanity.* Harmondsworth: Penguin.

Tanweer, H. A. (1992) *Race and Mental Health, MSc dissertation, Social and Economic* Studies Department. Bradford: Bradford University.

Taylor, C (1995) *Philosophical Arguments.* London: Harvard University Press.

Taylor, Charles (1975) *Hegel.* Cambridge: Cambridge University Press.

Thomas, P. (1991) Critical reception: Marx then and now, in, T. Carver *The Cambridge Companion to Marx.* Cambridge: Cambridge University Press.

Thompson, R. F. (2nd Edition) (1993) *The Brain: A Neuroscience Primer.* New York: W. H. Freeman and Company.

Thornton, L. and Brunton, P. (2005) *Understanding the Reggio Approach.* London: David Fulton Publishers.

Tileston, D. W. (2004) *What Every Teacher Should Know About: Learning, Memory, and the Brain.* California: Corwin Press, a Sage Publications Company.

Tubbs, N. (2000) From Reflective Practitioner to Comprehensive Teacher, in *Educational Action Research,* Volume 8, Number 1, 2000.

Tulving, E. (1972) Episodic and semantic memory, in E. Tulving and W. Donaldson ((Eds)) *Organisation of Memory.* New York: Academic Press.

Tulving, E. (1985) How many memory systems are there? *American Psychologist,* 40, 385-98.

Turner, B. (1987) *Medical Power and Social Knowledge.* London: Sage.

University of Derby (2004) *Key Note Project.* University of Derby Intranet, URL: www.UDO.Derby.ac.uk

Vernon, D., Metta, G. and Sandini, G. (2006) A survey of Artificial Cognitive Systems: Implications for the Autonomous Development of Mental Capabilities in *Computational Agents*. European Commission Project IST-004370 Strategic Objective 2.3.2.4: Cognitive Systems.

Vygotsky, L. S. (1962) *Thought and Language*. Edited and translated by E. Hanfmann, and G. Vakar, Massachusetts: The M. I. T. Press.

Vygotsky, L. S. (1987) *The Collected of works of L. S. Vygotsky*, vol. 1. New York: Plenum.

Vygotsky, L. S. (1995) 'Interaction between Learning and Development', in J. D. Demetre, *An Introductory Reader in Developmental Psychology*. Kent, UK: Greenwich University Press.

Warren, C and Karner, T (2005) *Discovering Qualitative Methods: Field Research, Interviews and Analysis*. USA: Prentice Hall.

Watson, J. B. (1920) Conditioned Emotional Reactions. *Journal of Experimental Psychology*, 3 1-14.

Wilde, L. (1991) Logic: Dialectic and contradiction, in T. Carver *The Cambridge Companion to Marx*. Cambridge: Cambridge University Press.

Williams-Siegfredsen, J. (2005) Run the Risk, *Nursery World*, 04/08/054. P. 25.

Winter, R. (1987) *Action-Research and the Nature of Social Inquiry: Professional Innovation and Education Work*. England: Gower Publishing company.

Woodhead, M. & Montgomery, H. (Eds) (2003) *Understanding Childhood—An Interdisciplinary Approach*. Milton Keynes, John Wiley & Sons Ltd. and the Open University. (Book 1).

Zuber-Skerritt, Ortrun (1992) *Action Research in Higher Education: Examples and Reflections*. London: Kogan Page Ltd.

Index